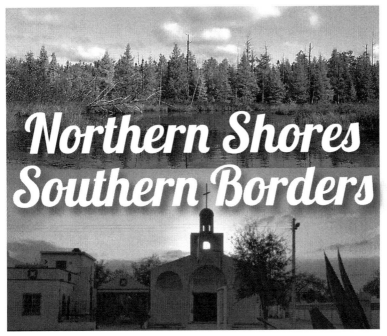

Northern Shores
Southern Borders

Revelations of a Bilingual Life

JANET KURTZ

Layout and Design by Chip & Jean Borkenhagen
River Place Press, Aitkin, MN

Contributing Photographer: Joey Halvorson Photography
(Back Cover Author Photo & Others)

Map Drawings: Robert Morgan

ISBN: 978-1-7339423-8-6
Library of Congress Control Number: 2020903412

Published by

40274 Diamond Lake Street
Aitkin, MN 56431
218.851.4843
www.riverplacepress.com
chip@riverplacepress.com

www.JanetKurtz.com

The final chapter was published in the April/May
2019 issue of *Lake Country Journal Magazine*.

This project was made possible, in part, by a grant
provided by Five Wings Arts Council, with funds
from the McKnight Foundation supplemented
with Legacy funds.

Dedicated to:

My mother, Phyllis M. (Wise) Kurtz
and in memory of my father, Donald W. Kurtz

Gratitude and eternal love for the foundations
you provided for my brother, Steven, and for me,
raising us to be mindful of our Mother Earth
and all of its inhabitants.

"No insisto en que sea una aventura completa, sino es el comienzo de una, porque así es como comienzan las aventuras."

"I do not insist that this is a full adventure, but it is the beginning of one, for this is the way adventures begin."

Don Quixote de la Mancha
Miguel de Cervantes Saavedra
(1547 – 1616)

Table of Contents

Table of Contents

Table of Contents

Table of Contents

INTRODUCTION
LA ENTRADA / THE ENTRANCE

This book is my journey through a maze. We all travel a path that begins with the well-worn routes of parents and those who went before us. One day, an opportunity, a seemingly chance meeting, a life altering accident, a foray outside of our daily perimeters veers us in another direction.

How do we decide which path to take? Is it, as Grandma might say, "by guess and by golly" or "divine intervention" or just "pure damn luck?" Regardless, each decision takes us to another room with more doors. Each door, a potential life changer.

The first fifteen years of my life were defined by the four seasons of the north. The first robin of spring, long summer days floating on a sun-sparkled lake, red maple leaves drifting to the forest floor, and the sensible desire to hibernate over winter. My social conscience evolved out of mid-sized midwestern towns comprised of middle class Caucasian Protestants. My choices were defined and certain behaviors expected. I wasn't aware of my comfort zone until I left it.

In 1968, while skipping along this path marked by my parents' guideposts, a fork in the road appeared. My stoic, outcome driven, somewhat stubborn German side encountered a ninety-degree turn into a magnificent south-bound trajectory. The new corridor was cut from towering, trimmed cypress hedges sculpted into passageways with arches, secret rooms, and hidden coves. At my feet, a pebbled Roman-style mosaic path invited me to step inside. I crossed the threshold. The scent of Norway pine gave way to whiffs of jasmine. I followed my nose along a trail that led through living hallways, no longer bordered with high-bush cranberries, but curved bougainvillea branches woven through trellises and oleander blossoms.

I was Alice in Wonderland! I entered a world of bright colors, trilled sounds, spicy foods, and guitar serenades. I was young, malleable, not yet cemented in my ways. I stuck my head out of my northern turtle shell with its carefully choreographed life and crossed into a space decorated with exotic purple jacaranda trees, six-foot tall red poinsettias, bright yellow and azure tiled fountains spurting skyward in airy patios. The German polka took on a wild, Mexican *Norteña* beat, a blend of "northern - sauerkraut" and "southern - salsa." Not a choice of either/or, but . . . both!

But wait, there was a rabbit hole. It wasn't all tacos and fiery flamenco. Around the bend, another reality erupted. It included poverty and hunger, inequity between multi-national stock-holders and their peasant laborers, bloody civil wars and fleeing refugees. Families were separated at U.S. border detention centers. Churches participated in an Overground Railroad to Canada. I became aware of U.S. interference into other sovereign countries. Each revelation taking me beyond giddy enthusiasm to a maturing, ever-changing world view.

One Friday afternoon in my Homer's Writing group (named after Donna's dog, not the author of the *Iliad*), I read my essay about a recent phone call from a neighbor requesting my services to translate for a Zapotec immigrant farm worker, lying on a gurney in the local emergency room after being kicked in the head by a cow.

"How do you end up in all these situations?" Maggie asked, perplexed and dumbfounded.

"Spanish," I answered without hesitation. There it was, the common thread woven into every fiber of my life.

According to my Latin American Literature professor, northern people prefer a linear story line, getting from A to Z, as opposed to the latino circular course. Perhaps that is why my stories lined up in chronological order. But stories get derailed, bent out of shape, and unexpectedly rerouted, often circling back to past occurrences for wisdom and guidance. That unavoidable "Latino Circle" kept spiraling to reconnect the backstory even as it progressed forward.

This book follows my circuitous life through unexpected intercultural events ever recreating and enlarging my worldview. It includes Spain's Moorish history, a medical mission to the Guatemalan Mayans, exchange programs with urban, upper-class Mexican youth adjusting to rural life in mid-Minnesota, Central American refugees fleeing on the Overground Railroad to Canada in the 1980s, uncomfortable ethnocentric awakenings and unpopular political truths. Continuous revelations changed my mind and my actions. A maze. Amazing.

My "northern - sauerkraut" roots provided a foundation of work, community and family ethics. My Spanish "southern - salsa" side gave me another perspective, another dimension, and another world. I chose curiosity over fear of the foreign. Each stranger—a potential friend.

I am pleased to walk this path with you. Come, let us begin.

Jan

THE FOUNDATION - OUR ROOTS
CONCERNING MEMORIES: STEPPING STONES

I went to my east porch and opened the door to let the late spring breezes in through the screen. I sank back into the old sofa and looked out over the garden and yard reaching to the woods. I closed my eyes. Behind my eyelids, foggy memories emerged, then evaporated into mental mist. Just as I opened my eyes a flash of blue darted across the sky. Was it the papa bluebird swooping after an insect for his brood or one of the blue jays that overwinters at my feeders? I reasoned that it was the bluebird nesting in one of my two boxes since the blue jays generally retreat to the forest when good weather returns. Yes, it must have been a bluebird.

Memories are like that. Memories are our perception of what we experienced. It is our truth drawn from educated guesses blended with emotions, maybe a photo, music, then enhanced by detective work uncovering exact dates or places. This process evolved as I followed the thread of people, meandering events, and decisions that wove my path into a bilingual, multicultural life.

Like the northern Minnesota porch in springtime, my stories are irrevocably fashioned by place and time. I am a product of the 1950s post-war baby boom, the 1960s social and political rebellions, and the gender role evolution of the 1970s. I am a product of my ancestors, part of the immigrant stream from Germany to Lancaster, Pennsylvania, then on to Illinois after the Civil War. My world view began with their decisions and genetics, including my height, another factor in the way I maneuver through this world!

I was born on November 20, 1952, to Donald, a young preacher, and his wife, Phyllis, a school teacher. We lived in a parsonage to the side of the Perkins Grove Evangelical United Brethren country church surrounded by Illinois cornfields. In the spring, my dad liked to walk the furrows left by the tractors, collecting flint shards and full-blown arrowheads. Other than these small fragments of another culture, my environment could be described in one word: White. White people, white bread, white snow. Even the immigrants of the northern Illinois villages of my parents' youth were Caucasian. Those German-speakers stayed low during World War II, assimilating to avoid detection. Despite my parents leaving home for their respective colleges in Naperville and Iowa City, the demographics remained the same.

FOUNDATION STONES: MY NORTHERN – SAUERKRAUT SIDE

My first memory of other cultures in the world dates to 1956 when we moved from northern Illinois to northern Wisconsin to build the family cabin. In Three Lakes, my father worked construction for Cy Williams, best known for being a professional baseball player with the Chicago Cubs and Philadelphia Phillies. The building experiences were helpful until that winter morning when he arrived at work to find the business burned to the ground. He took his lunch pail down the road to the Forest Service and was hired in time to eat with John Cooley, his new partner in porcupine reduction. My mother stayed at home with my brother, Steven, and me. Our new home was an older, two story rental house. We were cautioned not to play upstairs, where the owner stored her furniture, and to keep our distance from the Indians that walked along the edge of our backyard on their way to work.

At age four, I was too young to discern fear from distrust in adult voices when they spoke of "the Indians" in town. The Indians, the accepted term at the time, worked the potato fields and loaded sacks full of them into train cars at the railway station three blocks from our house. When we drove by the station, I didn't know if I should duck down and hide or press my nose against the window and sneak a peek. I peeked. I saw brown men, dressed in dirty brown clothes, lifting brown gunny sacks of brown potatoes. Some had long hair. Was that the difference?

I was six when we moved to Eau Claire, Wisconsin, where I learned the term PK, "preacher's kid." Dad accepted the youth pastor post at the First Congregational Church. Being a PK is a little like being a celebrity, or at least living under the public's watchful eye. The congregation patted me on the head as I grew from one grade to the next. I watched my table manners at Fellowship potlucks and tried not to get caught running in the church basement. Church members became my extended family, a blessing and a curse. As a child, I felt protected inside their bubble. As a teenager, normal pubescent behavior was deemed rebellious and unacceptable for a PK. I, however, was already on a path veering sharply away from beer, cigarettes, and off-colored jokes. I firmly believed my body was my temple and I kept a clean house.

Life in Eau Claire was tidy. It seemed the sidewalks were all straight, the skies were blue, and the green grass was mowed. I walked three blocks to school. My neighborhood was filled with nice friendly families. I didn't even realize I was a minority—a religious minority, that is. Evidently, Catholics had large families because all these kids flocking to my yard for kickball, Red Rover and hopscotch had scads of siblings. I was unaware of the potential religious rift until we reached the age of confirmation.

One Catholic friend, Ann, discovered I was merely dedicated and not yet baptized. She gasped and made it her job to protect my life until the water was sprinkled, just in case I might die and go straight to a place called purgatory. My only other awareness of Catholic differences was the quiet rumor that they could go out on Saturday nights, do anything they wanted, and on Sundays go to something called confession to be forgiven. That was frowned on by my father but seemed like a good arrangement to me.

Next door, Agnes, a Catholic woman, was married to Joe, a Jewish man. After my experience with Ann, I supposed that being married to someone of another religion must be challenging. This factor was brought up around the time of "the talk" before dating. Advice was clear. Stick to similar education, class, and religion in marriage partners. Race wasn't mentioned probably for lack of visible diversity.

I did have two friends who weren't qualified as WASPs (White Ango-Saxon Protestants), as friendships were not restricted by the aforementioned dating guidelines. When Susie and her brothers arrived from China with their thick Chinese-English dictionary, my group of friends embraced them. When Mary, a Navajo native, moved in, we were delighted when her birthday party introduced us to fry bread and she wore regalia from her culture. And there was my father's friendship with Joe. I never thought about his being Jewish until the day they tried to move our piano into the basement.

Our narrow hallway made it necessary to go out the back door and maneuver the upright into the stairwell from the direct approach. It was too tall and scraped along the ceiling. Dad took the crowbar and removed a few stairs before trying again. They were strong men, but no amount of wrangling moved the piano to the last step. The project was taking longer than expected. They sweated and twisted, but the piano stayed stuck in the stairwell.

By then, the sun was going down. It was a Friday. Joe stopped, patted Dad on the shoulder and said, "Sorry, but I have to leave. My Sabbath just kicked in." Dad's Sabbath didn't start until Sunday. He watched Joe exit the house and turned back to the piano.

I met my first African man due to church outreach. My parents were often called upon to host foreign visitors when they came to town for mission work. His name was Justus Kotanga, a musical name that rolled off his tongue with a rhythmic accent. His smile filled with brilliant white teeth, even whiter in contrast to his blue-black skin. I was probably about six-years-old, taking in non-judgmental details. I just wanted to show him my cat, Snuggles. I picked Snuggles up by her kitty armpits, paws dangling in all directions and tail hanging limp. He eased Snuggles out of my hands and balanced her on his forearm, tucking in her paws and cupping her chest in the palm of his hand. "This," he said gently, "is the way to hold a cat." Snuggles purred.

"Well, the audacity of that man," is what I felt, but I didn't know the word at the time. A complete stranger had upended my cat-handling confidence. Yet I adopted his method and now recognize his gentle touch with Snuggles—and with me.

In the second grade I joined the Camp Fire Girls, a group akin to and possibly a rival of the Girl Scouts. They sold cookies, we sold candy. They earned badges, we earned beads. Anyway, one winter day at our meeting, my little friends and I were excited when our leader pulled out a list of names including ages, gender, and country of origin. For twenty-five cents, we could purchase an address and have a pen pal. I put my money down and received an address for Sandra Chaddock from far-away England. At the time, I thought I knew English. That turned out to be only partly true.

That summer I spent a week at Moon Beach Church Camp in St. Germaine, Wisconsin. There, I met the camp missionary family that spoke with a "funny" accent and used some of the words I saw in Sandra's letters. They didn't look anything like the people in the photos Sandra sent me, however. They were from India. But, more confusing was the concept of missionary. I thought missionaries were "white, first-world" people spreading the gospel to darker-skinned, third-world countries.

My confusion cleared up that first evening at vespers. This family of four sat with us around the campfire and told their story. The children had beautiful skin color, frankly the envy of those of us trying to get a tan. The mother wore the most wonderful thing. It flowed as she walked. It's very cloth shimmered in purple and golds. She called it a sari and showed us how she wrapped herself in the nine yards of material. I couldn't image walking in such an outfit, but thought it lovely.

Her husband told us of his desire to be a missionary and his uncertainly about where he wanted to be sent. He asked his church leaders where they thought there was most need. Without hesitation, they said, "America."

"What? America? Why?" we asked him. "Because," he said slowly, "in America there is much temptation. There is much wealth and opportunity. People forget these are gifts of God. Remember your many blessings. It is very difficult to give your faith attention with all the distractions."

In the fourth grade, I met my first "foreign friends." Our teacher announced that Gisela and Carlos, from Belgium, would join our class after Christmas. They didn't know any English. How awful, I supposed it would be, not to be able to talk to anyone. I asked Mom for her college French book and took it to my room. Through phonetics and her help, I managed to memorize: *Comment Allez-vous, Aimez-vous l'ecole? Mon amie,* and *Je t'aime*, in that order. "How are you?" "Do you like school?" were natural openers. From "my friend" to "I love you" was a leap. I just wanted them to feel welcomed.

But French wasn't the direction I wanted to go. I really wanted German, the native tongue of my ancestors, but it wasn't offered until junior year in high school. I was given the official, albeit short-sighted, advice by the high school counselor to get my "two required years of language" out of the way early. I could move on to college, done with the deal. Spanish was offered a year before French and German, so there it was—Spanish.

STEPPING STONES TO SOUTHERN – SALSA SIDE

By 1970 I was headed to Mexico for my third time. I was seventeen and had finished four years of high school Spanish. During my three previous summer trips, I met authentic Spanish-speaking people, not just names in textbook conversations but a flurry of faces. Raúl. Beda. Pepe. Lucio. Carmen. Flesh and blood people from another country. Our friendships grew through snail-mail letters rimmed with green, blue, and red borders stamped with Mayan pyramids and Olmec heads.

I'd run to the mailbox hoping for airmail envelopes. When they arrived, I took them to a quiet place, tore them open and got out my dictionary. Squinting through their foreign penmanship and stumbling over native-speaker vocabulary, I put the puzzle of communication together. This wasn't for a grade. This was motivational learning at its best.

The letters began with flowery, courteous intro-paragraphs, '*Espero que esta carta te encuentre bien en compania de tu familia. . .*' I hope that this letter finds you well in the company of your family.' After wading through the body of the letter, I looked for clues to their feelings in the closure. Was it merely '*Hasta luego*' or the next level, '*de tu amigo que te quiere*', from a friend who loves you.' I yearned for news of dances, escapades at UNAM, the University of Mexico, and what was going on in Saltillo when the space I used to occupy among them was vacant.

Who knew that I might get good at this Spanish stuff? Why did my advisors tell me to stop after two years? Is language the only subject where accomplishment is not rewarded with praise and support to go on? Imagine two years of music for a budding musician and being told to quit. Only two years of football? Ha! This became an ongoing theme throughout my career. Ah, but back to the beginning.

My first Spanish teacher was Mr. Llewelyn Edming, a tall, slender man, with a stilted gait and flamboyant hand gestures. Later, I would identify these as characteristics of a gay man, but I was fourteen. What did I know or much less, care? He was jubilant about Mexico and filled lesson lulls with outrageous stories from his travels. I remember exactly four things from his class.

First, he brought us a big hunk of dried pig skin, *chicharón*, the real stuff, not the thick, multi-ingredient imitation. He cracked off little pieces for us to taste. I watched him make the rounds. He got to my desk. I put out my hand. I looked at the chunk he dropped into my palm and grimaced. It included a coarse, black pig's hair! Oh dear. I nibbled around it. It tasted like a hairy potato chip.

My second memory included a large, crystal-cut red brooch he wore from Mexico. He walked slowly through the aisles, repeating the vocabulary and giving us all a chance for a good look. Then the brooch moved. It crawled toward his collar. I was afraid to say anything. Was I the only one that just saw that? It looked like a big bug chained to a pin tethering it within a small area of his lapel.

Mr. Edming chuckled, put down his textbook, and unpinned a large beetle with colored glass glued to its back. He explained that it could live up to six weeks on the piece of bark that he had right here in this little transparent box he pulled out of his pocket. When not being worn, it could eat and sleep in the container, or so they told him. Then he returned to his desk for the Mexican jumping beans and told us about the little worm inside. Apparently not the same worm as found in the bottom of a tequila bottle. Mexican insects, it seemed, had many career choices.

Third, the annual International Foreign Language week gave us the chance to dress as flamenco dancers, beret-wearing French artists, and Latin students wrapped up in sheet togas. Mr. Edming came as a bull fighter, complete with the red cape and pink socks. We did the limbo, a dance I was built for, enabling me to win the 'how-low-can-you-go' competition.

And finally, there was book learning. We were given a primer, *Leer y Hablar* and taught through ALM, Active Learning Methodology, the most recent, hot language acquisition technique whereby we memorized conversations without comprehension. I recall only a piece of the first chapter's conversation:

—*¿Cómo están María y Luisa?*
—*María está bien, pero Luisa tiene catarro.*
—*Ojalá que se mejore pronto.*

It was years before I realized it included the challenging, upper-level subjunctive verb tense and that Mariayluisa, was . . . Maria y Luisa, two people not one. It was decades before I used the final phrase, "Hope you get better soon," when a Mexican checkout girl sneezed.

Somehow, with a confusing batch of independent, memorized situational clauses, I passed on to Spanish II. There, I met the formidable Mr. David Haakenson, who preferred to be called, *Jefe Supremo*, the supreme chief, the boss man. He expected us to know how to conjugate verbs and write them in our AMSCO workbooks in all humanly known tenses. I was sunk.

Yet on I went. I had to finish two years, after all. Turns out Haaky, as we called him, had a dimple and a twinkle in his eye. On Fridays, if we got our drills done early, he'd tell us to pull out the green-stapled song book. *Guantanamera, ¿De qué color es la piel de Dios?*, *La Bamba*, *La Llorona*, and *La Cucaracha* were among the tunes that became our own. Singing worked better than speaking.

COMBINED MEMORIES

Many memories have weathered the years. Are they accurate? There's a story of blind men led to various parts of an elephant, then asked to describe the animal. Their accounts accurately portrayed the trunk, a tusk or the tail, but were void of the whole picture. In writing my memories, I had the advantage of my mother's travel journal, my diaries, photos and friends' letters to fill in where my memory faded, providing a more holistic panorama of events.

I renewed contact with Lucio and Raúl. I pulled out my old LP records and was delighted to remember the words. After fifty years of Spanish, I am now confident that I better understand these words and have gained historical and personal insights. Spanish is the connecting thread running through the tapestry of my life.

Despite all this information, one unsolved mystery remains. How had my cautious, midwestern parents let me go out into the world so young?

"When you got something into your head," my mother informed me, "you wouldn't let go. Perhaps we gave in."

I prefer to think it was a midwestern miracle. Either way, it was a life changer.

"*Caminante, no hay camino, se hace camino al andar.*"
(Hiker, there is no road, the road is made by your walking.)
—Antonio Machado
(Spain, Generation of 1898)

Section I
Crossing Borders
Saltillo, Mexico, 1968-1970
&
Seville, Spain, 1972-1973

1

Capítulo Uno
Lorraine's Car Heads South

It was August 1968. In September, I would be a junior in high school, hoping to be allowed into the Spanish III class despite my low C grade. Perhaps that was why I was sitting in the back seat of Lorraine's car enroute from Wisconsin's sky blue waters to Mexico's cacti covered mountains. Or perhaps, as my mother recalls, I begged her to let me out of Middle America to taste the world my Spanish teacher, Haaky, "*el Jefe Supremo*," created with his travel tales.

For the past three days, Lorraine, a 40-something divorcée, and her 18-year-old daughter, Cindy, took turns driving us through the Iowa cornfields, the midwestern plains and into the deserts between San Antonio and the border. The scenery blurred into a mix of freeways, morphing together in repetitious offerings of fast foods, chain motels, and generic gas stations advertised just before the off ramps. Only the accents of the radio announcers gave a clue to our changing position until we reached Texas, where Spanish crept into the radio dial along with ranchero music. Heat waves wiggled off the car hood as we squinted into the flat desert stretches, counting off miles to Laredo, our border crossing.

Laredo is where they stopped us. Mid-morning. Dust. Hot sun. Long lines of noisy traffic waiting to cross the border in both directions. Finally, our turn. The Mexican official looked into the car and asked for papers. Identification. Letters of consent. Consent for what? For me to cross the border. Didn't my parents send a letter giving this woman permission to have me along? Kidnapping? What, me? Kidnapped?

El Jefe had taught us about *mordidas*, literally "the bite," a bribe seamlessly woven into the Mexican culture to speed up transactions. Was this one of those times to slip the official a ten? What if this guy turned out to be honest? *El Jefe* had also described Mexican jails. It wasn't worth it. Lorraine reluctantly turned the car back toward downtown Laredo.

Once in the town center, she parked the car and walked me to a small office several blocks off the main drag. It was dimly lit with a nondescript man sitting behind a desk. He asked a few questions and scribbled some notes. I vaguely remember standing in the shadows, wondering what he could possibly do to get me into Mexico.

When we stepped back into the bright sunlight, Lorraine looked down at me and quipped, "You can call me 'Mom' now. I have adopted you and here is the paper complete with the raised seal to prove it." What? Was she serious? She was clear on one thing. I was to keep my mouth shut at the border.

I did keep my mouth shut and this time we were waved through Customs to the highway leading into Mexico and the Sierra Madre Oriental mountains. We did not stop again until we were safely inside the city limits of Saltillo, our home for the next three weeks. Within an hour my shy, stoic German persona was bumped aside by a budding Latina alter ego, called into being just in time to save my newly acquired mother from "*Montezuma's* Revenge."

We arrived hot, tired, and hungry. How would we know where to eat? *El Jefe's* words came back to me. "Find a place filled with locals. They know." Up ahead, a small cantina's parking lot was filling. We pulled in.

The waiter led us to a table and plunked down three single page menus. Oh no! Being the only one with an ounce of Spanish, I would be expected to decipher the menus. I stared at mine. Not only were the words new to me, but the dishes were culinary concoctions that changed names according to the position of the tortilla. Were they stacked, rolled or folded? Were *carnitas* little pieces of pork or beef or chicken? Or goat, like the carcass turning on the spit when we walked in? So this is what *El Jefe* meant by, "Comprehension requires cultural context."

We looked around at other tables, at the counter, and at the brightly colored menu above the cooking grill before ordering. Everything smelled delicious. We pointed at pictures and took our chances. The *mesero* placed the hot platters before us and asked, "*¿Hay algo más?*" Three words. I could do that. "*No, gracias,*" we didn't need anything more. Not until a few bites into the meal anyway.

Lorraine's eyes widened. Her left-hand reached for her throat and the other waved wildly in midair, more or less in the direction of the waiter. I looked across the table at Cindy and then down on Lorraine's plate. There, on the bed of rice and *frijoles*, lay a bitten off chili pepper.

Tears streamed down her cheeks. The waiter ran to our table with a pitcher of water. *Agua!* Oh no, not *agua*! *El Jefe* told us that *agua* in Mexico was akin to arsenic for the unaccustomed gringo. That could lead to hours curled in the fetal position on the cool tiles of some Mexican bathroom floor wondering if you should insert your head or behind into the toilet first. It is said this is the revenge that the Aztec emperor, Montezuma, inflicts on all white invaders, due to the treatment he received at the hands of the Spanish *conquistadores* in the early 1500s.

Just as the *mesero* took Lorraine's glass to pour in the offending liquid, a memorized phrase popped out. "*Tráigame leche!*" I pleaded. "Bring me milk!"

Like magic, these foreign words sent a full grown man to do my beckoning. He turned heel and came back from the kitchen with *leche*, the preferred antidote to sooth the effects of spicy foods. Wow! No textbook dialogue was ever this exciting. Lorraine's breathing calmed. Around us, clusters of patrons returned their attention to their *arroz con pollo* and *Dos Equis* beer. I really was in Mexico!

My meager Spanish kicked in, but my math was hopeless. Who was going to figure out the bill? "Lorraine," I asked, "Do you have a calculator? We'll need $1.00, $5.00,

21

$10.00, on up to $100 converted to pesos so I can make a chart." We spread our foreign bills and coins out on the table. "These look like monopoly money," Cindy observed. "Look, a ten-thousand peso bill! I'm rich!" Just when we cleared that cultural hurdle, Lorraine looked at me and sighed, "How much are we supposed to leave for a tip?"

Out of the Frying Pan and into the Fire

Back outside, Saltillo was a maze of narrow *calles,* streets full of honking taxis, braying burros, and unpredictable pedestrians. Lorraine was now the sole driver under the Mexican auto insurance policy. I was promoted to front passenger seat, for map reading and to stick my head out the window to ask directions. Cindy was relegated to the backseat, in charge of finding traffic signs and street names.

"What street are we on?" Cindy asked before Lorraine entered the boulevard. "I don't see any signs."

"They are on the sides of the buildings," I said, again thanking *El Jefe.* "Check about eight feet up for the tiles that spell out the name. They should be on the corner buildings. The numbers are over the doors."

"But the school address has two numbers. Sixteen de *septiembre*, thirty-four," she read off the envelope.

"The street is *16 de septiembre*, one of their revolution dates," I said, again excited that I recognized something from Spanish class. "The number 34 is the building."

The streets meandered with no evidence of straight blocks. Lorraine pulled up to an approachable-looking couple and I rolled down the window. They read the note with the address as I asked, "*¿Nos pueden ayudar?*" "Can you help us?"

They smiled and rattled off a sequence of instructions accompanied by gestures and finger pointing. I captured the first phrase, smiled back and nodded thank you. It was enough to get us a few streets farther, where we would take the indicated right, or did they say straight ahead?

"Oh, man," I groaned. "I can't tell if they are saying *derecho*, straight ahead or *derecha*, meaning right. I will get us lost, or worse, change someone's gender!" Lorraine slowed and pulled over to the next potential guide. "And," I added before again rolling down my window, "*Jefe* said that these people want to be helpful if they know the directions or not!"

Following this routine, we stayed off the one-way streets, made it around Alameda park, and turned into the quiet, palm tree-lined boulevard where we finally found *La Universidad Interamericana*. The variegated green tile-covered façade seemed to indicate a small building from the sidewalk, one of those misleading Spanish architectural phenomena. Lorraine parked in the shade and then gave me a nudge toward the entrance. The massive wood-carved Colonial doors creaked open. Cool air flooded over us from the inner sanctum of a flower-filled patio stretching for more than a city block to the back wall that was topped with broken glass bottles.

The registration office was to the *derecha* of the entry. I introduced myself to the secretary and was more than relieved when she spoke English to Lorraine. By now, my head was throbbing from the clatter of two languages banging around like pool balls searching for a pocket. My eyes were scorched from squinting at the sides of buildings where shadow patterns played among the climbing red bougainvillea vines covering the street name tiles.

I closed my eyes and felt the darkness cool their burning. I wasn't aware of my stiff back muscles until they began to relax and my shoulders lowered into their normal position. I noticed my chin was still jutting forward in the strained-listening pose. Ah, but we had made it. Almost.

I felt a tap on my shoulder and there was Lorraine, with another piece of paper in her hand. It was the address of our hosts, the Fuentes family.

"And where do they live?" I was almost afraid to ask.

"Back," Lorraine grinned at me, "way back. . . on the other side of town."

MI CASA ES TU CASA

It was a large house, much larger than mine back in Wisconsin. It had two stories with solid brick on the first floor and white adobe above. It was roofed with tejas, red Spanish tiles, and encircled by a four-foot cement wall. There were two gates, one for the cars and one to the front door. The driveway gate was barred. Lorraine parked next to it.

As advised, we locked our car before approaching the house. There was a balcony atop the main entrance roof where a woman lounged in the sun. The front walk gate was unlocked. We proceeded to the carved wood front door. Finding no doorbell, I knocked.

It seemed a long wait, but the door finally opened revealing a short, rounded, very white, blond woman. Blond? Caucasian? "*Somos estudiantes*, We are students," I began. "Oh, come in, come in! The school called and I was expecting you. I am *Señora* Fuentes. Carmen," she finished in a sweetly-accented English. She sent a man to get our luggage and led us into the kitchen where she introduced us to several other students taking residence there.

Mary was from Minnesota and in her third of six weeks of study with the program. She would become our beacon, shedding light on many mysteries of this house and how to maneuver through the new lifestyle. Others were staying as many as twelve weeks. We were signed up for three weeks of morning classes and afternoon tutoring.

Señora Fuentes showed us upstairs to our bedrooms. They were spacious with large windows open to the air and light flowing over intricate Mexican tile floors and walls. We'd share an ample bathroom and a balcony.

"You need to know about the water in the bathrooms," she began. "We don't always have hot water. This little knob," she said pointing, "is what you turn on to heat the water. It will take about ten to fifteen minutes. We have a cistern on the roof to catch rain water for washing, so do not drink it. If you sing in the shower, keep your mouth down," she smiled. "We provide pitchers of clean water in your rooms for drinking and brushing your teeth. We can't have you getting sick!"

Next she handed us our towels. "When you are done bathing, leave the towel on the floor. The maid will get it." A maid? Just put your towel on the floor? My mom wouldn't have that!

"Also," she continued, "leave your beds unmade. The *criadas* will just make it over or take the sheets to wash, so leave them alone." *Criadas* is plural. How many maids are there around here?

She led us downstairs to an eating area with a large dining room table and six chairs. "Breakfast is served at 7:30. It includes eggs, refried beans, *buñuelos*/sweet breads, fresh juices, fruits, and coffee. If there is any special need, let me know so that I can tell the cook." Refried beans for breakfast? And a cook? Maids and a cook? I thought Mexico was poor.

Señora (Sra.) Carmen motioned to the chairs and invited us to sit for lemonade. "Would you like ice?" she asked, before three very light-skinned children came skidding up to the table. "These are my *hijos*, two sons and a daughter," she managed to say before they ran out the other door. "Oh, and don't order drinks with ice in the streets. You don't know if it was made with purified water," she said, placing chilled glasses in our hands.

At supper we were introduced to Dr. Alberto Fuentes, the *hombre de la casa*, the man of the house. After the meal, I followed Mary to the balcony and asked if she'd clarify what I thought I understood that day.

"Yes," she confirmed. "Dr. Fuentes and his wife are from a straight line of Spanish blood, Spain Spanish, not *mestizo*, mixed blood. He is a medical doctor and she works at a school. Yes, it is unusual for her to have a career, but Dr. Fuentes isn't the *macho* sort, insisting she stay home.

"As to the maids, follow what Carmen said because there is no point in you making your bed or cleaning up after yourself. You will get fresh towels every day. They will do the wash, fold your clothes, and put them away, too." Then Mary added, "Don't get too comfortable here, though, because we are all moving to the new house next week. It is amazing!"

Was it possible to have something more amazing than maids, cooks, and balconies?

A PERSONAL MAID?

Mary was right. The following week after classes, we were picked up and delivered to a new, under construction *barrio* that still lacked paved roads. Only a few homes had sprung up within the perimeters of the survey stakes, and ours was one of them. The Fuentes' new house stood out like a carved, shiny sculpture in the desert.

The side entrance opened into a large patio furnished with high-end lounges, a white wrought iron table, and a tiled fountain. The wall bricks were laid in lattice pattern, allowing in light and breezes. Beyond was a double door into the main house, which they opened into an entry where the floors shone like ice rinks. We followed Carmen from room to room.

"This is where we will be eating together," she said, with a nod toward the massive dining room on our right. "This room," she motioned with her left hand, "is for the kids and informal eating." She continued a few paces down the hallway with us following before saying, "Careful here.", Then she took two steps down into a smaller room with yet another table. "This is where the maids eat and have their sleeping quarters behind. It is closest to the kitchen and back utility patio."

I had heard about this. It was no benign architectural whim. This was a constant reminder that the maids were a "step down" and they had to step up to be part of the regular house. They did not enter by the front, but the back patio door, where laundry was done, often in a *pila* scrubbing sink, and hung to dry.

Later that day, we moved in and met the new maids, four now needed to cover the bigger house. Beda was to tend to me. She was responsible for my bedroom, my clothes, even my hunger. If I wanted a snack, she prepared it and brought it to me. She was fifteen. I was fifteen. She was from the *campo* outside the city of San Luis Potosí. The four maids, all cousins, helped support their extended family living in the country there.

No one had ever told me not to befriend someone until now. "We are not to socialize," Mary said after Carmen left us to unpack. "No boy talk, no giggles, no walks around Alameda Park, *nada*." Mary continued explaining the protocol. "Beda is working for you, not a peer."

I never viewed another fifteen-year-old girl as anything but my equal, except maybe for my unexplainable sense that I was in a lower class than cheerleaders. I knew what not belonging felt like, but Mom said I did not have to accept other people's assessment. I didn't have to, but Beda?

For her, this social status thing was built right into the architecture. Just as she had to step down into her quarters, I had been taught to make my bed, get my own snacks, and wash my dishes. I had no experience sitting at the table and being served by anyone, except maybe my mom. I didn't know how to pretend someone was invisible while standing right there.

It got worse after I started making friends at school. When they stopped by, one of the maids would answer the door, announce their arrival, and disappear. They returned with icy fruit *licuado* slushes and then went to market or to the kitchen to peel the potatoes and fry the fish for supper while I planned my next outing.

One afternoon, things shifted. After *siesta*, Beda, Mary, and I were alone in the house. She knocked on my door and asked if I needed anything.

"Yes," I said. "I do." I paused and pulled up a chair for her. "Beda," I started. "we are the same age and I am not used to being served. . . by anybody!"

"At my house," I continued, "I make my bed. On Saturdays I clean the whole house.

Every night I make supper because my mom is a teacher and gets home later than I do. My brother and I do dishes and sweep the kitchen. We hang out our own clothes to dry in our backyard."

I looked up and saw she was listening closely, nodding her head, understanding my Spanish even if not comprehending my life.

"Beda, I would like to be friends, but I don't know how to do that here. I don't want to get you into any trouble." I stopped.

She stood up, went to the nightstand, and picked up my hairbrush. She motioned for me to sit in the chair she had just vacated. She stepped behind me and started to comb my hair. It felt so good. She had such a soft touch. She gently brushed through my bobbed hair and patted it in place. She held up the hand mirror.

I looked at my reflection and then back at her and smiled. "Beda, my hair is so short and yours is so long and beautiful." I paused. "May I?" I held my hand out for the brush.

JAN COMBING BEDA'S HAIR.

She hesitated and then handed it over. I stood up and said, "*Siéntate aquí*, sit here."

I filled my left hand with her thick tresses and with my right, gingerly slid the brush through her Rapunzel hair. I made one pass after another through her waist length locks.

We relaxed into the rhythm of the brush. A forbidden giggle escaped. Her words trickled out. She had a boyfriend. He came to stand outside her window on his days off. Sometimes he threw a pebble to get her attention. I brushed. Sunday was her day off. They liked to stroll around Alameda Park until dark. She rode the bus to San Luis once a month. I brushed. She gave her *pesos* to the family. I continued brushing.

Her hair began to shine. I pulled it away from her face and stood to her side, allowing for a look in the wall mirror.

There, in the mirror, were the faces of two fifteen-year-old girls smiling back at us.

~ *Puente* – Bridge ~
(Diary entry, 1968; rediscovered in 2018)

Neither Mom nor I could recall just how it came to be that I was in that car with Lorraine and Cindy. Was it, as my mother remembers, my begging to go? As a teenager, wouldn't I have engraved such a yearning in my long-term memory? Like wanting to have a horse? Or marrying Michael Landon from the 1960s TV western, *Bonanza*? Wouldn't I remember wanting to leave the country?

Then, among my memorabilia, I found my 1968 school calendar and a typed journal page. On February 7, 1968, I was afraid to jinx my luck, but dared to write this down in my diary anyway:

I am a highly emotional girl and when I heard that news, my days filled with thoughts of leaving the family for such a long time, leaving friends and the like. Letters were going back and forth making arrangements and ironing out details and I sat in the midst, quite confused.

My mind couldn't cope with such things as my solo flight to Colombia where I knew no one. What would I do? What would it be like? Why! I couldn't even speak enough Spanish to get me off of the plane!

Shall I tell anyone? Shall I talk to my teachers? I decided I would not tell anyone until I was sure and I wouldn't tell my Spanish teacher until I got back.

After that was settled my delighted heart cherished the secret and made many a gray day glow with anticipation. I was not used to having things work out for me and this was too good.

My mother had now started correspondence with my mother-to-be in Colombia and things seemed to be straightening themselves out. One big question that my mother couldn't find peace with was my age. Wasn't I just a bit too young to be taking such a trip? Yes, but I wasn't going to tell her that!

I was going to be a Junior in high school though. At least that made it sound better. Time trekked on. January, February, and then we got another letter. Maria's family had moved to another city and Maria had to go home and help. It appeared that her visit would be put off, and perhaps, indefinitely.

I was still invited to go there for the summer and then plans would be made for Maria to visit some other time. Now, what were the new hooks going to be? There certainly were some and they were tough. Now I would have to make the whole trip, including a night alone at Miami, to this far off land. I would have to switch flights and wait for student stand-by. This changed the picture considerably.

My parents knew I was putting my whole heart and soul into going. They never made it sound impossible yet, my built up courage and self-reliance was dwindling fast. The question floated, ever present. One evening my parents came home from a teacher's get-together and called me into their bedroom.

End of note! Was that the end of Colombia? Was Saltillo a consolation prize? Whatever transpired, I became a foreigner in August of 1968.

Capítulo Dos
The *Gringa* Gauntlet

Regardless of how it happened, there I was strolling along the streets of Saltillo, a fantasy unveiling itself in every step. I was enrolled at *Interamericana*, a Spanish Language school for foreigners. I qualified and everything around me was also foreign. The shady boulevard, the feel of my sandals crossing cobblestone streets, the piercing pinks, tangerine oranges, and Caribbean turquoise paints that delineated one house from another. The crawling bougainvillea vines, sculptured bushes, even the bird songs were strangers to me. From *frijoles* for breakfast to dogs that understood more Spanish than I did, I was loving it. Me, two thousand miles away from my midwestern world, sauntering down the streets of Saltillo, soaking it up when . . .

UNIVERSIDAD INTERAMERICANA

. . . I tripped on one of a multitude of cement chunks raised up in the sidewalks by a protruding tree trunk. I recalled *Jefe* telling us to watch our step, but he wasn't talking pot holes and earthquake cracks. "Watch out for Macho Mexican Men," he had warned us.

I recovered my balance and looked up. Mexican guys were leaning on walls, park trees, at bus stops, and standing on corners, arms crossed, scrutinizing each *chica* from top to toe.

Up ahead a group gathered along the outside walls of the *Universidad Interamericana*, checking out the new Monday arrivals. From their lips dripped all array of unintelligible sounds, either whispered, whistled, or recited, as each female gingerly worked her way to the school's entry. At least this gaggle of *gringa* gazers made it easy to locate the *Universidad's* entrance.

Eyes down again, I edged my way toward the university door, when a long sucking sound brought me to an abrupt halt. *"Uuuuuf, apúntamela."* I heard it again. "Uuuuuuuuf. . ."I listened carefully and later repeated it to my tutor.

"Those are called *piropos*," she informed me. We started a list. *Apúntamela* meant: "Mark her down for me." Back home, these were considered to be "cat calls," a negative term for the invasive, creepy comments directed at women. However, in Latin America, *piropos* comprise a genre recorded and published, a vital part of the mother culture.

Being petite, I generally heard: "*¡Qué bonita, mamacita!*" (What a pretty little mama) and "*Chaparrita.*" "*Chaparrita*" was my favorite. It translated to a sweet form of "little woman," including a positive, endearing tone that I gladly accepted as my adjective.

"*¡Cuántas curvas y yo sin frenos!*" ("So many curves and me without brakes!") is fun and translates smoothly. "*Bendito sea el día en que tu madre te dio a luz.* Blessed be the day your mother gave birth to you" includes religion and compliments your mother, the most important person in Mexican lore. *Piropos* are a bittersweet mix of appreciation and invasion of privacy. At fifteen, I was already working on my feminine and feminist personhood. *Piropos* presented a duality. Compliment or crossing of the line? Either way, it was incentive to sharpen my Spanish listening skills and grow my vocabulary. Leaving my house to go anywhere included a gauntlet of guys and their personal *piropos* collection.

LA UNIVERSIDAD INTERAMERICANA
"Those were the days, my friend, we thought they'd never end."
Song by Mary Hopkin, 1969

The sign inside the school entry stated, "*Aquí se habla español*" and if you didn't understand that, the next sign was a warning: *No inglés.* This was, after all, a total immersion school in the heart of Saltillo, Mexico. Students had come from all over the world to improve their cultural and linguistic skills.

After the language level exam, we were given a class schedule and a slip of paper with a name and time. I was to meet Juana at 4:00 p.m. That made us Juana and Juanita. I took this as a good omen. She was my tutor for private conversational practice and help with homework, of which there was an abundance.

It took only one day of classes to realize I was in over my head. Grammar was already into the subjunctive. The idiom class would be memorizing phrases and the vocabulary class? The professor dictated fifty words a day to be put into sentences for the next day's quiz! My notebook soon filled with Juana's handwriting, speeding up our release into the streets.

My Mexican schedule had little in common with my life in the north. Morning classes lasted until 1:00 p.m. Then the Mexican mid-day feast was followed by *siesta* and afternoons with Juana. Nearly every night we gathered at the Roma, a downtown disco. On weekends, I had up to three dates a day. "Those were the days, my friend, we thought they'd never end, we'd sing and dance forever and a day. . ." Yes, *Qué tiempo tan feliz!* What a happy time!

LATE LUNCHES

The Mexican *almuerzo* was at 2:00 p.m., so the desire to eat was strong after a long morning. The school schedule did allow for a *descanso* break, giving us time to buy a snack and a *yogur para beber*. These yogurt drinks even came in chocolate and included acidophilus, an extra dose of amoeba defense. Yet, when I got back home for the midday meal, I was ready for any new dish placed before me from the Fuentes' kitchen. There were steaming lentil soups, stuffed peppers, Spanish rices, exotic fish and fresh, warm tortillas served with the chilled tan-colored *tamarindo* or red *Jamaica* juices. Thus began my lifelong yearning to have a cook.

Almuerzo was followed by another delicious time of day, the *siesta*. *Siestas* were made easy by overall cultural practices. Stores closed. Banks closed. Even the local cathedral shut its doors, despite disgruntled tourists who had "traveled so far" grumbling audibly about the inconvenient closings "just when I got here." These same sort of visitors were likely among those that thought mattresses would be an improvement over hammocks, the natural way to let cool breezes rock you to sleep. When the sun lowered and long shadows stretched down the streets, it was time to go back to school.

TUTOR TIME FIELD TRIP

ROSALBA WITH MY TRAVELING PUPPET, RANA, IN THE MEAT MARKET

The market had sections never found at home. The *carnecería* included entire pigs' heads, which the butcher gleefully held up in front of his face for a photo op. The chickens were fresh. I know because they were in cages until purchased and killed on the spot. The smell of fish led to the *pescadería*, where tiny dried shrimp in bags resided next to ocean white fish, eyes, tail and all, waiting for the *señora* to decide how many kilos before the machete-shaped knife sliced them up, to be wrapped in paper and carried home.

Piñata candy, found in sacks as big as pillow cases, was sold at the *dulcería*. Here I discovered that the small print really mattered. Many bags of suckers, wrapped candies, and gums included the word *enchilada* on the package. This literally translates to "in *chiles*," like Tootsie Roll Pop suckers, only with *chile* inside. This is great if you were brought up on them.

The most intriguing part of the *Mercado* was where *curanderas* shopped. These shamans, healers, and grandmas bought herbs, candles, and packets of powders according to their beliefs. Many remedies date to Aztec times and some have a modern twist, like the packets of powder promising to bring money if sprinkled from head to toe while chanting *dinero*. If sprinkled from foot to head and repeating *amor*, it attracted love. I bought some but never tested them.

There were candles to the *Virgen de Guadalupe*, patron saint of the Americas, and statues of Jesus Malverde, folk saint of Mexican drug dealers. I did not know who they were then, but they were everywhere. The skeletons of the *Santa Muerte*, angel of death, measured up to four feet tall, draped in all manner of trinkets. Loose leaf teas were mixed according to ancient recipes and weighed for sale. The smell of copal incense was the clue to finding this section.

Our two hours together usually included the time of afternoon tropical rains. We'd hop over puddles, run under palm trees, and make our way back to the *Universidad*. "How do you say that?" I remember asking. "*Lodo*," she answered, laughing as we looked at the mud covering our sandals. This is the only word I recall from the hundreds I wrote in the notebook.

We ran for cover inside the *Universidad* and found the other tutors gathering under the umbrella tables in the patio. It was time to meet everyone and make some plans! It was then I noticed the Mexican girls headed home while the boys asked us to go to the disco.

ANA, JUANITA, JERRE, PEPE, & JAN

Capítulo Tres
Mexican Dating "In the Day"

Saltillo, like most cities of Spanish origin, is built around a center plaza with a colonial Catholic church on one end and government buildings on opposing sides. The nearby *Parque Alameda* features flowing fountains, wall-climbing bougainvilleas, brightly tiled benches, and a maze of manicured pathways filled with families gathered on Sundays. Saturday evenings, it was the site of a centuries old courting custom.

This ancient ritual featured young men walking in a circle one way around the plaza while the young ladies promenaded in the opposite direction. Mothers and aunties kept vigil from their wrought-iron benches, watching for that subtle dip of the head toward their daughters. If the *muchacho* made eye-contact with the *señorita* on more than one passing, the *chaperones* might nod approval for him to tap her shoulder. If she accepted, they would meander off together, exploring the plaza in full view or taking a table where he'd invite her to a lemonade. Thus, the days of childhood clique clusters morphed into a potential romance.

The young men were expected to ask permission to proceed with the courtship. When a date was procured, he'd go to the house, meet the parents and usually leave with his date and one of her younger siblings. Children were preferred over aunties because they could be bought off with ice cream cones and told to wait on a bench while the couple made their rounds of the park unsupervised. The tall, groomed hedges and walls of climbing roses provided nooks for all manner of public displays of affection. Teenagers without *chaperones* were supervised by the local *policia*, whose job description included ungluing lip locks with a mere parental "evil eye."

Foreign girls like me arrived in miniskirts, tank tops and newly applied lipsticks without a clue regarding decent Mexican family traditions. The young males, used to their Saturday cruising circles, parental scrutiny, and little brothers tagging along, eagerly anticipated each Monday's influx of new, naïve foreign fruits, ripe for easy pickings. Working as a private tutor at the *Universidad* was the best job in town. It implied good character and a trust factor for the incoming female students, arriving ignorant of Mexican formalities.

I was among the naïve, but soon saw what Juana and her girlfriends put up with every summer. As a Mexican girl, she was painfully aware of the Mexican male migration toward incoming foreign females.

Mi Gran Noche
¿Qué Pasará, qué misterio habrá?
"What will happen, what mystery will there be, on what could be my great night?"
Song by Raphael

By Wednesday I had met Raúl, Pepe, Lucio, Roberto, Ricardo, and Nicolás, all up-standing tutors approved by the university for high standards, or so I supposed. Before leaving school, the tutors corralled us into a planning session for our get-togethers. Usually, we headed for the downtown *discoteca*, the Roma.

Jerre was the only guy from Minnesota, so he became our *angel guardia*/ guardian angel. "Us *chicas*" kept within his range until getting better acquainted with the locals. These Mex-ican guys wrote us poetry, brought roses, sang serenades, and loved to dance. Our resistance was low. The guys up north hadn't prepared us for this barrage of attention. We were cultur-ally and linguistically vulnerable.

The best advice had been, once again, given by my dear *Jefe Supremo*. "If you do not completely understand a question, never say "Sí" and I mean, *nunca, jamás*, never!" Such a simple thing, yet not always possible. How were we to know if we had misunderstood?

When at the disco, Jerre kidded us about bringing along a big dictionary, "To place between you and your dancing partners," he'd say with a wink. However, our favorite tune, "*La Minifalda de Renalda*" (Renalda's Miniskirt), was a bouncy polka tune, impossible for dictionaries. And yes, there were those slow dances. The guys wrapped our hands inside theirs, pressing them gently to their hearts and then softly sang their rendition of English into our ear. That last part was a disaster, but the hand-hold was sweet.

At the Roma, we foreign girls were usually led into the dark dancehall with someone's hand guiding our backs until we got to a table. They'd order us drinks, of which I knew nothing in any language. I was there for the love of being asked to dance every dance. I ordered my Coke, with the occasional drop of rum, a weak *Cuba Libre*. The joke was that there is no such thing as a *Cuba Libre*, because *Cuba Libre* means "Free Cuba" and that was an oxymoron.

One evening I squinted through the burning cigarette smoke searching for Jerre. I discovered him on his third-something-drink-with-tequila just as someone grabbed my hand. In a whish, all of us were dragged out toward the back door. Jerre behind me, his girlfriend, Terry, in front, with Raúl, Pepe, and Nicolás herding us down a dimly lit passage to the street behind. The running stopped a few blocks later at the park.

What the heck? My Spanish wasn't that good, but there was no hint of impending chaos. I had survived on a lot of good faith and trust each evening. Had I said yes to some-thing I hadn't fully understood?

Like the time I accepted that invitation to hike in the vineyards outside of Saltillo, thinking the whole group was going, only to end up alone with Juan. Or the time one of

Lucio's friends took me out to see where they worked and didn't mention Lucio was not coming. Just as fear struck, Lucio swooped in and saved the day. I was incredibly lucky.

We were all lucky again that night. When we caught our breath, Pepe started to laugh and Raúl just shook his head. "The *Policia*!" he panted. "The police raided the disco! They were looking for under-aged foreigners!"

Clearly, that would have been us.

HOMAGE TO JERRE

Each morning the shoe shine boys gathered hoping for our business. Jerre, the free spirit, lined us up and put them to work. When it was my turn, I was unsure that my white sandals warranted a shine. They barely had anything to cover and would get dirty by lunchtime. But, in the spirit of giving these *chicos* work, I put out my foot.

After ten minutes of applying creams, buffing, and a flourish of rags, the *limpiabotas* held up my sandal and grinned, "That will be *dos pesos*."

To my horror, my sandals were now yellow! Before I could react, Jerre chirped, "Where but in Mexico can you get a whole new pair of sandals for just two *pesos*!"

JERRE

In retrospect, Jerre's light-hearted reaction was brilliant. He had modeled the secret to travel and life. It's all about attitude and flexibility.

FOR THREE WEEKS

We ate refried beans every day, three times a day, even breakfast. They were tasty with *huevos rancheros* and fresh mango. We got used to having maids. Maids to cook, clean, fold our clothes, make our beds and lock the door behind us when we went out. We no longer did the chicken thing when we crossed the roads—that business about sticking our necks out, then retracting them, then squawking as we flew back to the curb. Mexicans say foreigners look like chickens when crossing in traffic.

When our time was up we hugged the *muchachos* good-bye and promised to write. I did. They answered. I understood that they missed me. I didn't understand what they wrote to me about the 1968 Olympics. The significance of Tommie Smith and John Carlos, two African American athletes raising their black-glove fists during the US national anthem was overshadowed by the Mexico City massacre in the *Plaza de Tlateloco*. Decades would pass before the truth of the snipers, the army, and the number of civilians gunned down would be released.

Lorraine, Cindy, and I retraced the highways back to Wisconsin just in time for September classes. I couldn't wait. *Jefe* didn't know about my three weeks in Mexico and I wanted to see his face when he did his ritual first day assignment. "Now," he'd say with his twinkling grin, "go to the front of the class and tell us about your summer... in Spanish."

When he called on me, instead of dying a Spanish Inquisition death, I threw my shoulders back, held my head high, walked to the front of the class, took a deep breath, and didn't stop for five minutes. His jaw was riding on his chest and my face hurt from smiling.

My secret was out. *Jefe* knew that I was beginning to *defenderme,* defend myself in Spanish. The four exchange students that year included Mechi, from Peru, and Lucia, from Colombia. My circle of friends embraced them into our birthday parties, school dances, ice skating, and game nights. The principal called on me when he needed translations. Lucia and I overtly wrote notes in study hall hoping some teacher would say, "Now, stand up and read that to everyone!"

I also practiced my newly acquired Spanish by writing regularly to Raúl, Pepe, Nicolás and Lucio. I wanted to go back. I got jobs babysitting and working with a veterinarian. While my friends bought up records, new clothes, and the latest fads, I put my money in the bank. Maybe I could go back in 1970 for my senior graduation present to myself.

Then, a miracle! The next summer, Dad and Mom decided our family camping trip through the Southwest could dip across the border into Saltillo. We'd borrow Lorraine's camper. When we got to the border... they stopped us. But this time, it wasn't because of me.

~ *Puente* ~
1969 – My Family Crosses the Border

According to my mother's travel journal, our family trip of 1969 evolved in an attempt by my father to cover a special place for all of us. His own wish was to go to Arizona and Carlsbad Caverns in New Mexico. Mom shook her head against all the miles of heat and cacti, but I reasoned that would put us close enough to Mexico to cross the border into Saltillo.

My brother, Steven, was totally involved with tropical fish. At age thirteen, he had already procured special permission to work at Michelle's, the neighborhood pet store. If we went to Mexico, we could return via the Texas coast and get some seashore time. At that point, Dad threw in New Orleans, as a carrot for my mother. Time didn't permit such a large loop, so Dad cut out Arizona and it was a plan.

Our usual modus operandi was a car, an umbrella tent, picnics, and hundreds of miles per day. This time, Lorraine offered up her camper, a major camping upgrade. We'd be off the ground, have beds, and be able to eat out of the rain. It was settled.

Each day Mom recorded our stops, where we visited, what we ate, and personal details of family travel. She described treeless campsites, swimming under the starry Texas nights, Dad and Steve's foray into Carlsbad Cavern's nightly bat exit, and the day we got to the border.

35

Capítulo Cuatro
Eagle Pass to Saltillo – Stopped Again!

It was hot and sunny, as only the Tex-Mex border knows how to be. The sun glinted off of the five lines of cars being waved through the checkpoint or, like us, being pulled over to the side. A rather round man in a tan uniform asked Dad to roll down the window so he could look inside the car allowing more hot air into our un-air-conditioned vehicle.

"What does he want?" Mom asked me, the resident Spanish speaker. "Something about papers for the camper. He wants Dad to get out of the car," I guessed, then sat back, wondering if I should get out, too.

As Mom remembers it, Dad did not want to involve me. He was adamant, for reasons he alone knew. This marital disagreement added to the heat felt in the car's interior.

Fifty years later, rereading this passage in her travel journal, she leaned in toward me and spouted, "Why couldn't my stubborn German Kurtz husband just let you do some translating?" Then, throwing her hands into the air, she continued, "Why did he have to pull the 'Father Knows Best' bit?" Her voice rose, memories returning, fresh, clear, and surprisingly raw.

Personally, I remember getting hotter, waiting helplessly next to Steven, who stared out his window toward the Customs station. The official took his time under the blazing sun. He motioned for Dad to open the camper. He looked inside, right and left. He stuck a billy club into some crevices, poked the mattresses, scratched his chin and tweaked the end of his moustache.

From the backseat of our steaming car, I could only wonder what it could be this time and hoped that my dad held his tired temper.

At some point, I was out of the car, following my father, who was following the official. Once again, I found myself in an office, waiting to enter Mexico. Once again I was thinking about everything my teacher, Haaky, *el Jefe Supremo*, had taught me about Mexican culture. Does this guy need something or want something?

I listened to what he was telling Dad. No progress. Hoping my dad would forgive me for breaking the Bible commandment about obeying one's father, I blurted out, "*¿Qué necesita usted?* What do you need?" Then, hoping my three years of Spanish were serving me correctly, I translated his answer, "He wants to know why we don't have a license for the camper."

"In Wisconsin it's not required for vehicles under twelve hundred pounds," my dad responded.

"You'll need one here or a document proving what you say," the official countered. Then he detailed how to get to the Chamber of Commerce office to obtain a notarized statement verifying that claim.

Déjà vu. Last year, Lorraine, Cindy and I were turned away at the Laredo crossing because I did not have a permission letter from my parents to cross. Now it was the camper! As Dad and I returned to the car with this unpleasant news, we ran across the man who had sold us the Mexican car insurance for our four days south of the border. After a short explanation, the salesman took care of the notarized paperwork, relieving us of the trip back downtown.

The border official was not pleased. He shook his head, scratched his chin, and frowned. According to him, the document wasn't official if not from the Chamber. He hedged.

My sixteen years of life experiences had not prepared my brain for this new terrain. I was now out-of-body, observing this scene from somewhere up in the ceiling corner looking down on two men. Their voices faded into background noise as my mind rushed around looking for an out. At that moment in time, the Border Patrol uniform effectively made the big, round Mexican, the boss.

Still floating over the scene, it came to me. What if we pay this guy a *mordida*? Of course! He is waiting for the cultural greasing of the palm. All of this fluff about the license might be a stall! I bet $10 would clear this up fast. Or would it take $20?

But alas, what if this guy was an honest cop? I again recalled *Jefe's* caution. Would my suggestion land Dad in a Mexican jail? *El Jefe* had described those in some detailed horror to make sure none of us would ever do anything landing us there. It was certain death by stale *tortillas* and *cucarachas*.

I took a deep breath and pulled on Dad's sleeve. He leaned down. I whispered in his ear. "Give him a ten. Just put it slowly on the desk and wait."

He did. I held my breath. The ceiling fan slowly rotated, shedding revolving shadows over our waiting. We stood there. My dad and me, accomplices. The patrol's eyes swept across the desk. He stood up. He showed us to the door.

Dad and I return outside to the blazing sun. We get in the car. He waves us through. He turns to the next car behind us. Dad eases on the gas. We don't look back. We breathe.

Meanwhile, back in the car...

Mom wrote: Thursday, June 12, 1969

> While Steve and I waited at Customs, we saw a terrifying near-accident. Some man came roaring down the street in his car and nearly ran over a mother and her two children. It was the narrowest escape I've ever seen and Steve and I were both badly shaken just witnessing it. Nobody seemed to stop at the stop signs or have any regard for traffic regulations. From that point on, all of us (except Janet) were in a state of tension for our own safety. As we left Eagle Pass, it was frightening to drive because the houses were built right out to the street. Children and animals seemed to dart out of nowhere, as well as other cars. When we finally got out of the city, it was a little better, but so hot!

The terrain between the border and Saltillo is desolate. If you like cactus-covered mountains, heat, and miles of miles, you might have a different adjective. The up side of these long stretches can only be put in perspective if you've driven the congested, chaotic traffic of large cities. Pulling a camper through towns clogged with honking taxis, braying burros, and darting pedestrians exacerbates the situation. On a good day, my father hated driving a small car through cities of over 40,000. I look back on this portion of our family trip as the ultimate act of fatherly love. Oh, and motherly love, too!

Mom's journal continued:

> The landscape was more of the same—cactus and dry land. Only it got hotter and hotter. The houses along the way were mere hovels made of clay. They had windows and doorways cut out, but no glass or doors in them. Steve was all for getting back to the U.S. and so were the rest of us, except for Janet. I felt sorry for her as it was a grueling emotional experience for her to endure the tensions of customs and the cutting remarks of her family. All this was a far cry from her "beloved Mexico" of last summer.
>
> The trip from Eagle Pass to Saltillo seemed never-ending. We couldn't travel fast because of the heat and fear of hitting animals or people along the road. Finally, we arrived in Saltillo about 7:30 p.m. We wound up at the Huizache Motel, a lovely place consisting of a series of apartments and carports ringing a city block with a beautiful inner courtyard and swimming pool. Our apartment has two large bedrooms, a kitchen, bathroom and center hallway—all for $10 per night. It's part of the older section which is two stories high and has white iron balconies. All the windows have grille work on them. We met the family next door. They were from Missouri and plan to spend 2 1/2 weeks in Mexico. Around 10:00 p.m., we went to the motel restaurant for sandwiches, but Janet and the girl next door went swimming instead.

MOM, STEVE, & JAN IN HOTEL
KITCHEN

Even I was relieved when Dad parked the camper in the back lot of the Huizache Hotel. It would stay there while we roomed in this cozy family lodging with pool. We were all convinced that driving as little as possible would improve our chances of survival. Time to teach them about taxis.

TAXI TIME

Taxis rival carnival rides. They go fast, stop quickly, may or may not have a working clutch, and come with protective religious icons dangling from the rearview mirrors. You simply stand on the curb, or a few feet into the street if you are desperate, raise your arm and make a sort of peace sign when the taxi comes into view. If their light is on, it is occupied. Step back quickly.

There are many taxis available in the busy areas of town. If you want to be safe and sure of car and driver, you call an official company and they will come promptly. Promptly is not a Mexican trait, but for public transportation, it does happen.

Mom and Steve were the first to venture out with me. I hailed a taxi from the corner, asked the driver what he charged to get to the Municipal Market, and in we went.

"Now," I said to Mom, "you need to make sure they put on their meter so you don't get overcharged." I felt so worldly.

We settled in back and he screeched into traffic. Mom grabbed my forearm. He raced into a little crack that opened up between the cars. He zigged while other cars zagged. "Is this man trying to kill us?" Mom squealed, tightening her grip. We wove in and out of lanes. There was honking involved. "Don't they have any traffic laws in this country? Is he drunk? Insane?" He pumped the brakes. "Are we going to get out of this alive?" she gasped, as she completely cut off all circulation to my arm. Steve clung to his door's handle. The statue of *La Virgen*-of-Something-or-other swung wildly back and forth from the rearview mirror, which he used to glance at us. Was he grinning?

Mom's journal record of this ride ended in two words: "Terrifying nightmare!"

Her nightmare was my dream come true. This was Saltillo! I was back! There was the market, just as I had left it. I could stop trying to explain everything to my family because they were here, with me, in the taxi! Only when it came to a full stop did Mom release my arm and her breath. I counted out my *pesos* and stepped into this world I thought I had left forever when I said good-bye last August.

My heart drank in the scene. A large man grasped his huge bouquet of brightly colored helium balloons floating for sale above the businessmen seated in front of kneeling shoe shine boys. A flow of humanity moved between cold *licuado* tropical fruit drink stands, *elote* on a stick, (boiled corn smothered in melting butter and sprinkled with red chile pepper,) the pink cotton candy, and the news boys hawking the Daily *Prensa*.

I looked back into the taxi and saw Mom and Steven frozen in their places. I reached for Mom's hand. Steven was still clinging to the far-side door handle.

"Come on," I coaxed them. "This is going to be fun!"

THE MARKETS

Describing a market is, at best, a one dimensional effort in a multisensory world— the clamor of vendors, the pushing of people, the smells. The fish market blending with the dangling cow carcass, its blood being washed down the middle of the aisle by a young man in his once-white apron, now marked with red handprints. Mickey Mouse *piñatas* dangling overhead with a collection of bulgy-eyed clowns, traditional stars, and big bananas waiting to be picked for a birthday party. On one side, mountains of dark *moles*, that mixture of chocolate and chiles used in chicken recipes. On the other, pyramids of oranges, tomatoes, mangos, and papayas reaching for the sky. "Follow me," I yelled out, looking over my shoulder to see where my mom and brother were.

They were not immediately enamored. "Are we going to buy our groceries here?" Mom wrinkled her nose. "No, we'll find a supermarket, just like home. I don't know enough about buying in kilos to trust myself," I assured her. "I'm not sure if the food prices are fixed, but either way, I can't do the math conversion, much less in another language."

I led them out of the daily clamor and into the touristy section. The difference here is the vendors follow you out of their shops, reducing their asking prices the farther away you go. Being pursued did not increase Mom's and Steve's comfort level. Acclimation comes at a personal, private pace. I needed to slow down and let them explore. It worked.

Mom began looking at some trinkets and followed her curiosity into a vendor's stall. A smiley, big-bosomed woman sat inside on a stack of *sarapes*, watching a tiny television. She lifted her eyes from her *telenovela* and greeted my mother with a, "*Buenos días, señora.*" To which my mom replied, "*Bonjour,*" then looked at me. "Why does that happen? Why does French always come out?" Then, she turned to the woman and tried again, "*Buenos días, señora.*"

The flood gates opened. With smiles, touching fabrics, nodding over colors, and writing down prices on her sheet of paper, the anxiety evaporated into exclamations. "These people are nice! They are very patient and helpful. Let's go see what they have over there."

The shopping spree was cut short by hunger. "What is that being grilled on the spit," they asked. "*Cabrito*/goat. They slice off enough to put in the hot *tortillas* she is taking off the *comal*, that flattened pan set over the fire," I explained. Our stomachs growled.

"I know this all smells great," I said, "but Haaky warned never to eat the food in a market. Our gringo tummies just can't compete with south-of-the-border amoebas. Markets don't have the hygiene standards of the restaurants. We can find a place where locals eat or go to a *supermercado* and take food back to the Huizache." Mom voted for that option.

After grocery shopping, our second taxi returned us to our hotel via those narrow streets that force pedestrians to step into door sills when cars pass by. He ignored stop signs and honked his way through intersections. When the *taxista* parked at the Huizache, Steve bolted for our *casita*. He went straight into the bathroom, locked the door and swore he was not coming out until it was time to leave this country!

Dad looked at the closed door and back at us, arriving with our packages and food. Regardless of what had transpired while he was napping, there was no way Steven would, even if he could, spend three days locked in a bathroom. With this, Dad turned his attention to us, now dropping our bundles onto the beds. He finally looked at me and whispered, "What happened?"

"Taxis," I whispered back, then started pulling my treasures out of their sacks.

"Look," Mom said, pointing to her new blanket. "The vendor told me that the blankets woven with the red, white, and green stripes of the Mexican flag are Saltillo's signature *sarapes*."

I was busy taking my two Aztec onyx bookends out of their nest of newspapers, pausing to read the sexy movie ads. "We have to go back, Dad. They have onyx chess sets in all sizes. I think you should get one." The bathroom door opened a crack and Steve's nose peeked out.

"It was different to bargain," Mom chimed in. "Different, but fun. It made me feel like I was getting a good deal. I finally figured out the *peso* to dollar amounts. I'd go again!"

"There is a place in town where they do glass-blowing demonstrations. It's where I bought the wine decanter and glasses last year. Would you be interested?" I asked, vaguely aware that the bathroom door was opening.

Then there was Steven, headed out of his self-imposed exile toward a box on the floor. "I want to show you what I bought," he announced to Dad, who was pleased that no other parenting beyond patience had been necessary.

The New Fangled Camera

The next day we got to see Dad's Texas purchase, a new-fangled technology called a Polaroid. This camera would develop our pictures within minutes, right there in our hand. We wouldn't have to wait for weeks to know if we had gotten the shot! We'd try it out at what the tourist brochure touted as "the best view of the city," from atop the old *Fábrica de Sarapes*.

Mom wrote: Friday, June 13, 1969

We went to a fabulous Shop with a serape factory in the back. Before I had nearly enough time to browse, we were conducted on a tour through the factory. It was very interesting. All the workers are paid by the piece. The guide did the dye work. The workers who made the serapes were men. Their designs were lovely. They worked with fantastic speed. The workers who tied off the ends were women. The guide took us to the rooftop for a view of the city. He pointed out sixteen Catholic churches and five Protestant churches. He was a very nice man and tried hard to communicate in both Spanish and English.

I recall watching two ancient men tossing their loom shuttles back and forth between the threads, playing the feet pedals like a pump organ. Geometric designs emerged along with donkeys or quetzal birds. Then up the stairs we went to the roof with the advertised promise of the best panoramic view of Saltillo.

Mountains embraced the brown adobe city. In the distance, we could make out the Rio de Janeiro styled *Cristo* statue on a far mountain peak. The red-tiled roofs spread out over the valley and climbed into the *Sierra Madre Oriental* mountain range. Dad held up the camera for our first shot. He placed us with the mountains behind and said the mandatory Mexican, "Whiskey—pronounced, wee – ski," producing the expected sappy smiles as he clicked. We circled around the camera for the countdown. Dad pealed back the paper and . . . nothing. Another shot. All black. Again. Black.

Disbelief. Disappointment. Disheartened. Later that day, the local camera store informed us the shutter had a malfunction. Mom wistfully noted in her journal, "It would have been a nice picture."

Capítulo Cinco
La Familia Mexicana más Mis Amigos

Having my family meet Raúl, Pepe, Lucio, and my Mexican family, the Fuentes, was beyond my dare-to-dream list. Yet it was happening! They were all here, just like we had planned in our letters. With their guidance, we took the car back into the streets. They yelled out simultaneous directions while I used my knowledge from last year to sort out the *derechos* (go straight) from the *derechas* (go right), hoping Dad was watching the stoplights. Steve's two years of Spanish were kicking in, giving him a sense of autonomy over his situation.

Mom wrote: June 14, 1969

> Awoke at 7:00 a.m. Had breakfast. Then, Don took Steve and I to the market. We had a great time shopping; Steve really got good in bargaining and was very useful with his Spanish. He bought a sombrero, bongo drums, small serape, ash tray, salt and peppers. I bought a large pottery jar, small pottery jar, onyx book ends and two plates.
>
> Don, Janet and Raúl went to Raúl's friend's house to see his collection of Indian relics. He was a young man and had a fabulous collection. His father was a professor and had worked with the National Geographic Society on archeological expeditions.
>
> After lunch, we took a taxi to the Fuentes' home. It's a beautiful new structure across the street from the hospital where Dr. Fuentes works. Carmen was very friendly and spoke excellent English. Mary, from St. Paul, who rooms there, joined us in the living room. We were served tacos and Cokes.

REALLY—TAKE IT!

It was at Carmen's that Mom stumbled onto a generous Mexican custom behind the *mi casa es tu casa* saying. Carmen gave a tour of her year-old home, with the patio's burbling fountains, the glazed black marble floors, the gold fixtures, and the maid's quarters. This surpassed anywhere we would ever live and Mom took in every detail.

43

CARMEN WITH MY FAMILY BY HER HOUSE

"Look at the dining room chairs," she pointed out. "They don't tuck them under the table like we do. They are sideways. You come in, sit down and slide under. What a great idea! Why don't we do it that way? We could learn something."

She followed Carmen from room to room, complimenting her on her taste and floor plan until they finally came to a handcrafted clay water pitcher, painted with white daisies.

"That is such a beautiful piece!" Mom exclaimed, noting that daisies have such simple elegance.

"It is yours," Carmen said, taking it off of its shelf. "Please, take it as a gift from my house to yours."

Mom was horrified to think her compliment had landed her a gift. I expect she answered something like, "Oh no, but I couldn't. No, really, I couldn't." But it was hopeless. Carmen insisted and oh, yes, she could accept the offer. Thank heaven Mom didn't compliment Carmen on the patio's tiled fountain! As for the pitcher, it still resides on my kitchen shelf.

MOTIVATED TO SPEAK

After bargaining at the market and getting to know some of the "locals," cultural barriers dissolved. The first harrowing moments of "those crazy drivers" gave way to jumping into taxis. The market, with its overwhelming sights and smells, became a destination. My amigos, "the boys," that brought the heart of Mexico to me, now warmed the hearts of my family. My parents accepted my comings and goings in this culture with less trepidation.

Mom's June 13th afternoon's entry continues:

> From there (the Serape Shop), we finally got to the market place. I bought a green pottery jar, Steve got little onyx bookends and Don got a billfold. We 'lost' Janet and the boys temporarily when they went ahead. . . but we soon got together again. Then, we took the three boys home and went back to the hotel.
> Janet left early because she had a date with Raúl to go to the Interamericana University dance. I went to bed immediately after supper. All of us were exhausted—except Janet, who got in at 2:00 a.m. She reported a good time with good music, dancing, etc. We missed something good, but that's O.K.

My family's next step? Communicate without me translating.

Mom wrote: June 14, 1969

It was 7:00 p.m. till we got home. Janet was expecting Pepe soon, so she didn't go to the motel restaurant with us. When we were almost finished, Lucio walked in. We sat and talked a long time using his limited English, Don and Steve's limited Spanish, sign language and drawing pictures on the napkins. He went with us to our motel and visited until 10:00 p.m. He's truly funny and a fascinating fellow.

The hieroglyphic napkin pictures survive to this day in Mom's scrapbook.

OUR SUNDAY DRIVE

On this occasion, I was available for translation but we got lost anyway. Raúl and Pepe showed up for a promised excursion outside the city limits to a favored destination for Sunday picnics. I translated directions to Dad as Raúl and Pepe tried to remember the route between bouts of guitar playing and continuous singing.

RAÚL AND PEPE LEANING ON DAD'S CAR

Mom described it this way: June 15, 1969

This was the day of our picnic in the mountains. Raúl and Pepe had volunteered to take us to a spot where there was a nice stream and caves to explore. That whole day was somewhat jinxed. We had to move from our apartment to another. . .the weather had apparently, been hotter than usual and there had been a run on the ice market. We gave up and headed out.

45

Raúl had brought his guitar, so the two boys serenaded us with Spanish songs as we drove along. All of this was most enjoyable until we had driven over 60 miles and still weren't there!

Finally, we stopped and Raúl asked a fellow along the highway where the place was. We had passed it about 40 miles back! This gave us some understanding of another difference in the way many Mexican live from what Americans do. Their concept of time and space appears to be less accurate than ours for at least two reasons. First, they live in a more leisurely fashion which doesn't seem to be dictated by the clock. And second, many of the Mexicans depend upon buses and taxis for their transportation. They aren't nearly as aware of mileage as someone who drives his own car. Of course, the boys were very chagrined and remorseful about the whole thing. Raúl assured us that in Mexico, they always shoot people for things like that.

When we arrived, many Mexican families were there having fun just as Americans might do on a Sunday afternoon. The main difference was that there was a large flock of goats which browsed at will and sometimes interrupted lunch-time for the picnickers.

Mom generously concluded: "At least, we saw more of Mexico than we had expected."

FAST FORWARD TO 2019 – WHAT WAS THAT SONG?

While reviewing her journal, Mom and I compared our mutual stories. "Don't you remember?" she asked me, incredulous. "How could you not remember that they sang the same song over and over? It was popular in the U.S. and Mexico. You must remember," she insisted.

"Was it "Louie, Louie?" I hummed a few bars.

"No."

"*La Bamba.... Para bailar la bamba se necesita un poco de gracia. . .*"

"No."

"*La Cucaracha*?" I sang out the whole first verse.

"No" she said, exasperated. "They sang and sang. Raúl played guitar. We just kept driving. I figured it was a "Mexican culture thing," you know, like time. It just passes. They don't arrive on time, what's that called?"

"You mean *la hora latina?*" I surmised.

"Well, when Raúl realized we had traveled way past our turn-off, he gave me a serious look and said, 'They kill people for less here in Mexico.' Remember?"

"No, but he might not have been kidding," I noted.

She knit her eyebrows and tilted her head, so I explained, "He said this only eight months after the October 1968 *Tlateloco* massacre. There was a pre-Olympics demonstration meant to call the world's attention to the oppressive Mexican government. The military and police of Mexico City swept into the *Plaza de Tres Culturas* to crack down on protestors and shot hundreds of them, many university students the same age as Raúl. They still haven't agreed on the number of dead, rumored to be much higher than the official three to four hundred."

On that note, we paused. I searched the web for popular tunes of the 1960s. The illusive song remained a mystery until the following week.

I was back at my house, listening to my Sandpiper's Spanish album from that era, delighted how the lyrics returned to me. While singing along to *Guantanamera*, the phone rang.

Without so much as a polite hello, Mom shouted into the phone, "I know it!"

"Know what?" I asked, totally lost.

"The song!" she said, with a tone of having won the lottery. "I am listening to a Latino music show on public radio. Listen," she commanded and began to hum.

I couldn't believe my ears. Mom was humming the same tune I was, in that very moment, singing with my stereo.

"*Guantanamera*!" I exclaimed, still amazed at the improbability of what just happened. "Hold on a minute, Mom. I'll put on my record and you see if it's the same one."

"That's the one, *Guantanamera*," she reaffirmed. "They played it over and over. Mystery solved!

But Raúl's 1969 remark about "killing people for less (than that) in Mexico" remains a mystery. On that summer day, I was sixteen, rolling down some highway outside of Saltillo, apparently singing *Guantanamera* with my friends. Politics had not yet entered my life. In a few short years, that would change forever.

BACK TO 1969

Mom wrote:

> At 3:30, we went to the pool and eventually, Lucio came. The boys took turns playing the guitar and singing. After a while, a soccer game started involving three other young fellows. They were excellent players. Don played, too. If this had been in the States, the gardener would have been upset, seeing these boys run through the flowers and tear up his work. Here, the gardener cheered them on! They retrieved the ball from rooftops and, when it went into the pool, Steve jumped in. At 7:00 p.m., we came back to our rooms for re-packing. Janet, Pepe and Raúl were going out for a walk at 9:00 p.m., but Raúl didn't come till 10:20. He was loaded with

gifts for us: A sombrero for Steve, records for Don and Janet, bull horns for me. I was surprised at the selection until I recalled that it used to be a custom for the bullfighter to present the horns of the bull he had conquered to his "lady fair," so I decided this was an honor after all. The best we could do in return (which was not expected of us) was to give each of the boys either a compass or a flashlight. Lucio had been lost in the mountains for 8 days, so he definitely wanted a compass. We sat around the kitchen table and talked while we had a late supper. Janet went out again and returned at 1:00 a.m.

That night, Raúl took me to a dance at the *Interamericana* school. Maybe we met up with Pepe or Nicolás, as it was my last night in town. Maybe he held my hand on the way home. I don't remember. The walk from *Interamericana* to the *Hotel Huizache* wound through Alameda Park, past the manmade lake with its fountains. Street lights shimmered over the tiny waves made by the lovers rowing in rented boats. Music wafted out into the downtown streets from bars and night clubs. One of the songs cried out by a hired mariachi wailed, "*Volver, Volver. . . a tus brazos otra vez.* Oh, to return to your arms again." I had never been in love, but their notes clearly portrayed heart wrenching pain.

It was better for me, this custom of group dating. Raúl, Pepe, and Nicolás accompanied me all over, sometimes alone, but mostly together. Lucio was not part of the clique, showing up whenever he wanted to practice English or have a few laughs. I was just glad that my family had now met them and experienced this other life I had so unsuccessfully attempted to describe—a life so contrary to almost everything we knew.

At sixteen, I was skipping along my life's path, oblivious to its leading me into my future. It never occurred to me that it was also changing my mother's world view.

At the end of her first full day in Mexico she had written:

> Once I was safely in bed that night, some of the humorous side of the day's events struck me. It occurred to me that our first reactions to Mexico —"the land and its people"—would make a hilarious comedy in the hands of a gifted scenario writer. Here we were: a family of four from a background of respect for law and order, conscious of the use of time and money, products of a Protestant religious heritage and a Republican political heritage, in a setting where all these values were nullified by another way of life.
>
> Now I knew what it felt like to be a foreigner!

On her last night in Saltillo she observed:

> As we said our good-byes to each of these three boys that night, we realized that they had "made" our stay in Mexico. They showed us the good side of their people, the side that the tourists just passing through probably never see. They redeemed their countrymen in our eyes. I hope we did as well for ours.

Monday, June 16, 1969, we left at that mystical hour just before dawn. A veil of light crawled over the mountains bringing the road before us into view. Saltillo slept in our rearview mirror. Just like that it was over. Eyes closed, I curled up in the back seat, reliving the scenes of my recent past while my brother looked ahead to his future on the beaches of Galveston.

~ *Puente* ~
Determined to Return

During my senior year, most of my high school friends were buying Beatles albums and trying on the latest bell-bottoms while I saved my money. Babysitting was not lucrative at fifty cents an hour, regardless of family size. The job description ranged from diaper changing, dish-washing, and in the case of one family, singing "Tiny Bubbles" to their kids at bedtime. I went to the school counselor and was told to look at their jobs card file.

There was a position open at a veterinary clinic within bike-riding distance. With all that diaper changing, I was qualified to clean kennels. It was an after-school job that grew to include Saturday mornings. It ended up requiring a harder heart than I had.

The kennels were mostly filled with dogs brought by the dog catcher, the street strays. They had one week to be claimed, adopted, or euthanized, that "polite" word for being killed. My duties included releasing them to outside runs, replacing all newspapers, mopping the floor, feeding them, and getting them back inside. If a particularly rowdy, wary or uncontrollable dog was boarding, the veterinarian gave me a heads up. Except for the Sunday the Great Dane got loose and greeted me by pouncing his paws on my shoulders and drooling on my head. I continue to prefer lap dogs.

All Saturdays included the killing needle. On that day, I was elevated to office duty, complete with white nurse's cap. We closed at noon after the paying patients left and turned ourselves to the task of euthanasia. After work, I cried. I learned to grit my jaw and close my mind, a protective tool I used later in life. I was saving for Saltillo and questioning if the "means justified the end."

South of the border, Raúl, Pepe, Nicolás, and Lucio helped me with my Spanish via the letters they sent regularly. I read them with my dictionary in hand. I verified verb tenses in my AMSCO workbook. I double-checked my word order. . . noun-adjective is not backwards, it actually makes sense... tell me what you are describing and then describe it!

My bankroll, such as it was, and my confidence in going on my own, grew. I had mostly viewed myself as a naïve, Midwestern, seventeen-year-old protected preacher's kid. My whole life was guarded and scrutinized by an entire congregation. The PK identity didn't exist when I boarded my first airplane, alone in another country, imagining adventure.

I had two things going for me: I successfully completed four years of Spanish and Carmen, my Mexican mother, agreed that I could stay in their downtown apartment right on the Alameda. Mary, now in her third summer with the Fuentes, would be my room-mate. Beda, my maid from 1968, would be sent from the big house to serve us.

The trip was confirmed. I packed only my most modest mini-skirts, a homemade dress (cheaper than store-bought), a notebook, dictionary, camera, and address book. My flight would lay over in Kansas and Texas before landing in Monterrey, Mexico. Getting to Saltillo would have to figure itself out enroute.

That August, Mom, Dad, and Steve drove into the Nicolet National Forest to the cabin of my father's making. I was only six-months-old when my mother first held my chubby little hands and dipped my feet into Lake Julia. This summer was the first in my life I did not head to my beloved north, but flew south instead. This summer no one was holding my hand when I boarded that plane. I was on a mission. My "sauerkraut" persona was developing a flip-side: "salsa!" Two lives for the price of one. Bring it on!

FAMILY CABIN IN NORTH WOODS OF WISCONSIN

DAD ENJOYING THE VIEW FROM THE POINT

6

Capítulo Seis
8 de agosto, 1970

Excerpts from letter written to family on first flight to Mexico, age 17.

Dear People,

I'm at least going to start out with good intentions, so. . . I got on the plane an hour ago and we are now slowing to land in Kansas. Wow! I'm sitting with a wonderful lady from St. Paul going to Mexico City for a seminar. She teaches at St. Catherine's. Name: Mrs. Lennon. Take off was beautiful. Skyline and then clouds—all below us. Breakfast was ham and eggs, biscuit, orange juice and milk served over Mason City, Iowa at 8 o'clock.

This descending is another story. We are falling 25,000 ft. Yep, that's Kansas City below at 8:30. Now I can see the country side. It's green clumps of trees, miles of homes, long highways! I'm sitting by the window in front of the wing and have a pretty good view of things! We are making this landing in three minutes!

I'm beginning to like this mode of travel. The people are friendly and—get this—Mr. Nelson, the Chippewa Falls Spanish teacher is on this flight. Things are happening so fast. Looks like we just fell into a river! I went back and had a nice chat with Mr. Nelson. Get this, he is coming back from Toluca the same day I am so we'll be getting together then. What a funny world!

Back to last night. Jerre and Fernando got me (from bus station). Jerre was a great help (at airport). He knew just where to go and what has to be done once you were there. We stopped for coffee and were early at the gate. You don't even go outside. It's right from the building to the plane.

Now it's 9:10 a.m. I just can't comprehend it. . . the flight, the lift off, everything. On air pollution—planes are bad news. . .

Dallas! We changed crew—got a more reckless driver—and went swooping out of the airport. This was the cocktail flight, but I passed those up for 7-Up. Mr. Nelson and I got off the plane at Dallas and looked around. It's a great airport—air-conditioned. Already things were more Mexican.

Forty minutes later I left Mrs. Lennon and Mr. Nelson to brave it alone.

Things are much better this way. I mean gradual adjustment. With Jerre to start me off, a friend from Chippewa, and now alone. I think I have the hang of it. My Braniff plane is just pulling out now.

On landing there were four huge rabbits running around. I hope some-one is at Monterrey to get me. I'm going to sleep well tonight and wonder how I made it. It's a little boring to think that all I've seen of the territory covered are the insides of a plane and two airports.

I am now seeing some people that I saw before at the Mexicana check-in desk. Well, they just sat down and started talking to me. They don't have reser-vations but they are waiting to go to Monterrey and then, if they make it will continue—to Saltillo. They've heard of the Fuentes but don't know them per-sonally. If my friends don't come for me, maybe I'll be able to go with them.

Oh man, we're on Mexicana now. There should be a ride at Monterrey cuz I met a woman and her daughter who are going to the same school and we shall go together. Now to get through customs. OH, what a lovely day. When I see their familiar faces I might just die—but oh how happy.

The pilot is slapping everyone on the back and the one guy didn't fit in the plane is in the cabin! Imagine! Oh Mom, oh Dad, oh Steve. . . I'm here!

Nicolás, the sweetheart, was at the airport. It didn't take long to get through. The guy at the *aduana* said I had pretty eyes and passed me with-out checking a thing. I'm right across the street from the Instituto, one block from downtown and two blocks from the park. It's the cutest little apartment. We have it nice including sitting room, kitchen, bedroom and bath. It's sweet and lovely. There's just the two of us and a maid. It's fan-tastic. Well, Nicolás is coming in 25 minutes and I have to change clothes and go to the Correo to mail this first.

Love & *Buena Suerte* and Good Times and . . . WOW!

Jan

THIRD TIME'S A CHARM

There it was. The very letter written during the take-offs and landings of my very first plane ride. Grammar got overrun by raw enthusiasm and unabashed awe.

I hadn't remembered that Mr. Nelson, the Chippewa Falls Spanish teacher, was on that same plane. What were the chances? The people I met at the Texas airport reappeared in the streets of Saltillo with open-armed hugs, influencing my fresh emerging world view.

How things have changed! We no longer get to stay with loved ones at the gate until boarding nor wait there to give them hugs on their return. That day, we scurried onto an

Aeromexico plane and witnessed something I would never see again in my life. The plane seats filled around me. No more space. The shoulders of a young man on stand-by slouched, his hopeful eyes glancing between the stewardess and posted wait list. She looked up and motioned him to follow her into the plane. She knocked on the cockpit door and the pilot's head appeared, then nodded yes. The young man entered and reappeared only after we landed in Mexico. That seemed wild even then!

The descent into Monterrey was also wild. The plane lurched and took a few bounces when it hit the tarmac. The wing flaps opened with a swish of air, slowing our speed. One final bump and we were coasting toward our gate. Simultaneously, the whole lot of them applauded. Was that usual? Were they happy to be back in their homeland or relieved that the bouncy approach resulted in a safe landing?

I looked out the tiny window, a teenager on my first flight, now in a foreign country, alone. I was blissfully unaware of anything but proceeding. My ride to Saltillo fell into place when Nicolás showed up and got us bus tickets. How lovely. I smiled at passengers, stewardesses, and customs agents, receiving smiles in kind. Smiling continues to work for me.

How incredible to be a free agent, without school, without expectations, but with a personal maid and my friends. I barely recognized my own life!

THE APARTMENT

My apartment was located on the second floor of what had been an office. The entry led to a waiting area that still had several couches and a desk. Behind that, the stairs led up to our living quarters. There were two bedrooms, a bath, kitchen, eating area and balcony.

Mary was again attending school. Beda, my friend the maid, and I fell into a comfortable routine of mealtimes, outings, and shared activities. The apartment was conveniently located on *Calle Victoria*, a main street within walking distance of the Alameda, school, and the market.

This little apartment belonged to the Fuentes family and became my home for two weeks. They had other students at the "big house" with Beda's cousins covering maid services there. This was the third summer Mary and I lived together in Saltillo. We were practically sisters.

BEDA

Beda, my maid from 1968, had been sent to the downtown apartment to cook and clean for Mary and me. Unlike our first meeting, restricted by unwritten rules between social classes, we were now without supervision. We lived together. Yes, she made the breakfast, but she also sat down and ate meals with us. Yes, she answered the door when the guys showed up, but she stayed to laugh and be teased. Yes, she did our

BEDA

wash, but I helped hang it up. This was a much more comfortable arrangement for me. Plus, she introduced me to her cousins. Finally, some girlfriends!

Beda was in charge of the apartment. Sometimes, Alberto Fuentes Jr. joined us for *almuerzo*. He came downtown often and didn't always have time to get home before his next obligation.

On those days, I remember giant hamburgers instead of the usual Mexican cuisine. Both the Coke and catsup had very different tastes than at home.

Beda lived in the maid's quarters in the "big house" out in

JAN, BEDA & "THE MAIDS"

Barrio San Lorenzo. She worked from breakfast to after supper at the apartment earning $20 a month. As she didn't have a room here, she'd hit the couch for her rare siestas. Then, we'd met on the balcony overlooking Calle Victoria and the *movida*-action on the street.

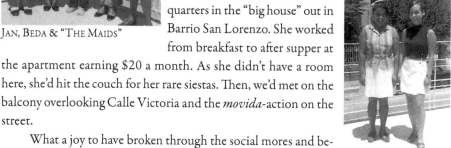

What a joy to have broken through the social mores and become friends. Now we often combed each other's hair, shared stories about "the boys" and her large family.

BEDA AND JAN

LUCIO

The handsome young man at the bus station with Maria, Beda and their cousin is Lucio. Our friendship grew out of his interest in Cindy during the 1968 stay. I was the translator, a loose term for my abilities that first year. Cindy was otherwise taken, but Lucio remained. He was gallant, funny, the artist who drew on napkins for my parents in 1969, an all-around delightful guy, and faithful friend. He made me laugh. How refreshing.

LUCIO

Lucio was a gentleman, inviting me to a gala event, movies, and for walks. While others sought a good-night kiss, he was my solid, go-to *amigo*.

Lucio would show up and be a clown. He enjoyed taking a seat at the reception desk and playing the part of a secretary, client, doctor, but rarely just Lucio. Mary was his frequent side-kick. Sometimes he'd drop his guise and allow his endearing self to show through. Even my mother recalled that side of Lucio.

LUCIO & MARY

I was thrilled whenever he invited me to be part of what I viewed as a Mexican custom, not a date. It was times like this that I had to pinch myself. I danced, laughed, flirted, tasted life. Spanish was exciting. Never at home did I get attention like this! *Gracias* for being a total gentleman, Lucio.

LUCIO & JAN AT PARTY

RAÚL, PEPE, AND NICOLÁS:
THREE MORE GENTLEMEN

RAÚL

PEPE

NICOLÁS

These pictures show the only time that these guys weren't smiling! It seems the days of the old tintypes had not gone away by looking at these 1960's class photos of my three friends. Raúl and Pepe were tutors at *Interamericana*. One of them had been paired up with Jerre Suski, my self-proclaimed chaperone the first year. I never understood how it worked, but I got the perks. Each day, one or more invitations came my way and it didn't seem to matter if the other guys knew. I had been raised to respect one guy at a time, so had to do some self-adjusting. Raúl and Pepe or Raúl and Nicolás were the frequent combinations.

Then my teacher's explanation came back to me. Groups. The Mexicans date in groups, so I was not breaking some social code. I could have three dates a day, divided amongst three friends, and hurt no feelings. In the evening, we usually all went out together. Thus it was that I came to have Raúl, Pepe, and their good friend, Nicolás, come into my life.

For two weeks I floated around Saltillo, comfortable with my Mexican life. The last day, Raúl and Nicolás took me to Monterrey's airport and put me on the plane.

Before I left, I wrote the following, copied here in its original text:

Queridos padres y hermano,   August 1970

The last of my letters I guess. Things have been going fast and furiously. The days are so full and interesting it's hard to believe. I'm trying to keep a diary but I'm only on Sunday and its Tuesday. This morning I went to Lucio's office. Later, Beda and I went to the *chicharo* for groceries and there were taxis on the corner so I hopped in one and went to the *Favorita*, a beautiful *fábrica de sarapes*. It's a friendly little place that offers everything at great prices. I bought a poncho sweater type of deal. It's tan with roses and other decorations. It's hand knit and pure wool, perfect for fall and early winter. I also got some onyx figurines and a little something for the *sala*. I still have to get presents for Doll and Barb, a purse for myself, maybe a record. I'm spending a lot but I figure that's what money is for. I hope you like what I've gotten you. It's been hard to get things for Dad and Steve but they have a lot of things here for women! I'm bringing some candy home. It's really different—fruit—but, good. I might bring some of "Mama's Tortillas" but I'll have to buy a big bag to get everything back home!

Lucio and I might go to his school this afternoon so I'll be taking more pictures. This is the season of the *Pelones*—the "bald ones"—shaved for their first year's initiation at the university. You can see long black hair all over the place. They ought to do that in the States! Lucio wants to go swimming but he's caught quite a cold and had to go to the doctor last night. Yesterday while downtown, I saw the *Señora* I had met in San Antonio and oh was it great. She came running over and gave me a big hug

and started rattling off about everything. She held my hand the whole time and gave me a kiss before she ran to a waiting cab. That's why I love it here. In Eau Claire, we might have nodded recognition, if even that. Here, I let everything happen and it'll turn out O.K. Don't wish the days away. They're too beautiful.

Love, Juanita

RAÚL, JAN AND NICOLÁS AT THE AIRPORT

I boarded that plane, heading to a future that included college. Somewhere. But I wasn't done with Saltillo. I'd be back.

BECQUER STATUE; PARQUE MARIA LUISA, SEVILLA, SPAIN

LOIS, JAN, & MAGGIE

~ *Puente* ~
Making Choices
Seville, Spain, 1972

Hamline University was my final choice. Terry, a friend I met in Mexico, invited me to visit a Spanish class led by her favorite professor, Dr. Barbara Younoszai. We walked into class, took a chair, and waited. I was totally unprepared for the soft, silky Spanish that came like a lullaby through Dr. Barbara's lips. I had come, after all, from three years of *El Jefe Supremo*, Supreme Chief of Memorial High School's Spanish Department. He carried himself with strength, confidence, and spoke with conviction readily available to those of height and bass voices.

I eased myself back and listened. This soft voice was equally confident and self-assured. She answered questions with questions. Verb conjugations purred out over us, unlike the rat-a-tat-tat I was used to. I watched her float from one student to another, bending over shoulders to check workbooks, tapping incorrect answers with her pencil. Her smile lit her face and made her eyes twinkle. That, I recognized from *Señor* Haakenson. She was my new home.

After Spanish, social work was my second interest. It seemed reasonable to combine these two subjects and become a bilingual social worker. Hamline thought it reasonable to assign me a Sociology advisor. This ended quickly. At our first meeting, she reviewed my transcripts, looked up and announced that I had completed my foreign language requirements and need not register for more. Spanish was, in reality, the only thing I was good at. How could she miss my request for a Spanish minor? She was quickly replaced with a Spanish advisor.

In this way, I got a variety of "-ology" classes and a plethora of Spanish literature, Latin American history, linguistics, and phonetics, as well as upper-level language classes. I entered freshman year unaware of Golden Age Literature, the Generation of 1898, the lists of South American dictators backed by U.S. administrations and the *pluscuamperfecto*, yet another verb tense. I was aware that Hamline offered a junior semester or year abroad. I choose a semester. The Spanish option was Seville.

In the fall of 1972, Lois H. and I, buoyed by Dr. Younozsai's soft, encouraging voice in our heads, left for Spain—Lois for the full year and I for one semester, both of us equally naïve as to where this might lead. The future had not occurred to us.

I vaguely recall our families seeing us off at the Minneapolis-St. Paul airport. Jim, my boyfriend of three months, was there. I waved to the assembled and turned toward the plane. We met Maggie, a third girl from Minnesota, while boarding. Her nose wrinkled up and eyes sparkled when she laughed. We hugged.

The next hours are foggy memory clips of darkness, cold, noise and a sense of being thrust out of my comfort zone. It was an unruly night flight due to its passengers, other college students headed abroad, literally tasting their freedom via alcoholic beverages. For long hours I tried to cover myself with a thin airline blanket, wondering what I had gotten myself into.

Capítulo Siete
Madrid in August

Down a narrow street off of the *Puerta del Sol* plaza, a tall, lanky American man stood at the ancient hostel's reception desk holding up keys and calling off our names. Dr. Jerry Johnson, our local advisor/professor and leader of twenty-five college juniors from almost as many states, sent us to our rooms. Before we were allowed to get sleepy, he took us into the streets of Madrid. His first job was to put us through an orientation meant to toughen up the faint-of-heart and avoid homesickness. Activity is the best antidote and he was taking no chances.

Once regrouped outside, he handed out Metro maps and led us into the bowels of Madrid. We paused in front of the Metro ticket vending machine, memorized his steps of putting *pesetas* in this slot and pulling tickets out of that one. We poured down the steep stairs and flowed onto the platform. "Listen up," he yelled over the rumble echoing down the tunnel toward us, "when the train doors open, get in as fast as you can and move out of the way. Everyone needs to have their whole body inside before the doors shut." He paused while visions of trapped appendages flailing outside the train car washed over us. The train screeched to a stop. The doors slid open. We made a dash. We were in.

"Up here," Dr. Johnson said, pointing to the top of the car's wall, "is the route of the line we are riding. Notice the names at the end of the lines. That is how you identify which way you are headed." He continued the lesson, "When it gets to the station where you want off, a slight flick of the door handle will open it. Get off as quickly as you got on, for all the same reasons."

The train swayed around a corner, sending me into my peers. As a person of small stature, reaching the rings above was impossible and the other choice seemed to be snuggling under some stranger's armpit to grab the pole. I choose that over falling into someone's lap.

After transportation, the next most important lesson was acquiring food. Dr. Johnson suggested the *Menú del Día* as the "best plan for our *peseta*." It included several *platos* courses plus bread, house wine, and often dessert for a price beating *a la carte* orders.

"Note that I said house wine, the *tinto de la casa,* not mixed drinks." He looked at each and every one of us. "Cocktails and liquor are very expensive. Wine goes with the main meal here or with *tapas*. Without drinking age enforcement, you may be led into temptation."

He looked at us again. "Steer clear of drinks that involve a lighted fire on top."

We followed him down the *Calle de Alcalá* to the *Plaza de Cibeles*, where a statue of Cibele, Greek goddess of fertility, raced across the waters in her chariot pulled by two larger than life-size lions. Traffic circled the *glorieta*/round-about. Little birdie chirps marked the seconds one had to make it across at the stoplights. "The chirp is designed for the blind," Johnson informed us. It also helped me scurry across when I couldn't see the remaining seconds flashing next to the red lit hand on the pedestrian signal.

There were blind people in the streets, but not necessarily with white canes and red tips. Some wore sandwich boards and yelled out lottery numbers. It was, and still is, their government given right to sell lottery tickets. Another lottery trivia involved pre-pubescent boys singing out the winning numbers daily at noon.

Dr. Johnson's long legs kept the pace moving forward. I scampered to keep up while looking at tall buildings sporting gargoyles, turrets, balconies, and all manner of past-century design. I recognized some of Mexico's post-Aztec architecture. The term "flying buttresses" made us giggle. The image of public hangings in the *Plaza Mayor* made us cringe.

We circled back to the *Puerta del Sol*. "This," Dr. Johnson was saying, "is the exact spot from which all distances are measured in Spain. When you see a sign saying '100 kilometers to Madrid,' it is from there to this circle," he concluded by stepping inside of the emblem marked on the sidewalk. Looking straight ahead, Madrid's iconic coat of arms statue, the *Oso y Madroño*—the Bear and the Fruit tree—sat on its island surrounded by rivers of traffic. "How does a bear figure into the center of this metropolis?" someone asked Dr. Johnson. "Centuries ago, this was the king's hunting ground," he answered, sweeping his arms wide. "This was all forest once."

After a few days of orientation, Dr. Johnson put us on the train to Seville. The *RENFE* took six hours, which gave us some time to reflect on our next phase. The cars swayed and chugged along the track. Clusters of city buildings changed to rolling olive groves and back again. We nodded off with the rhythm of the rails. We crunched on our almond and fig snacks. Stops at various towns unloaded people and products unto platforms. The conductor checked our tickets again. Finally he called out Córdoba. Only one more hour to go.

The train stopped at Seville's *Santa Justa* station. Dr. Johnson gave us a piece of paper with the address of our new home before leading us outside to hail taxis. I was put in the back seat with two other students, Darrell and Jennie. They looked at me. Jennie squeaked in a semi-terrorized voice, "Would you please do the talking?"

I showed the *taxista* our pieces of paper and leaned back between them. The taxi sped through streets, down alleys, and along boulevards with palm trees. People blurred by. We crossed a river. Perhaps this was residential. Tall apartment buildings with small shops on the street level. A market. He took a right and parked. He motioned for Jennie and me to get out. He got our suitcases from the trunk, took our *pesetas* and left us on the curb, waving good-bye to Darrell disappearing around the corner.

"Is this it?" Jennie asked, handing me her slip of paper. "I guess," I replied, shrugging and unfolding my note. We held them together. "Looks like the same street, same building number, different apartments." It seemed that Jennie and I were going to be neighbors. I was as glad and relieved as she was.

LOIS & JAN STUDYING

Capítulo Ocho
September in Seville

MY SCHOOL – *LA FÁBRICA DE TABACOS*

"The *Universidad* has 110 patios," Dr. Johnson informed us. "Try not to get lost." Fortunately, our small troupe of U.S. students was relegated to only a few classrooms, the libraries, (yes, plural), the cafeteria, bathrooms, and Dr. Johnson's office. But first we had to get there. He distributed the *Plano de Sevilla*, a map of the town center, and wished us well.

The residential area where the taxi dropped Jennie and me that first day was *Los Remedios*. The river we crossed was the *Guadalquivir*. Most of us were scattered around that neighborhood, with several exceptions, including Maggie. She lived in *Triana*, the colorful *barrio* noted for gypsies, wild dancing, bullfighters, and a church built for Ana, the mother of Mary. Of course Mary had a mother! As a Protestant, this was news to me.

It was a straight shot from my apartment building to the *Remedios* bridge, down the boulevard past *María Luisa* Park and across the street to *La Fábrica de Tabacos*, best known for the opera *Carmen*. The walk took me about 45 minutes, which I did four times a day.

We walked to school, then home for lunch, then back for afternoon classes. As part of our U.S. university programs, we registered for a full course load taught by Spanish professors in Spanish. Spanish History, Linguistics, and Geography were among the required courses. I added U.S. History as an elective, thinking I might have an advantage. Instead, I was humbled by my lack of a world view, especially where my own country was concerned. Not only did these students develop their perspectives of the United States through a European lens, seeing our foibles, idiosyncrasies, and confusing conflicts of interest from a distance, but they were native speakers. They fluently pronounced their debates and wrote papers with excellent grammar and syntax. I should have signed up for flamenco dancing.

After class, the routine included more walking, this time to the downtown for *tapas*, drinks, and maybe to finish some homework. Tapa-hopping meant walking from one bar to the next seeking out the best fried fish, exotic olives, or tastiest *ensalada rusa,* a sort of potato salad. This cultural activity took several hours, with more sitting than walking. Calculating meandering distances wasn't possible. The time it took was a more accurate measure. At around 9:00, we were home for a light supper of soup, yogurt, or a wedge of potato *tortilla*, not Mexican, but Spanish. Key words: eat and walk.

Key question in Spain? Was I using "Mexican" or "Spanish" Spanish? In Spain, *tortilla* is the culinary term for an omelet, unlike the Mexican flat, corn tortilla. My vocabulary and accent were first honed in Mexico. To this day, Spanish friends "correct" me when my "Mexican" comes out first. *Caminar* or *andar*? (to walk). *Beber* or *tomar*? (to drink). These are like the regional "pop" or "soda" choices in English. As to the accent, it is more a "poh-TAY-toe/poh-TAH-toe" distinction. Be clear on one thing—Spaniards do NOT lisp.

MI CASA NO ES TU CASA

My Spanish mother was not the host mom I expected. That first day, she greeted me with a perfunctory kiss on the cheek, showed me to my room, and said she'd call me for supper. That, as it turned out, would be the totality of our relationship. She kept house for five of us; her husband, Rafael, their toddler son, Rafaelito, and two paying students, of which I was one. She was in the business of renting out her rooms for extra money, period.

For one month, I did the best I could. At first, she did try to find out what foods I liked. She made a great *tortilla* with tiny shrimp, so out of a desire to be helpful and easy, I told her that was my favorite. Later she accused me of costing her too much because shrimp was so expensive. I expected to be part of a Spanish family. What I got was a landlord.

As an entrepreneur, her name was listed as one of many "places with spaces" available when hotels were full. Many Seville housewives made extra cash providing rooms, especially on major holidays. It wasn't uncommon for me to traipse over cots of strangers when crossing the living room to my corner bedroom. On one such night, she introduced me to Bob and Jim, two young, handsome businessmen just in from New York City. I gave them a friendly, Midwestern welcome and asked if they wanted to know anything special about Seville.

"What we need first is a good spot for supper tonight," Bob began. "Do you have any suggestions?" Oh, did I. Every day I walked by places that enticed me, but my student budget stopped me at their entrance.

"There are so many possibilities. Would you like to be on the river or downtown?" I asked, thinking that would narrow the list of options.

"Along the Guadalquivir River," Jim jumped in. "Anything right on the river?"

"The Rio Grande is a lovely looking place right on the banks of the Guadalquivir. I say 'looks' because I haven't actually eaten there. It sure smells great when I walk by," I added. "They have an indoor restaurant, but most people eat on the decks overlooking the water," I told them. "I've watched the rowing teams practice from the *Isabella II* bridge. Across the river is a docking spot for the tourist flamenco showboats. At night the music

63

floats out over all the shoreline restaurants during their two-hour cruise."

"Sounds perfect," they agreed. Then added, "Would you be our guest?"

"Really?" I hesitated. "Are you sure?"

"We need a guide, right Jim? Bob asked him. "You said you haven't eaten there yet. What do you say?"

I said, "Yes."

I informed the *Señora* I would be eating out, put on a nice dress and led my two countrymen onto the streets of Seville. They followed me down *Calle Virgen de Luján* to the river. The lights were just beginning to come on, throwing an eerie glow over the waves left by a fishing boat. Across the bridge, the Seville of centuries was gearing up for another night. On our side, the restaurants were frying fish and slicing *Manchego* cheese.

"I just love this time of evening," I sighed. "Look over there," I pointed. "The *Torre de Oro* is all lit up. There used to be two of them, one on either side of the river. In Columbus' time there was a huge, I mean gargantuan chain between the two, stopping all ships arriving from the Americas. They did an inventory of incoming treasures there. At least that is what they told me. All sorts of fifteenth century journals and papers are still saved at the Archives of the Indies by the cathedral over there," I now pointed at the spires rising into the spotlight beams. "It's the third largest cathedral in the world. Worth the visit."

In the early evening, the ambience changes from people on a mission scooting by to a lazy flow of friends finding a place with aromatic *tapas* and a favorite wine. Jim and Bob wanted to sample the *pescadito frito*, fried fish, and local sherries. We dipped into a side-street bar filled with Moorish geometric tiles and boisterous Spaniards out-shouting each other.

"What are they yelling about?" Jim asked. "Are they fighting?"

"That's called gesturing," I laughed. "They are disagreeing on something that happened in a soccer game."

Bob and Jim decided to split a *ración*-serving of *bocarones*, fried anchovies. "Aren't you joining us?" Bob asked.

"I have to save room for the real meal," I explained as I watched them finish their wine.

We returned to the street and continued toward *Triana* along the palm-lined promenade. The streets filled. Some bars were overflowing. Customers spilled out onto the sidewalks.

"How much farther?" Jim asked, as we edged around the crowd.

"About five minutes to the place I suggested. If you look in and don't like it, we'll go along *Calle Betis* to the end and stick our heads in at the other places along the way. You can read the *Menú del Día* signs propped in their windows to check the specialties and prices before going in. Less embarrassing than if you get in and can't afford it," I concluded.

"Well, we probably have more money than time," Bob commented. "Let's just go for the Rio Grande."

We crossed the street at the *Plaza de Cuba* and saw the Rio Grande sign flashing.

"There it is," I said, "The *Menú* plaque is by that gate, in case you want to have a look."

Without a glance at the *Menú*, they walked straight to the maître d and indicated a table on the riverside of the open deck would be good. By now, the night sky was black, spattered with twinkling stars. The river was a glitter of reflected lamp lights. The slow moving current carried two tourist flamenco showboats full of hand-clapping, boot stomping, skirt swirling gypsies past our deck, filling the air with heart-wrenching chords.

"Cuando paso por el puente, Triana, contigo vida mía con mirarte solamente, Triana me muero de alegría... Triana y olé!"

"What are they saying," Bob nudged me.

"Oh, that is so difficult," I shrank back. "All I can catch between their Andaluz accent and spreading one word over an entire octave is patchy. To me, it is a love song to this place. To Triana. The *faroles*/lamp lights, the bridge, the gypsies singing, an old woman vendor calling out her wares along the street. Something about *buñuelos.* Maybe she's selling bread."

The bilingual menu helped me escape any more translations. I waited for them to choose before gauging what the budget range might be. They ordered high-end sea foods and a bottle of good wine, or so they said. I didn't know. I only drank house wines mixed with spritzers, not the thing to request at this fancy place.

"Don't you drink?" Jim asked me when he ordered their bottle. "We're in Spain, after all."

"I'm fine with my glass of sparkling water," I assured him, "as long as it doesn't come from the river! I don't think they even swim here."

Their conversation grew louder with each course and its companion beverage. I began to look at my watch. I had class in the morning. As a non-drinker, I could only guess their limits. At least they were paying. It was a fifteen-minute walk back to the apartment. It was getting late. I could feel it. It was time to leave.

The night river breezes refreshed us. I pointed out the *Plaza de Cuba*, now ablaze in street lamps. I kept to the populated pedestrian paths at this hour. The floating flamenco cruise boat headed to its dock. I picked up my pace.

I unlocked the apartment entry to let us in. The *portero*/doorman shot a *mal de ojo*/evil eye, towards Bob and Jim, now swaying after me to the elevator. Geez, what must he be thinking? This doesn't look good.

We squeezed ourselves into the tiny four-person space. The doors closed. Their wine breath drifted down on me. I fidgeted for my keys. The door clanged open. It was good to be free of the elevator and in the hallway.

I unlocked the door to a dark apartment. Everyone was asleep. I hoped *Señora* hadn't put them next to me. Oh, no. They followed me down the narrow hall to the living room. They were in the room next to mine. At their door, Bob leaned into me. "Would you like to join me and Jim in our room for a night cap?"

The voices in my head struggled between Midwestern good-manners and self-preservation. "No," I said firmly, then added, "thank you." I jumped into my room and nearly shut the door in his face. I felt my heart pounding.

Outside my door, they were whispering, hissing between their teeth. Arguing, yet not loud enough to wake the others. I waited on my side of the door. I decided not to dress for bed, but instead, opened and shut some drawers. They moved into their room, that space on the other side of this thin wall.

I turned off the light and held my breath. I crawled under my covers. I couldn't make out what they were saying. Then, the banging began. Fists on my wall. I heard, "Jan, come on over here." A pause and then louder, "Jan!" followed by more thumping on the wall.

I remembered the room key *Señora* kept in my night stand drawer. I hadn't locked my door before. I had to find it. Would it work? I quietly pulled the drawer open and felt around. It was there. The key! I tiptoed to my door and slid my hand around the knob. I found the lock! The hole. I slipped the key in, turned slowly, and heard a clink. The lock slid into place just as the banging arrived at my door.

One of them juggled the door knob. He tried it once, twice. It held. He cursed. My jaw clenched. My fists clenched. My shoulders tightened. I listened. More rattling of the doorknob. Then silence.

I sat on the bed in darkness, covers pulled to my chin. Another jiggle on my door knob, then I heard him step away. Their door creaked open and slid shut. More grumbling. Bed springs creaking. I held my breath. I stayed motionless until soft snoring gurgled from the other side of the wall.

After long hours, morning light returned. I dressed for school, grabbed my backpack, peeked out of my door, and made a dash across the living room, past my breakfast and out the door. I didn't care what they intended last night or if I just had a vivid imagination, but I was done with that hotel house. I went straight to Dr. Johnson's office.

I poured out my story regarding the hotel/*casa* and how my very own countrymen had, in my opinion, tried to break into my room last night. Of all people! I thought I could trust my compatriots. I had offered a helping hand, not an invitation to be abused. Regardless, I needed out of there immediately. Dr. Johnson leaned into his desk and picked up the phone. I watched him dial.

"I found you a home a few blocks from where you are now," Dr. Johnson informed me when he hung up. "There is a fine *Señora*, a widow. She lives with her son, Mario. . . about your age. She rents to three other Spaniards, all students. No tourists!" he added, slapping the desktop. "Mario is coming for you this afternoon. Be ready."

Now all he had to do was call my current *Señora* and tell her I was leaving.

9

Capítulo Nueve
October – *Virgen de Luján* Street

She was furious. I packed my bag through a barrage of insults. When Mario, my new Spanish brother, arrived she nearly threw me out the door at him. He took my large suitcase and I, my carry-on. The street noises did not cover the sound of her wrath. From the balcony, she raised her fists and voice, calling me, among other things, a *puta americana*, an American whore. There I was, walking away with a young man, likely proving her case to all the listening neighbors.

Turning the corner and getting out of her sight was an indescribable relief. Mario looked over sympathetically and walked faster. Soon we entered his building and his elevator. When we got to the 7th floor his mother greeted me warmly and my second life in Seville began.

SPANISH MOM (RAFAELA) AND JAN

Señora Rafaela, as I called her, was rounded, probably in her late 50s, greying hair and a quiet, grandmotherly smile. She led me inside, explaining that I would be in Mario's room and he'd move in with Pascual, a student from Alicante. She assured me there would be no hotel overflow here. Mario introduced me to Chiqui and José Luis, brothers from Puerto de Santa María. I guessed my new brothers were in their early twenties. My twentieth birthday was coming up in November.

"Do you have a boyfriend?" was one of their first inquiries. I took out my one photo of Jim, placed it on my desk, and answered, "Yes." The teasing began almost immediately. They moved from Jim to my Mexican accent. In the days to come, they began calling me *la mimada,* the spoiled one, because *Señora* – Sra. Rafaela made my meals before feeding them. I was unaware of this, thinking that the table for two in the kitchen alcove wasn't a fit for all of us.

There was a large round table in the living room. When it got cold that winter, Rafaela placed a heavy tablecloth on it that

JIM DOTH

reached to the floor. She put an electric heater underneath and we'd sit with the cloth draped over our knees, tucking our hands below for warmth. When she did serve food there, we kept our hands above table, as it was bad manners to have them in our laps. The round table was a great place to converse, play games, watch TV, snack, and, of course, to stay warm. But most of all, it was time for them to tease me with word plays, double meanings and jokes that needed specialized vocabulary and cultural context. In their defense, it was all done in good fun.

LA JAULA

Besides the kitchen, the eating alcove, and the living room, there were four bedrooms, two baths, and a balcony/*terraza*, where Sra. Rafaela kept rows of planters. She spent her days cooking, cleaning, watering her flowers, and knitting on a machine in the living area. Despite the fact that we often spent afternoons together, I never learned much of her story. She never spoke of past nor future. She was a widow. She had a daughter up north, expecting her first child around Christmas. Mario was her son. She liked to knit. I asked if she'd make a short pull-over sweater for me, in part, to help her financially and in part to have a memento from "my Spanish mother." She agreed.

She was a good cook and I was well fed. I became a fan of *café con leche* with a lot of milk and sugar. I drank that and ate my morning *Magdalena*, a sort of Twinkie sans the filling, for breakfast. That had to hold me until the 10:30 break at school, when we went to the cafeteria for a sliver of potato omelet served in a *bolillo*/bun. That was to last us until the 2:00 p.m. *almuerzo*. My time in Mexico had prepared me for this eating schedule.

After this big meal of the day, I headed to my small but adequate bedroom for *siesta*. The walls were covered with Mario's postcards. A single one mattress bed, small desk, metal bookshelf, and chair completed the furnishings. At the end of the narrow space, a single window let in natural lighting. My only personal decoration was Jim's photo. The "boys" made a big scene of bowing to it and asking his permission to enter when they wanted to visit.

My tiny bathroom barely had room for a miniature sink, toilet stool with water tank and chain above on the wall, and narrow shower. *Señora* showed me how to light the hot water heater and was clear about short showers. Shampooing involved turning the water off and saving up for the rinse. If you didn't abide by the natural law of water supply, you simply ended up covered with drying soap. It is a clear case of natural consequences. Cold water or no water.

My move to Sra. Rafaela's changed everything. Her *piso* was a place of laughter, shelter, steaming lentil or chickpea soups and yet she called it *una jaula*, a cage. *"Eres una pajarita en una jaula de lobos,"* she would tell me. "You are a little bird in a cage of wolves." We smiled when she invoked her saying in various tones of voice. There was the scolding tone when the guys ganged up on me. There was the cautionary tone when they wanted something from me. There was the endearing tone when they invited me to go out with them in the evenings. I liked being *La Pajarita*/Little Bird. Gratefully, they never behaved like wolves.

JOSÉ LUIS & MARIO

CHIQUI & JAN

PASCUAL W/ GUITAR

THE *BARRIO DE SANTA CRUZ*

On weekends I ventured off, away from my neighborhood, toward the *Real Alcázar de Sevilla* and the Gardens of Murillo. There was no humanly possible way to ingest all the history hidden under the soft golden sand of the pathways. I was dimly aware of the Roman ruins of Itálica, unearthed outside of Seville, hidden below these streets. Shards of pottery, tiles, and religious icons still showed up with each new construction.

Geometric tiles covered park benches and palace walls, racing along passageways and up to carved Moorish scripts praising Allah. The Mediterranean blues, scorching yellows, and rose red *azulejos* tiles covered the walls, walkways, and splashing fountains of cool, hidden, inner courtyards. Orange trees grew inside the *Patio de los Naranjos* below the *Giralda* and throughout the winding trails of *El Barrio de Santa Cruz*, providing year-round shade and humor. Locals pick out uninformed tourists by their squinty eyes and pursed lips. Not all oranges are for eating. These fruit trees produced marmalade, not fresh juicing oranges.

Massive red and pink bougainvillea thickly climbed up whitewashed and golden painted walls. Black wrought iron balconies reached out close enough for the neighbors to kiss. The whole point of walking through the *barrio* is to lose yourself—literally, go get lost. Each turn presented another photo op, but I had the luxury of having six months. I didn't have to take the picture and hurry off behind a disappearing tour guide.

Walking alone was another luxury. Although I wanted to describe all this to my parents at home, on these walks I didn't have to find adjectives. After getting over the initial feelings of panic at not knowing exactly how to get back out of this maze, I relaxed. There were hole-in-the-wall shops for consumerism and bars for the hungry and thirsty. Bars with tall, dark, wooden counters I could barely see over. Bars with stout men wiping out glasses with white dish cloths and scribbling prices on the countertop with chalk every time a client ordered more. Bars with shiny floorboards creaking or crunching, depending on if it was allowed to discard snail/*caracol* shells there or not. The back walls had long, horizontal mirrors reflecting the patrons, *vino tinto* in their raised hands, making a toast. This was *the Barrio de Santa Cruz* that I loved. The barrio where I returned in the evenings after school with Chiqui, José Luis, Pascual, and Mario.

OUT WITH THE GUYS

In ancient days, the clink of armor and the clang of swords were among the sounds heard here. Christians, Jews, and Moors all passed through these byways leading to their respective mosques, synagogues, and later, the cathedral of Seville. The Alcázar once housed Pedro the Cruel, who is said to have walked these streets in disguise at night, spying on his subjects to detect crime or disloyalties. Carmen, of gypsy Tobacco factory fame, certainly flitted and flirted through here on her way to work. Why not? It was as likely as me, a Midwestern preacher's kid traipsing after four Spaniards from bar to bar, singing and playing music on a Saturday night.

During the day, the palms and sweet smelling myrtle bushes filled with bird song, but at night, it was guitars, lutes, and castanets. This is where Mario, Chiqui, José Luis, and Pascual took me along to the ancient bars and classic hole-in-the walls, playing for *tinto* and *tapas,* bought for them by appreciative bar patrons. Under the moonlight, dancing between shadows, chasing Chiqui's laughter and Pascual's sensual rendition of "The Girl from Ipanema," was an unimaginable dream compared to my protected life in the Midwest. The guys could have left me back at the apartment to languish in homework. But no, when the mood struck, they grabbed their guitars and called out, "*Vámonos*! Let's get going! It's *cachondeo* time. Time to live it up!" And we did.

10

Capítulo Diez
November – On the Road

Classes were interrupted by occasional vacation days. I didn't know what there was to see, but instinctively knew I had to take advantage of these stretches to explore beyond Seville. Students from our group would chat over sangria, discuss destinations, and then fall into travel partnerships. After one such conversation, Marty, a girl from New Mexico, and I ended up on the road to Lisbon.

PORTUGAL AND BEYOND

Buses were reasonable and frequent, so we boarded. Our trepidation about not knowing Portuguese was short-lived. Those living in the countryside had some difficulty with our Spanish, but city dwellers must have had more experience. They spoke Portuguese, we spoke Spanish, and all went well. Marty knew what she wanted to see, so we headed for the *Torre de Belem* and surrounding tourist points of interest. I followed. We bought shrimp by the kilo, sat on a hill with a view of the ocean, and peeled into the prawns until we burst.

After Lisbon, we headed northward, destination Salamanca. I guess the transit wait did not suit Marty, because I found myself standing next to her on a highway with our thumbs stuck out. This terrified me, but it terrified me more to be alone in Portugal. In my world, hitchhiking, known here as "auto-stop," was forbidden. My parents' voices screamed in my head never to do such a thing. Too late, a big semi pulled up and Marty was already hopping in. At least she sat next to the large, looming driver and I could cling to the door handle.

When he dropped us at the next town, I headed straight for the rail station. We caught a train that got us to Salamanca around midnight. Even at that hour, several innkeepers had people standing there with placards advertising their places. We slung our packs over our backs and followed a woman in a limp house dress to her residence and gratefully slid under a thin blanket into sagging single beds. In these travels, we graded places, not by the number of stars, but the number of blankets. This was a "one blanket" which was fine for the fall weather. As our travel experiences accumulated, late night arrivals and desperation led to even lower standards, as happened at our next city, Madrid.

We stepped off the train at 10:00 p.m. into a nearly deserted station, two teenaged girls, backpacks, late night, European capital city. Again, my parents' voices echoed from the deep recesses of my head. "But Marty and I have already been in Madrid," my inner voice popped up. "We know how this works," it proclaimed confidently. It was 1972 and Francisco Franco was the supreme dictator, after all. He was in his fourth decade. He didn't allow any deviance from his strict expectations. His *Guardia Civil* walked in pairs throughout the country, from metropolis to village, night and day, wearing hats called *tricornios*, three-cornered, like the children's song. The back was flat so that, according to my friends, *La Guardia* could lean up against buildings while observing the passing populace and their hats wouldn't fall off. They kept the streets safe, or so those who supported Franco claimed. It was mythology, according to those opposed to his reign in Spain.

It is a fact that they were the *orejas*, the ears, of Franco's government. They patrolled the streets, keeping the citizenry in check, but also listened in for any controversial conversations. At the *Universidad*, some students were involved in underground, anti-governmental newspapers. One friend of mine, Antonio, a student in our mutual American History class, was involved in something. It was not uncommon for him to speak in hushed tones when we met at cafes or tell me to keep walking while he faded back to have a conversation with someone who was sitting on a park bench. He warned me not to speak my mind in class, because one never knew which student might be working as an *oreja*.

These were very strange concepts for me, a girl who thought her freedoms of speech, movement, and liberty in general, were a given. Yet my own country was mired in the muck of the Vietnam War. My Spanish friends proved far more knowledgeable in world affairs than we, their U.S. peers. Our debates over Vietnam and freedoms revealed my ignorance and naivety. How could we defend our belief that we had free speech while watching the news from home on Spanish TV? True, Spain only had two channels, but the newsreels showed teargas, police baton's smashing into students' heads, and screaming chaos across our country. So this is how the rest of the people on the globe got their impressions of us. The world's view had never occurred to me. Was there such a big difference between the *Guardia Civil* in the streets of Spain or National Guard called out to the protests in our cities?

For now, in Franco's Spain, I respected Antonio's judgement and caution. Yet the irony did not escape me. The same vigilance that denied Antonio's freedoms of speech and assemblage, also kept me safe after midnight. Another revelation. Another learning experience. Antonio was working for a new day. Franco would die soon and Juan Carlos, Franco's self-appointed successor, was set to return as King of the Kingdom.

The Kingdom – HIST: 101

Oh my, how the Spanish professors loved to draw timelines on the boards including names of territories, peoples, entire tribes. Tribes. The word brought images of Ojibwe and Potawatomi, not Germanic. Europe had a tribal group called Goths, whose family tree morphed into Visigoths when they got to Southern France and the Iberian Peninsula. The professors wildly chalked the boards full of city-states and listed names of the counts, princes and emirs that ruled, showing Christian and Moorish roots.

The Moors, or Musulmanes, crossed the Strait of Gibraltar and filled the peninsula with lavish architecture, running water, baths, libraries, and religion. The Christians weren't pleased. Was it the bathing? Too much touching? A problem the Christians would later have with the Native Americans (Indians) when they "discovered" the New World.

Regardless, one day the Christians embarked on recapturing and reuniting all the peninsula's territory. In northern Spain, c. 720, Pelayo pitched his first battle of the *Reconquista* in Covadonga. Centuries later, in 1492, Isabella and Ferdinand finished the quest by winning the last battle in southern Granada, thus making it the longest war in human history (711 – 1492).

With this history lesson fresh in our minds from a recent lecture, Jennie, Maggie and I returned to Granada.

FROM CLASSROOM TO THE STREETS

Jennie and I stood gazing at the statue of Columbus kneeling at the foot of Queen Isabella, wondering aloud how a woman managed life in the fifteenth century.

"Well, it had to help that she was a queen," Jennie observed. "Her castle in Segovia sure had a nice view. Do you think she really wanted to marry Ferdinand? That business about uniting her kingdom of Castile with Ferdinand's Aragon doesn't exactly sound romantic."

"At least she was older and owned more land than he did," I noted. "That gave her more influence. Bet that is why she got to ride her white horse down here with the troops instead of staying at home in the tower."

"Funny they never mentioned that back in the States," Maggie mused. "All we ever heard was that Columbus got money from her for his three ships. It never even occurred to me that the Nina, the Pinta and the Santa Maria were Spanish names! Or are they Italian?"

We looked up at Columbus, head bowed, kneeling at the edge of her long gown.

"I wonder if this was before or after his voyage," I mused, then added, "Any chance he came back to say thank you?"

"Ha!" Maggie grinned, "more likely he's back for more money."

"Don't you wish we could have intercepted them in history and told them what was going to happen? Maybe stop some of the bad stuff?" Jennie stared up thoughtfully, then continued, "It's scary. Two people met, made some plans, exchanged money and, to this very day we are all affected by the moment this statue depicts. It might have seemed in-consequential at the time, but good grief!"

"Are you thinking just of the Americas and the Indians, diseases, and the rapes that resulted in the Mestizo race, 'cuz what happened right here in Granada wasn't pretty either," Maggie wisely interjected. "Geesh, Isabella came riding in on her white horse and expelled the Jews and the Moors. She started the Holy, get that? Holy Inquisition."

Our guide at the Alhambra had spun a vivid tale of the Moors watching the Christians coming from their vantage point, high on the hill inside their alcázar palace. The Alhambra, rising out of the mountain's red rock, was a fortress and home with delicate garden mazes, eunuchs playing lyres to the sultans' harems, fountains splashing everywhere, water even flowing down stair banisters. The Alhambra castle, engraved with Islamic script, honeycomb ceilings, reflecting pools, brightly colored courtyards, was Boabdil, its last sultan's, last stand.

The guide entailed, with some relish, how Boabdil ordered his men to boil oil, climb to the tower walls, and wait. They carried their "Ali Baba" curved swords and clenched daggers between their teeth. He finished the story with Boabdil hunched over in shame as his mother shook her finger at him, likely hissing between clenched teeth, "Do not weep like a woman for that which you could not defend as a man." Ouch. How completely humiliating. The quote is posted for all to see along the highway running south of Granada.

The three of us turned our attention from Isabella with Columbus still on bended knee to our map. This was our second time in Granada, the first being that school field trip complete with the melodramatic guide. This time, we intended to shop!

"Where is the Jewish section?" Jennie asked. "I remember some nice shops. I'm looking for that gold inlaid jewelry, what was it called?"

"Damascene?" I asked. "But, wasn't that from Toledo?"

"Yes, those famous conquistador swords," Maggie reconfirmed.

"One of my friends wants me to bring him one of those six-foot swords!" I said. "They'll never let me on the plane with that!"

"Buy him a damascene sword in miniature. A letter opener," Maggie grinned.

"There it is," Jennie interrupted, pointing to a spot on the map. "The Jewish section. It's called the *Realejo*."

~ *Puente* ~
What Happened Here Centuries
Before We Went Shopping

Our professors' lectures came to life as we turned down the narrow streets of shops. Who had walked here in 1492? The Moors and Jews inhabited the place, but the Christians were in pursuit. Not only was reunification on Isabella's agenda, there was a Pope pushing for conversion. Queen Isabella and her Grand Inquisitor swept in with "Convert, leave or die," the campaign slogan of the day. Some Jewish folk hid their menorahs and fell to their knees, crossing themselves to avoid torture. Some Moors packed their bags and crossed the Strait of Gibraltar. Some Christians and remaining citizens lied about their neighbors' feigned conversions to obtain their property. Like Maggie said, "Not a pretty picture."

Isabella and Ferdinand became known as: *Los Reyes Católicos*, the Catholic Monarchs. Their conversion and unification efforts earned them this dubious title, used with great pomp and godly authority. This was only the beginning of the conversion movement. When Columbus returned from the Americas, the scourge would travel overseas.

This is my revised edition of what the professors presented in the *Universidad's* history class. Spaniards are faced with the paradox of their New World "discovery" juxta-positioned with what they did once they got there. There is no amount of diplomacy that can cleanse the real version, so don't try. Everyone is a product of their historic times. To her benefit, the Queen did view the natives as human beings. Bartolomé de las Casas, a Dominican priest, presented volumes of passionate discourse defending them, with the ironic footnote that Africans would make better slaves. The Viceroys weighed in on the side of Indians being beasts, as it eased their economic consciences.

CATHOLIC KINGS AND "GRANADA" BOXES

The shops whispered their histories as we wound our way through the Jewish *barrio*. When our money ran low, we switched to window shopping along the streets in the general direction of our one-blanket hostel.

"Isn't that the *Capilla Real,* the Royal Chapel?" Maggie asked, pointing across the street at a large church. Jennie checked the map to confirm.

"Let's pop in," Maggie suggested. "Isabella and Ferdinand are buried there."

Autumn's chill seeped into our bones, colder still when we stepped across the threshold into Isabella's mausoleum chapel. We zipped our jackets. Our footsteps echoed into the rafters of her Gothic styled resting place. The aisles formed a cross, with her deceased family gathered, lying in state to the right. There, the *Reyes Católicos*, two figures carved in stone-cold elegance, look away from each other, yet forever together. We followed the sign pointing to a short staircase leading beneath the tomb.

Below the ornate burial monument were simple, wooden coffins, side by side, so humble, so alone. There were four boxes. Isabella and Ferdinand, accompanied by their daughter, Juana, known as *Juana la Loca*, Joan the Mad, and her unfaithful husband, Felipe, *El Hermoso*. He could not stay in her bed during his lifetime, but now sleeps next to her for all eternity.

None of them could have predicted that the Inquisition would last for 300 years in their "newly discovered" America, or that the class and religious divisions espoused in the 15th century would haunt the entirety of the Americas throughout history, up to today. A direct link exists from the social divisions earmarked by the racial and class terminology of Isabella's time to present day racism, xenophobia, and rejection of immigrants at our nation's border to these wooden coffins.

We gazed upon their caskets in the barren underbody of the cathedral. So this is how it ended for the Queen that financed voyages that burgeoned Spain into a kingdom where the sun never set. Spain finally fell, but the effects of colonialism rippled on.

Jennie broke the silence. "She didn't live to see the results of financing Columbus. I wonder if she knew how her gallant representatives cut off the hands of Indians that didn't meet their monthly quota of a hawk's bell of gold. Do you think she really believed her royal representatives when they reported converting the Indians, or did she know the truth and preferred to look the other way?"

"Who knows? Exciting times, albeit with mixed results," I concluded. "What would the world be like if the *conquistadores* went into new lands with a sense of awe and excitement instead of greed and mandated conversions?"

"They did have to pay off their war debt," realistic Maggie interjected. "What if Latin America got to keep all of their resources instead of being drained of their gold, silver, not to mention Incan potatoes to Ireland and Mexican *tequila* for margaritas?" she finished with a twinkle.

We took one last look at the wooden boxes filled with royal dust. Maggie, Jennie, and I climbed back into the sanctuary where afternoon shadows stretched into dark corners. Votive candles flickered ghostly shapes on the wall behind the altar. Stale incense lingered from an earlier service. "Let's get back to the hostel," Jennie shivered, shaking a cool draft off her shoulders. Was it the evening air or perhaps 15th century phantoms passing between us?

THE ALHAMBRA

The *Reyes Católicos* couldn't have imagined that one day, the magnificent Moorish Alhambra would fall into shambles. Hundreds of years passed. Winds howled through the lattice hallways and the sun faded the geometric tiles. Bats moved into the honeycombed *Bóveda* ceilings and cats crept into the corners hunting mice. The gardens overgrew their mazes. The clipped hedges went rogue. Itinerant vendors, waifs, dogs, and gypsy fortune-tellers left their mark in the once magnificent Moorish palace.

Not until centuries later did the Alhambra return to the light of day, due to Washington Irving, an American author meandering the streets of Granada. He cleaned up a room, moved in, and wrote his *Tales of the Alhambra*, 1832, a Moorish flavored collection. Amidst the chicken squawks, gypsy dancing, and sun-faded colors, he wove the sheer belly-dancer's cloth back together. He added curved swords and white steeds. Thanks to his book, the Alhambra palace and the *Generalife* gardens were brought back to life.

During our class trip to Granada, the guide painstakingly rattled off dates, art terminology, and detailed trivia about the Alhambra and *Generalife*. This time, we moseyed through at our leisure, feeling the fountain spray on our faces and sniffing the roses and myrtles, free of facts! When the cypress sent out long afternoon shadows, we headed for "Granada Box" hill, that narrow street winding down the mountain on its way back to town and the *Plaza Nueva*.

On our shopping list: Granada's specialty—inlaid woodwork. We remembered the hill between the Alhambra and *Plaza Nueva* was lined with shops. Inlaid tables, coasters, music-boxes, trays, jewelry chests, all demonstrated by local artists squinting into magnifying glasses, clasping tweezers in their dominant hands. We ran between shops, comparing prices and retail.

"I am looking for a medium-sized box for my rings," I reported to one vendor, after running back up to his shop. Jennie looked over my shoulder as he brought out a range of sizes and prices. Then, on cue, she casually mentioned in my direction, "Jan, I saw one just like that for about half the price a few doors down."

Without a pause, he took the box and started walking toward the door. "Come with me," he said, "That sounds like my sister's shop. We'll see if these are the same or maybe I can explain the price difference."

His middle-aged, ample-bosomed sister greeted him with a big smile and zealous hug, then turned back to us. "We give you a good price. Look across the street there. See that man bent over the work bench? He is our brother. He makes most of our products. We can mail them to your home. Please, please, go over and see how he does it. Anything you buy from him or us, well, it is all in the family."

Jennie, Maggie, and I exchanged bemused glances. So much for all our bargaining efforts. It actually removed some of the stress. We got to the business of buying.

The whole afternoon filled with chatter. Did you see that? Should I buy this? Would this be good for my mother? Do I have room for this in my backpack? Do you have any extra *pesetas*? We entered every shop on that hill—satiating our shopping desires before returning exhausted to our hostel.

We fell through the door, dropped our bursting bags on the beds, and let our treasures cascade out. "Put your stuff out so we can take a picture," I said. "I'm giving most of this away but I'd like to remember what we bought. Good grief, Maggie. Yours take up half of the bed!"

"While you two sort this out, I'm going to wash my hair and some undies," Jennie announced.

JENNIE & MAGGIE WITH
GRANADA BOXES

77

"Have you seen the size of that sink?" I asked. "I don't think all of your hair will fit!"

"Yeah," Maggie agreed. "But here is the perfect place to dry your laundry," she said, pointing to a three-dimensional plaque of the Virgin Mary, hands clasped in pious prayer, hanging on the wall behind her.

"Wouldn't it be sacrilege if Jennie hung her panties there?" I asked Maggie.

"Depends on which religion you profess in this town," she quipped, dimples deepening into her impish grin.

Age ≠ Maturity

Maggie had a point. Which religion? Jewish? Christian? Islam? There was so much missing from my formal, one-dimensional education. What about points of view? What Isabella saw as saving souls, the Jews experienced as annihilation. What Columbus saw as discovery, the Arawak experienced as invasion. The Vietnam War was going on with protesters, conscientious objectors, and world rulers ordering more bombings for peace. Really? Bombing for peace? And reunification? Of Spain in 1492 or Vietnam in 1972?

Thousands of nameless mothers were hiding their children. What's the quote? "Learn history or be doomed to repeat it?" I thought I hated history. Now I wasn't so sure. I was nineteen years old. My K-12 curriculum included United States history. Memorizing dates and names of numerous wars for quizzes. I didn't recall multiple points of view. I was registered for some conscience-raising education courses in the Spring. But my learning wasn't waiting. I was walking the same streets as Isabella II. In my first two months, I crossed Roman bridges, stood inside of jaw-dropping Moorish palaces, entered Jewish synagogues, stared at masterpieces by Goya and El Greco, and observed Franco's dictatorship up close. Experiences outpaced book-learning. Maturity raced ahead of age.

The Birthday Bath

I exited my teenage years in Seville on November 20th. Catch that? I'd turn twenty on the twentieth. To some in my group, that was a big deal, a "Golden Birthday." It was not part of my childhood mythology. On this birthday, my family was on the other side of the Atlantic in Wisconsin. They'd send a card and call long distance. That was a big deal. Calling Spain was expensive. In my six months away, I only called them three times. It meant I had to go to the *Telefónico* building next to the Post Office, pay some money, get into a booth and wait for the operator to call the number before ringing me!

My U.S. friends of the "Golden Birthday" belief began brainstorming options to make my day special. I reasoned that being in Spain was special enough, granting that some commemoration would be appreciated.

"What do you miss the most from home?" Jennie asked one day before the event.

"I really miss not being able to have a good hot soaking bath. One of those nice, long, relaxing baths, preferably with bubbles. At Sra. Rafaela's, we only have showers and the water always runs cold or out!" I moaned.

"So a birthday bath it is," she said somewhat triumphantly.

"How does that work?" I asked.

"Well, my family is going to be out-of-town for a few days. I'll just see if it is okay and then we'll pick a time," she answered.

She asked them, we picked a date and time, and they left town. I was to bring a towel.

To get into most apartments, one had to go past the *portero*, the man in charge of the entry door. He knew everyone who should be there, took packages, wrote down messages, and generally guarded the place. I was hesitant to go alone, as this was the building I left earlier under the screaming character assassination of my first *señora*. I did not want the *portero* or anyone else in the building to think I was sneaking back in. Jennie agreed to meet me on the *planta baja*, street level, and ride up with me.

"Are you ready for your birthday bath?" she asked in English so that no one would understand.

"I guess so, although this feels pretty weird," I confessed.

"Not to worry," she assured me. "No one is home so you have all the time you want."

We rode the elevator to the sixth floor, unlocked the door, and went in. The place was deserted, as she promised. She led me straight to the main bathroom and stopped.

"Shut your eyes," she commanded.

I heard the door creak and felt her give me a nudge. "Ok, now open."

The bathtub rim was decorated with scented candles. There were flowers in a vase on a stand and a bottle of bubble bath on the sink. She had thought of everything!

"Now," she began, "I'll show you how the faucet works. I lit the hot water heater hours ago, so that should be good. Use it all up! It's your birthday."

After showing me how to regulate the hot C for *caliente* and cold F for *frío*, lighting the candles, and opening the bubbles, she stepped back to see if she had forgotten anything.

"Looks like you're ready," she said and she turned the water on. "You just get in and give me a call when you're done. I'll be out in the living room in case you need anything."

What could I need? The water was coming out hot and full force, an anomaly for Spain. The scene was set. I undressed and dipped my toe into the filling tub. I added a generous serving of bubble bath, stirring it to a froth with my hand. Then I let myself sink in.

Oh my, was that divine. I relaxed into the hot scented water. It kept on coming, covering my toes and creeping up to mid-tub, an amount I never allowed myself at home. It occurred to me that I really didn't know how many gallons the heater held and cold water might start to come through. I reached over to turn off the faucet.

I turned it and turned it and . . . it just kept turning. There was no "righty-tighty" to this knob. The tub kept filling, but the water wasn't hot anymore. I looked up. I looked down. I panicked. I was in someone else's tub, in someone else's house, and I was about to flood their bathroom! I pulled the plug.

"Jennie," I screamed. "Jennie, come quick!" I got out and grabbed my towel as she burst into the room.

"What's the matter?" she stared at me. "Are you drowning?"

"Not yet," I said, "But soon! The water won't turn off and it's about to overflow!" Jennie looked at me and tried the faucet. It went round and round, but did not slow the water, not even a little bit.

"Quick, get a pan," my brain kicked in. "Get a big one, or two! We can bail some of this water into the bidet." Finally, the bidet would come in handy! "Get me a saucepan," I repeated. She stopped staring at me and took off for the kitchen.

She returned and thrust a pan in my face. By now, I had my clothes on and could use two hands. With one, I kept working the faucet and with the other began to frantically bail. I couldn't have bailed faster if I were in a sinking ship. The bidet gurgled.

"*Ay, Dios mío,* oh my God," one of us exclaimed. "Jennie, we can't do this all night. Call the *portero*. Maybe he can come up and fix this thing."

She ran back to the kitchen, picked up the phone and called down. I waited and bailed for what, as they say, seemed forever.

Finally, she came rushing back, but no *portero*.

"Jennie! Where is the *portero*? What happened?"

"Oh," she groaned. "Since my family is not here and we are two single girls alone, he refuses to come up. He said it just isn't done!"

"What the. . .? Even in an emergency? What are we supposed to do?" Now it was my turn to groan.

"He did explain how to turn off the water to this apartment," she whimpered.

"Do we know where the pipe is? Do we need tools?" I knew just enough to be worried.

"Look," she continued. "It is going to take the two of us. The main pipe is located outside the kitchen window in the air passage. I will have to lean out and you need to hold on to me!"

I was imagining a series of unpleasant endings including a possible six-story plunge.

"Okay," I took a deep breath. "We need to get ahead of this bailing. Let's pour as much water into the bidet and sink as we can, then make a run for the kitchen."

That is what we did. We even filled the two pans before sprinting out. Jennie got to the window and managed to nudge it open. She climbed on the table and stuck her upper body outside the window while I held onto her legs.

"It's stuck!" she shouted. "The lever probably hasn't been moved in years! Maybe it's rusted shut." She twisted and grunted again.

"This cannot be happening!" I yelled back at her. "Do you feel comfortable edging out a little further, you know, to get more leverage? I'll hold on really tight," I promised, wrapping my legs around the table's base.

Another major grunt from outside the window and another yell. "I did it! It is shut! The water should be stopped!"

I pulled her in and we both raced back to the bathroom.

It had stopped! The glorious water had stopped! We were trembling. We let out a scream and hugged each other. We danced. Then we looked around. The candles were melted, the bubbles were circling the drain, the sink was empty, and bidet chugging. We stared at each other. I took my towel and began mopping the floor. She shut the bottle of bubble bath and picked up the candle remains.

Then we started to giggle. It came in bursts. Uncontrollable. Into tears. Tense muscles released. The horror of moments before turned comedic. We held onto each other, giggles washing over us in waves.

"Jan," she finally managed. "Jan, I did not give you the most relaxed, luxurious birthday ever, but I gave you one that you will never forget!"

And to date she still holds the prize.

Crossed-Cultural Communications

My birthday wasn't over. Jennie and I finished cleaning and left not one trace of the flood before heading to my apartment. Perhaps my "Spanish brothers" were there and we could salvage something of this birthday. It has seemed odd to me that they hadn't mentioned anything to me all day. I expected at least a guitar rendition of *"Feliz Cumpleaños"* out of them. It was evening and only Jennie had acknowledged my birthday, my Golden, no less.

I was relieved to see Mario, Chiqui, Pascual, and José Luis sitting in the living room when we arrived. In her best Spanish, Jennie relived the whole birthday bath incident, to my chagrin and their delight. Then, there was a lull. They sat quietly, expectantly. What were they expecting? I was expecting an invite to go out for my birthday. The day was almost over!

Pascual broke the silence. "Juanita, are you going to invite us out for your birthday?"

"Who, me? I have been waiting all day for you to invite me out," I admitted.

"Here in Spain, it is the birthday person who invites their friends. We've been waiting all day for you!" they explained with melodramatic long faces.

"I had no idea!" I looked at Jennie and shrugged sheepishly. Picking up my coin purse of *pesetas*, I looked back at them. "Let's go hit the streets of Seville! My treat!" After all, I was celebrating my first "grown-up" birthday in Spain. Not too shabby!

Capítulo Once
December – *Los Pueblos Blancos*

There was another Janet in our group. No one ever confused us. She was the tall blond spelunking Janet. I was the short brunette Jan with a phobia about caves dating back to Tom Sawyer.

After some brainstorming over a *jarra* (pitcher*) de Sangria*, Janet, Jennie, Darrell, and I looked south for a new travel direction. "My grandmother has a condo on the *Costa del Sol*," Janet piped up. Well, that gave us a destination! The route there went through *Jerez de la Frontera* and *Arcos*. Why not? On our next school break, we took off.

The Spanish word *jerez* was mispronounced by the British, giving us the English word: sherry. *Jerez* was one big vineyard filled with distilleries of the quaint and prolific sort. It was our first stop even though none of us were wine connoisseurs. The large empty *Tio Pepe* barrel standing on end brought our walk-about-town to a stop.

"Jan, look there! That *portero* has a big wine barrel for an office. Maybe he'll get out and let us take a picture," Jennie said, pushing me toward the guard. Evidently, this was not the first tourist with her idea. He graciously stepped out of the barrel and motioned me to take a seat and pick up the phone. She snapped my picture, then asked about tours.

Most tourists were back to their everyday lives by October. Only a small group of us assembled to go with the next guide. It began with explanations of grape vines, cuttings, and names. Some grapes produced the *oloroso*, an aroma laden wine, while others were lighter colored and sweet. All news to me.

We passed a fleet of small tractors pulling loads of grapes toward the buildings where processing tubes and gurgling vats were at work. We trailed the guide down a

JENNIE IN BARREL PHONE BOOTH

corridor of century old white arches stretching above enormous vats of fermenting spirits. The open air softened the acrid whiff of souring fruit.

In the *bodega* warehouse, each darkened oak barrel rested on its side, waiting silently through the ages for the moment it would be tapped to mix with a current batch. Our shoes clicked over the worn stone floors. The guide stopped at a spigot, turned the knob and released a trickle of amber juice into a tall wine glass. He talked about how the liquids combined to produce entirely new wines. We gathered around a smaller barrel resting on its side while he popped open a hole on top, dipped in a long instrument with a small cup at the end, lifted it into the air and let spill a flow of dark emerald liquid from two feet up into the mouth of the waiting glass below. "Passing through the air is part of the process," he explained before placing his nose over the glass rim.

He took a long whiff then circled his glass in the air, swishing the wines into their new blend. He closed his eyes reverently when he put the glass to his lips. He took the smallest of sips and swirled it around inside his mouth, inhaling deeply. Then he spat it out! "The tasting is done with the nose and in the mouth, not the swallow," he advised us.

"Just like José Ignacio, 'The Nose' Domecq Gonzalez," I poked Jennie in the ribs. "He is a famous man from right here in Jerez! The guy has a nose like a beak. It's curved perfectly for dipping right inside the top of dainty wine glasses. My beloved Spanish teacher, Haaky, showed us the video back in high school. 'The Nose' swirled, swished, held his glass up to the light just like this guy. He'd talk about the fruit, the aftertaste. He sighed like he'd gone to heaven after he spit it out. So it's all true!"

I slowed my excitement to a hallowed pace. "Jennie, it's a religion," I whispered. "Think of it. These barrels contain liquids produced over a hundred years ago. Like sacred sacraments taken from the 17 and 1800s dripped into today. This taste never existed before and will never, ever again be tasted. *Imagínate,* imagine that!"

I tuned back into our guide. "Now," he was saying, "We will go to the tasting area and you can see for yourselves."

In a cozy corner of the large *bodega*, small tables were topped with dozens of various sized wine glasses. As a milk drinker, this collection of glassware reinforced my feelings of ignorance. In Spain, I was guided to order *Mosto*, as milk just wasn't done with meals. *Mosto* is the grape juice before it goes into the vats and barrels for fermentation. It has a nice color and tastes a bit like apple juice or light cider. If we ordered the *Menu del Día* that came with the cheaper table *tinto*, red wine, it was permissible to add sparkling water, 7-Up, or even Orange Fanta, creating a *tinto de verano*, summer wine. This wasn't the time nor place to add pop.

The waiters arrived at our table, white towels draped over their forearms and wine bottles in hand to pour sample portions into their proper glasses. Jennie and I looked at each other, eyes widening. "Are you going to spit it out?" she asked me. "I feel like a counterfeit connoisseur. If I swish and spit, I'll feel like, like. . . I'm putting on airs." I moaned.

"So?" she asked, "How many here know what they're doing? Who says we can't learn to become wine experts?" She lifted her glass and chinked it into mine.

After swishing and spitting a half dozen, what I am told were, fabulous sherries, brandies, and whiskies, I finally landed on one I liked. *Málaga Virgen*, a *moscatel* I could live with. Sweet, dessert, sipping *moscatel*. It was the time in the tour when everyone was supposed to take a bottle of their favorite and head to the cash register. It would be nice to have, but I could not be hiking around with a bottle in my backpack. It was then that Darrell pointed to the *botas*, wineskins, neatly showcased by the register. Perfect!

I bought a bottle of *Málaga Virgen* and a wineskin. Once outside, I poured my blessed *moscatel* into the new wineskin, slung it over my shoulder, and was off. Only two problems with that. One, I didn't know how to drink from a wineskin without drenching myself. That is cured with practice. The second problem also involves curing . . . curing the wineskin.

RECIPE FOR CURING YOUR AUTHENTIC, GENUINE,
MADE-IN-SPAIN GOATSKIN BOTA

Warm *bota* in the sun until pitch softens inside. When pliable, blow into it, inflating it to full form. Fill with cold water and let sit for a day or two. Drain water and refill with cheap wine. Leave that wine in for a week or so. Drain and pour in the wine of your choice. If you use your *bota* regularly, you have completed the process. If not, drain, unscrew the top, and leave open while storing. Repeat this process when you use it again.

Or, avoid this and buy a *bota* with a latex lining!

OLIVES

The four of us traveled on to Arcos, a village with an expansive Roman bridge and extensive panoramic view. We picnicked there before continuing to the coast. That was where we learned about olives. Olives were everywhere. The countryside was filled with either grape vineyards or olive groves. I had seen pictures of people on ladders, shaking olive branches and gathering olives in the netting below. That was the entirety of my knowledge until. . .

. . . we went to the market in Marbella. Darrell and I were commissioned to get olives while others went for hard breads, Manchego cheese, fruit, and wines, the usual picnic fare. But oh my, the assortment of olives. Bins and bins. Multiple colors of greens and blacks. Large ones, small ones. Nothing in jars like at the grocery back home. We stared at each other and back at the array of choices. We bought a kilo of something and took it to the hotel where Darrell decided to soak them in the sink.

Oh what an unpleasant moment when we bit into them at supper. We looked at each other, all wide-eyed, puckered, and spitting. We didn't know that olives, not unlike pickles, needed to spend time in crocks, marinating in some recipe of herbs, vinegar, something! Cucumbers become pickles and olives, well they needed to become OLIVES. What was there to do but laugh at our ignorance? The water soaked *aceitunas* got composted and we didn't look back. Next morning, we were determined to find Janet's grandmother.

GRANDMA

I have a certain stereotype that goes with the word "grandma." It is loosely based on both of my grandmothers. Nellie was short, plump, feisty, a good cook and vegetable gardener. Grandma Edith made brownies, crocheted and embroidered when not bent over her roses. They wore house dresses and spent summer evenings on the front porch in Illinois towns of under 300. Imagining them in a condo on the Mediterranean coast was a not a match.

However, Janet did have a grandma living on the Mediterranean coast. We packed up our bakery and fruit purchases, reread the handwritten address, and headed out. We found the apartment complex, climbed the stairs, oo'd and ah'ed at the swimming pool and other amenities before pausing on the landing while Janet rang the doorbell.

We waited.

"You did tell her we were coming, didn't you?" Darrell asked the here-to unspoken question. "You did tell her there would be four of us?"

On the third ring, we shrugged and turned to go back down the stairs when the door opened. A beautiful, tall, slender, middle-aged woman stood there wrapped in an elegant, could it be silk, dressing gown. Was this the right place? Was this Janet's grandmother?

The woman waved us into the entry. She looked us over as Janet humbly held out the stained bag of sweet breads and mumbled something about breakfast. I had the distinct feeling we were a surprise.

"Grandma" motioned for us to take seats on her semi-circular couch. I handed over our offering of fruit, which she took along with the bread bag to her kitchen island. Something was sizzling on the stove.

Jennie leaned over to me and whispered. "I smell bacon! We haven't smelled bacon for months!"

We watched her tear off some paper towels and put them on a plate before placing the first strip down to drain. We reluctantly removed our eyes from this delicacy to scan the rest of the spacious apartment.

The floor plan was open, airy, light, and reached out to a large balcony terrace, where the doors let in the Mediterranean breeze. Was there someone back there? My eyes widened and I tried to direct Jennie's attention with a hopefully inconspicuous nod of my head. At the far end of the living room, a door opened releasing a trim, well-groomed man, dressed in a loose white shirt and khaki pants. Our eyes locked onto him and then back to each other. We knew this wasn't Grandpa because Grandpa was. . .well, dead.

Grandma returned in a swish of silk with a platter tastefully displaying our food offerings. We gingerly placed a few items on our saucers and accepted her orange juice. The conversation was a blur, but it wasn't long before Janet made excuses for us to get on the road. We piled our little dishes on the tray and probably said something like, "It was nice to meet you" before getting to the door.

Several long quiet blocks later, Jennie and I stopped. She turned to me and blurted out, "Boy, when I grow up, that's the kind of Grandma I want to be!"

"Me, too, Jennie!" I grinned. "Me, too!"

JAN'S GRANDMOTHERS:
NELLIE KURTZ (WITH GIGI IN ARMS) & EDITH WISE

12

Capítulo Doce
January – New Traditions

There really were chestnuts roasting on an open fire in Triana! I thought that was only in that Christmas song. I followed my nose to a corner barrel that was steaming and surrounded by a small crowd. I took a peek inside and there they were! The steam and aroma warmed Seville's streets, that actually do get chilly during December.

The candy shops were selling something called *Turrón*. Sra. Rafaela said I must be sure to taste it, but warned me not to break a tooth. I tasted the hard and soft versions of this almond brick candy and bought some to take back home. Home in the States, that is.

It was time to think about home. Home to my "real" life at Hamline, in a dorm, with classes totally in English. I was conflicted. What was "real life" anyway? My mind shifted back to buying gifts. Christmas was part of my "real life" on both sides of the ocean.

El Corte Inglés and *Galerias Preciados* were the two major department stores in all of the big cities. *El Corte Inglés* had a branch downtown, not too far from school. I would go alone and take all the time I needed. I hated shopping, but this would be a scavenger hunt. I made a list. The store was clearly marked by floor and department. The basement was foods, so I could get the *turrón* there. A specialized tourist area offered fans, T-shirts, little stuffed bulls, flamenco dancer dolls, calendars, mantillas, the works. I usually didn't go for souvenirs, but frankly, this was a one-stop-shop, good prices, and one bill. I also wanted some of the kitchenware like *Señora* used to flip *tortillas* and make *paella*. That would be on the top floor.

I stepped onto the escalator and rode to my first stop. I glided off and began my tour of the aisles, up and down, nose to the shelves. At some point, I looked up and noticed a long robe slip out of sight. Hmm. I reasoned it was maybe someone from Morocco wearing a caftan. Seville is close to Gibraltar and gets African visitors. I put my head back down and continued browsing.

A few minutes later, I saw the back of this same caftan at the end of my aisle. Was it coming toward me? I turned and walked in the opposite direction. I took a quick look back. It was a man. A very black man. With a beautiful, almost blue black face.

The third time, he showed up in my aisle. Was I was being followed? It wouldn't be the first time. I started to consider my options. I looked around for clerks. No one. There was a woman's bathroom one floor up. I was close to an escalator. Exit plan.

This scenario of the mind was taking on a life of its own. There he was again. He put something on his head. A turban? He came toward me. Closer. He passed me! He went right on to the end of the aisle and entered an open area. His long robe literally flowed around the corner. I waited. He didn't return. I heard kid noises. Now I was curious. I took a deep breath and edged my way to the place he last occupied. What I saw next horrified me! I was mortified at my own fear and ignorance.

The aisle opened into the toy department. I watched this robed, turbaned man move to a throne in front of a line of children. He sat, arranged his garment, and called the first child over. He was Balthazar, one of the Three Kings, the black one no less!

Oh for. . . This guy was one of the Three Kings! My heart sank as the little cranky woman in my head wagged her pointer finger at my chagrin. The joke was on me and it wasn't funny. I was judgmental and, truth be told, a tad racist. I was relieved, but not proud.

GOOD LUCK GRAPES

Grapes. The price of grapes had gone through the roof! Economics teaches about supply and demand and grapes were in demand. New Year's Eve was a week away and everyone needed grapes.

Much to our surprise, the guys had taken the lead in planning a party to see in the New Year. It would be at our house. I have no recollection of Sra. Rafaela being around, so maybe that had something to do with the location. The guys invited Lee, who was now dating Pascual, and Jennie, along with several others from our U.S. group.

I was to shop for grapes. Mario instructed me to buy enough so that each guest would have twelve. I had never counted grapes before purchase and wasn't about to start. I finally got an estimate on how many guests, then joined the crowds in the grape line. I bought heaps. New Year's Eve arrived and so did the invited. About fifteen minutes before midnight, Mario, being the host, gathered us around a large bowl on the floor.

"The way this works," he started his speech directed to the non-Spaniards, "is this. We all sit around this bowl of grapes. I'll turn on the TV and they will be showing the *Puerta del Sol* in Madrid. We don't have Times Square, but our big clock is there. Each time the clock strikes, everyone takes a grape and plops it in his mouth. With each strike, take another. Do this twelve times and, at the stroke of midnight, anyone who has managed to eat all their grapes will have a full year of good luck!"

"Or choke to death," someone whispered.

So it was that we assembled on the floor and perched ourselves out over the bowl. Mario turned on one of the two stations available in Spain at the time. Just as he said, the crowds were packed like sardines into the *Puerta del Sol* square, cameras panning over them to a huge clock.

MARIO & GROUP OF US SHARING GRAPES

The clock struck, putting our Spaniards into motion over the bowl. We followed. A second strike, a second grape. A third strike and a third grape, this one having to share mouth space with unfinished pieces of its predecessors. Strike four. My mouth was full. I looked up to see how the others were doing. José Luis, Pascual, and Mario were concentrated on the bowl, but Chiqui was staring at me. I didn't know if I could contain myself. We all looked like greedy chipmunks.

Strike five brought the first snort. Someone began to laugh. Everyone was trying to chew fast, but it was so hard to keep up. By strike six or seven, some were too far behind to get back in the race with time. Partially chewed pieces began to exit laughing mouths, producing more laughter.

At some point, I chose life over a year of good luck. By the stroke of midnight, most of us were wiping our eyes or holding our stomachs. Mario had not told us how this might end. This was not such an easy custom after all.

It was not the only custom introduced that night. In the spirit of fair play, Jennie cleared her throat, called us to attention, gave everyone a serious nod, and then took something out from behind her back. She lifted a prickly leafed plant up and held it over her head. "Now," she said, "I'd like to tell you about mistletoe."

MAGGIE, CHIQUI, & JAN DANCING

MARIO, PASCUAL, & CHIQUI BID JAN FAREWELL.

JOURNEYING BACK

At the end of January, Maggie, Darrell, and I were returning to our home campuses in Minnesota for spring semester. Lois and Jennie stayed on, hanging out with my Spanish brothers. There would be more evenings in the *Barrio de Santa Cruz*. They would be there during the April *Feria* and Holy Week. One day, Lee and Pascual became engaged. Antonio would write me letters.

The whole gang threw us a going away party before putting us on the night train. We waved at their shrinking figures disappearing down the track. We turned to enter our sleeping berths. In the middle of the night, we passed through Madrid's city lights. We felt the bump when the train cars changed rail size in the Pyrenees and woke up to *café au lait* in Paris.

Maggie knew some French, so we let her order our food. Thankfully, many menus included pictures. I recognized "*oeuf*", the word for egg, but couldn't pronounce it. I could point. It was about all I could afford. Maggie knew about Monet's Water Lilies and led us through the avenues until we got there. She was our guide in the Louvre, taking us to the Mona Lisa before leading us to the top of the Eiffel Tower. Maggie made Paris! Then we boarded our plane.

Across the ocean, my parents waited at the airport with Jim. He had talked them into riding back with us to Eau Claire and staying a few days. What would it be like to pick up a three-month romance after a six-month hiatus? He got in the car and talked non- stop about his ski trip to Jackson Hole, oblivious to my life-changing experiences in Spain.

My parents and friends couldn't really comprehend the effect those months had on me, either. Returning to campus was like being a minnow thrown back into the lake. I looked and swam like all the other fish, but I was changed. It wasn't physically evident. No one could see that I missed speaking Spanish every day, that I salivated for *tortilla* sandwiches, and yearned for a night walking the *Barrio* under the influence of jasmine and guitar. Every day in Spain, I lived in moments that promised new discoveries. Home was routine. Except now, it wasn't daily—it required planning my future.

~ *Puente* ~
Back on Campus

Back on campus, life returned quickly to the rote schedule of dorm food, library study, and six blocks of the same buildings. My dream-vision balloon lost even more air when I met with my advisor that spring. She looked at senior class options and my transcript. She took a deep breath and informed me, "Not much you can do with Spanish, except maybe teach."

I didn't believe it and wrote to numerous Twin Cities companies, looking for bilingual work. I was convinced that being bilingual had value. Maybe enough value that a company should pay extra to get an employee that didn't need to hire a translator. Pillsbury, 3M, General Mills were all branching out into Latin America. Couldn't they see a good deal in a "two for one" employee? Wouldn't it be a great advantage to communicate directly in a geographical area extending to twenty countries and a vast piece of the United States?

As it turned out, they weren't that future focused. Advocating the worth of bilingualism didn't get me hired. I buckled and wrote again, suggesting they could hire me to teach their employees Spanish, as well as culturally correct mannerisms for their business transactions. Either I was naïve or they were short-sighted, or both.

Being physically short stopped another career choice. I had a brief dream of becoming a stewardess. That included Spanish, travel, and meeting new people. It was a "short"-lived dream because the job description had a height requirement. I hadn't figured on being two inches below their limit.

There is no comfort in being "ahead of one's time" nor being physically disqualified. Being a visionary is hard work. Being a product of one's historical era can . . . suck. Interviewers could still ask women if they were married and when the first baby was planned. At least the teaching field no longer fired pregnant women.

My advisor's words haunted me as I returned to her office and registered for the teacher track. I wanted to graduate with some job skills. I took the coursework and got my license.

Section 2

Graduating into "Real Life"
Birth, Death, and Detours

~ *Puente* ~
The Boyfriend - Vows and Deals

JIM & JAN

Yes, Jim Doth was waiting at the airport after that long distance relationship in an era of snail mail. Phone calls were out of the question expensive. In Seville, he spent nearly six months perched on my desk in the form of a four-by-four photo. His letters, however, rarely appeared. It turned out he used regular, not airmail stamps so his correspondence took long ocean cruises before arriving. His news was scarce, but he did say he missed me.

His life of work, friends and weekend entertainment had stayed static. My six months was literally from another world. We picked up our pre-Spain dating, with his forging toward a committed relationship while I concentrated on graduating with a Spanish major and Education minor. I was brought up with college as part of the "expected given" with marriage and family to follow, not precede.

In May 1974 I graduated from Hamline, but not before Jim came bounding up the stairs of Manor House dorm with a little velvet box in his hand, proposing before I had ordered my graduation robe and tassels. I accepted the ring with the clear understanding I needed to concentrate on my undergraduate work. I was determined to have my diploma first.

That September, Jim and I were married in the First Congregational Church in Eau Claire, where I had grown up. We honeymooned at my beloved cabin and then moved into 1511 Webber Street in White Bear Lake, a former cottage that suited our remodeling abilities and space needs until the day Jim was introduced to his newborn nephew, Matt. "I want one of those," were his exact words, when he picked up his brother's son. "Not until we have gone to Spain," was my response. "I want you to understand that part of my life," I declared, standing my ground.

In September of 1976, we were on our way. I planned total immersion for my husband. By the end of the first week in Madrid, he had toured the Royal Palace, gone to a bullfight, and realized that he was on Spain time. His strong will had to wait for me to translate. I had to explain the menu and that the food would be served when it was good and ready. Being louder wouldn't speed it up. Being dependent on my skills was a new concept. There was a subtle shift in our interaction. Without Spain, Jim wouldn't have experienced the added value of my Spanish.

The second week, we stayed with Antonio and his wife, Maribel. They generously drove us to *La Rábida* monastery from which Columbus set sail, filled us with *tapas* and acquiesced to riding with us around *Parque Maria Luisa* in a touristy horse drawn carriage. Oh, the mortification! A sign of true friendship. Antonio was a great host and Maribel became a lifelong friend, providing me home, hospitality, and multiple adventures in the years to come.

After Seville, we rented a car and headed to Gibraltar for the day cruise to Tangier. I dropped my passport while waiting in line for our tickets. A cheery Englishman picked it up and handed it back. In this way, we met Clive and Rita Payne.

JAN, MARIBEL & JIM IN SEVILLE

Their company made the day in Tangier a true adventure. He was a world traveler, laden with cameras, including movies. He shooed away the official guides in favor of a young boy, Mohammed, dressed in a well-used Bob Marley T-shirt. Mohammed spoke broken English, which he used to lead us down narrow, packed streets of the *Kasbah*. He took us through spice markets piled with curry, cardamom, and cinnamon. We followed him into pre-arranged shop-stops where merchants unrolled hand-woven Berber rugs with international shipping available. He knew where the official guides took high-paying customers for lunches in restaurants serving curried chicken followed by the belly dance performance. Their tambourines and silver-covered teeth flashed as they circled us sitting cross-legged on the floor. This foray into Morocco accentuated what Jim was experiencing every day in Spain. I had forgotten the discomfort of dependence on others in the baffling, incomprehensible din of foreign language and culture. I was relieved to reboard the boat headed back north to Spain.

We disembarked at Gibraltar and agreed to meet Clive and Rita in Marbella the next day. I was working for Hilton Hotels at the time and received free lodging at their Marbella property. Jim bought me a bikini in the boutique. The Mediterranean was as blue as the photos. I tried to hide in the churning waves until I got used to being as exposed as the locals. After lunch, the four of us were serenaded by a *Tuna*, a 14th Century troubadour-style Spanish-student trio. Jim reveled in his story-telling. Clive laughed. Rita grinned. We ended with sunbathing around the pool before exchanging addresses and farewell hugs. They headed north to Seville and we continued along the coast to Málaga, our port of departure.

In Málaga, I had reserved a room in a *Parador*, one of the renowned places of history and, usually, elegance. From our perch over the city, we watched men racing around the bullring below with a wheelbarrow sort of contraption including attached bull horns. So that's how matadors practice their passes. We hiked the castle walls and returned to explore

95

our spacious suite.

The bathroom was nearly as large as our cottage kitchen and living room combined. Jim was intrigued by all these bidet things next to each toilet, which we found to be perfect sock-soaking sinks. When we entered our breath-taking accommodations, he made the rounds, including bidet inspection. He twisted the handles to see if the water worked and, to our amazement, it rose up like a geyser. I mean, to the ceiling, a ten-foot fountain, straight up. It hit the ceiling and came back on us like a summer shower.

Jim quickly turned the faucets in the opposite direction, bringing the splash down to the inside of the bidet bowl. Wide-eyed, he looked out over the wet floor tiles where the wild waters circled around a center drain, and then glanced back at me, standing in the corner, gasping.

"Soooo," he said letting out the syllable in a long breath, "so, you're telling me that people actually sit on these things?" With that visual, we both burst out laughing.

The bidet incident "ended" our three weeks in Spain. We retreated to our balcony as dusk embraced us. We raised up our last *copa de vino* in a toast to our fairytale life before returning to what we called reality. I wistfully packed the Mediterranean bikini, knowing that October was waiting back home in Minnesota. What I didn't know was that I would never fit in that bikini again.

By the end of October, I wasn't feeling well. By the end of November, my Spanish designer pants were tight. Along with our memories, gifts, and souvenirs, I was carrying a baby, "Made in Spain." *En fin*, I got my trip and Jim got his son. That was so like him!

13

Capítulo Trece
Planning Life – Good Days

I did not get my first teaching job the conventional way. It came as an urgent need, from a tragedy, the word used most often to describe this stage of my life. But first, the blessing.

When we got back from Spain, Jim left his job at the National Guard Armory to become a realtor with Burnett Realty in White Bear Lake. He thrived under the tutelage of two realtors, Joe B. and Michael. Joe had sold us our house on Webber and, with a baby on the way, found us a larger rambler on Roth Place. Doth on Roth, no lie.

We moved in during the coldest January in memory. Twenty consecutive days of way-belows—twenty below on average. I was working at Hilton Reservation service, parking on Harriet Island and taking my pregnant self across the wind-swept bridge to work. My three memories of January: Ice, wind chill, and fixing up the new house.

Jim was passionate about his new job. No more uniforms for him, no sir. Oh, and no more saying, "No sir." He was done with the military. He bought a business suit, a new (to us) car, shined his shoes, slicked back his hair, and put up his first "For Sale" signs. I wrote ads for the Sunday newspaper and took freshly baked goodies to the open houses. Perhaps it helped.

By January, he had been awarded his first "Employee of the Month" plaque. This was good, as we were now living off of my meager wages and his commission. I planned to work until the end of May, allowing about two weeks before the baby's due date. Jim was driven by excitement and a need to have some money in the bank before that happened.

And then it happened. A month early. He had taken me dancing. I could hardly move, such was my waist's dimension, but I loved to dance. At 2:00 a.m. I was crawling on the floor. He called the midwife. She verified that I was in labor. Then came the "Paul Revere" ride across the empty, winding, dark highways of St. Paul into Minneapolis, me grimacing, letting a mantra of: "I can't do this" and "Not now, I haven't quit work yet! The nursery isn't painted. I'm not ready" escaped through my clenched teeth.

He dropped me at the hospital ER doors and parked the car. I waddled to the registration desk, fumbled for my insurance card, then saw him running to my side. I was terrified my water would break or that I'd start yelling. They made me walk to the elevator. They replaced my clothes with one of those tie-in-the-back gowns and put my things in a small room. Then, I was told to walk up and down the hallways, right past the nursery where, soon, a baby would be labeled "Doth" in one of those bassinets.

I wanted to let go my scream, but the woman in the next cubicle was already winning the yelling competition. Was she trying out for a Stephen King part? I didn't want to go to the place where she was! Then, a nurse came to me and patted my hand sympathetically. "She is deaf and doesn't know how loud she is." Oh, whew! Like that made it all better?

At 4:30 p.m., my sweet baby was born. They handed me a boy. "Look again," I demanded, so certain I was of having a daughter. I had no clue what to do with a boy and it was a boy. A scrunched up little five-pound ten-ounce critter, slightly yellow. Next thought: I wasn't going to let any government take a child of mine off to war. No military conscription for this little guy.

Next morning, Jim took the swaddled bundle to his chest and they both went to sleep. I couldn't remember any of the names we had on the list and the list was back home. When Jim woke up, he looked at me and said, "Gregory." I knew for a fact that was not on the list, but had no energy to refute him. Gregory it was. Jim hopped on his newly purchased motorcycle, the one he bought without consulting me, and zoomed to his parents' home to spread his side of the story.

Gregory was jaundiced, probably due to being a month early. They didn't let me take him home for a week so, I drove in every day to nurse him. I left bottles for the night staff and returned the next morning. It was May and unusually cold. While I waited between feedings, I knit him a blue bonnet to wear home. When he was discharged, the temperature was in the 90s.

JAN & GREG

JIM & GREG

14

Capítulo Catorce
May 23, 1978 – A Very Bad Day

The next year was a blur of changes. Our daily schedule went ballistic. Jim was gone at all hours, showing houses, doing paperwork, and going door to door looking for sellers. He had tunnel vision on a quest to learn and thrive. He was now the only breadwinner. We took a few days to go to the cabin that summer, but mostly he focused on work.

His tunnel vision probably caused the accident that day. He drove right through an intersection and totaled the car. He was not hurt. This time. Several months later, just two weeks after a big family celebration for Gregory's first birthday, he wasn't so lucky. That day changed everything forever.

On May 23, 1978, he jumped on that motorcycle I hated and left for his Burnett Realty baseball game on the other side of Minneapolis. "Put on your helmet," I yelled from the porch steps as he roared out the driveway, leaving me to finish the packing for our trip to the cabin the next morning.

Jim literally left the lawn mower in the middle of the backyard as if summoned by some irresistible, uncontrollable force to hop on that bike and ride off. I finished cutting the grass from the spot where he left the mower. I put Gregory in his crib and the luggage by the door. It was nearly 9:00 p.m. when I finished all the preparations and went outside to sit under the budding maple tree. I turned to look at our house of less than a year. The deck Jim built, the trestle for the clematis, the grape arbor from the last owner, the picket-fenced yard, the garden and dog kennel attached to the garage, our perfect family starter home.

Shadows lengthened, but what I saw next, rising over the garage gate wasn't a shadow. I saw what I describe as a vision of Jim, rising larger and larger over the backyard where I sat frozen under the tree. I remember the pink color of his muscle shirt and blue of his jeans fade off into the night air as the apparition evaporated invisibly while slowly rising over the garden. My body knew something was terribly wrong. I ran to the phone, dialed up Joe, and asked where Jim was. Before Joe answered, another realtor burst into the kitchen. Tom had driven by an accident on Highway 694. He thought it was Jim.

It was. At age 25, at 9:30 p.m., I began calling. First my parents, then his family and my friends. It became a rote message. "Jim was killed tonight in a motorcycle accident," I heard myself saying over and over. Michael, a realtor friend, had already gone to the morgue to identify him by the time I got the knock on the door. Two obligatory policemen read me their perfunctory lines right out of the movies. "We regret to inform you."

After my parents arrived it was decided I should try to get some sleep. I could not go to my bed. Not without Jim. I was led to the guest bedroom. Despite the extra covers, an inner cold numbed me. I listened to the rumblings of people in my house, grief entering each room.

The next day I found a funeral home, touched Jim's icy face and soft, wavy hair, picked a suit, left the wedding ring on his finger, and fed his baby boy breakfast. I chose a casket, ordered some flowers, and asked Dorothy to go with me to my doctor's appointment. Before I got checked in, I was offered sedatives. I refused. I had come for a pregnancy test. You heard me. A pregnancy test. It was negative. Some folks thought that sad. I was not. Seriously, would I want to be a 25-year-old widow, single mom of two? Jim's DNA was more important to the future than my well-being? I went home to our one-year-old son.

There I was notified that the cemetery was full, but there was a newer one next to Century College. I could buy a site there, maybe two, in case I wanted to be buried next to him one day. I don't remember the funeral nor the interment. It was rainy. My dad reported to me that, when the minister sprinkled the dirt over Jim's casket, the sun broke out. I only know that the following week we had a succession of thunderstorms. My basement flooded. A neighbor was hit by lightning and killed. I took the lightning and thunder as Jim's rage. The rain, his sobbing. The wind, howling separation. It was dark, scary, unrelenting. I huddled with my child, wrapping him into his baby blankets and rocking us both, back and forth in the creaking rocker, trying to fill the hole in my chest.

~ *Puente* ~
Death – The Word That Burns Your Tongue

Six feet under. Bought the farm. Kicked the bucket. Pushing up daisies. Gave up the ghost. Croak. In my culture, euphemisms are employed to neutralize or avoid saying *it*. Death. The word that, according to Mexican lore, burns our tongue.

In the weeks that followed Jim's death, people didn't know what to say around me. Advice was to get rid of Jim's clothes, the sooner the better, it seemed. Just as baby Gregory's clothes entered my life and washing machine at his birth, I noticed Jim's clothes vanish from the laundry shortly after his burial. A whiff of his cologne would start my tears and stop my heart.

I was broken in so many ways, but I did not want to drive to Minneapolis for grief counseling. That meant traffic, a babysitter and it wouldn't bring Jim back. That was the root of my problem. My everyday life companion, the one with whom I shared my thoughts, joys, hopes, and . . . The one who would have been excited at Gregory's first tooth, first words, first steps, wasn't there. He was irrevocably gone.

A neighborhood pastor spoke of Satan waiting to tempt me in my weakened emotional state. Late at night, when I couldn't sleep, his words haunted me. I did not believe a devil lurked outside my bedroom door, but other phantoms of my own imagination frightened me. Sometimes, I thought I heard Jim come through the kitchen door and down the hall, like he used to after a late night with clients.

My church did offer a grief group. Those who had already "lost" someone paired up with the recently bereaved to help them through the six labeled stages of grief: shock, denial, anger, bargaining, depression and acceptance. The woman assigned to me cried throughout our first and only visit. I bought a book by Elisabeth Kübler-Ross outlining near-death experiences. Somehow they were comforting.

One day a salesman came to the door and asked for the man of the house. I stood there with my baby balanced on my hip and simply said, "He is dead." With a stutter and a white face, he backed off the steps and nearly ran down the sidewalk.

It occurred to me that wearing black, like in Spain, would be a helpful sign to outsiders. I remembered the photos of middle-aged, rounded widows dressed in mourning, sometimes for years. At least an arm band would be helpful, like they used to do when soldiers died in war. It would notify people that this specific person was grieving.

During the months that followed, I began to notice that some people, including Jim's family, did not come over as often. When I entered a room, conversations fell to whispers. Laughter stopped. People didn't know what to do with me, a twenty-five-year-old widow and single mom. Both categories were rare in 1978. Young widow. How does that work? Widow was one thing, but young and single were complications.

During the first year, I became aware that I shouldn't talk to other women's husbands. At the church's official Couple's Club, I presented an ethical dilemma. They invited me to attend, but didn't know where to seat me. A single woman doesn't sit between a wife and her husband on the couch. I was offered the folding chair.

One Sunday morning, I noticed the pew where I customarily sat was occupied only by women. One divorcée, three elderly widows, and a yet unmarried, twenty-something female. I later learned this was a common church arrangement. It even had a name. The widows' pew. Subtle. What else had I missed, subliminally woven into my culture?

Denial. We surrounded ourselves by death, we just made it fictional. Death was portrayed on television, in the movies, and at Halloween. We paid at the box office to watch ax murderers and bloody butchering. We sat terrorized, scared witless. Halloween brought out ghosts, goblins and bloodsucking vampires peering out of their creaky coffins. The Grim Reaper, a faceless ghoul in a hoodie, was coming to get us with his scythe poised to cut us down.

With this specter haunting my every hour, it became impossible for me to venture into future planning. I was incapable of taking the long view. I knew that tomorrow was not a given. It was extra. How could people plan a vacation for next summer, much less retirement? Were they naïve? They could be dead by then.

The positive to this perspective was living in the present moment, the mantra espoused by that era's New Age gurus. The downside was a panic to live frantically in the face of impending demise. This produced a frenzied filling of my days. I could not face a lull . . . that empty moment when grief might catch up, tackle me, and render me helpless to my pain.

JIM'S GRAVE

15

Capítulo Quince
Día de los Muertos/ Day of the Dead

After four years of living in the tornado that had become my life, I found an alternative method of facing death and dying in the Mexican tradition called *Día de los Muertos*. It was one of those syncretic blends of Aztec afterworld and the Catholic All Soul's Day. It offered me solace, an intentional ritual of remembrance and the acceptance stage my own culture so blatantly lacked.

Instead of the Grim Reaper, *Día de los Muertos* introduced me to *La Catrina*, a jovial, life-loving skeleton clothed in flowing gowns and outrageous hats. She is, in fact, the "life" of the party. She and all the ancestors return to earth on November 1st and 2nd to visit their families, who have prepared a marigold path to the tamales, tequila, and earthy temptations they miss. She "embodies" love of life. Her very image is a reminder to relish living, from the mundane to the magnificent. Oh, how she loves being back on Earth to enjoy a morning *café con leche* and hear the caged canary in her flower-filled patio sing.

MARU WITH A CATRINA

JAMY WITH A CATRINA

My culture offered, "Eat, drink and be merry, for tomorrow you may die," Ecclesiastes 8:15. This Biblical refrain comes, not from joy and pleasure, but from a cynical voice bemoaning "all is in vain" so why not just party? Mexico's message was: "Death is your constant companion," a pre-Columbian sentiment codified by author Paulo Coehlo. Befriend death and realize the defining factor between you and dying is but a breath away. So, breathe deeply!

Coehlo's entire quote reads, "Death is our constant companion, and it is death that gives each person's life its true meaning." Jim's death changed me, and irreversibly, my life. *Gracias* to discovering another culture's traditions, I no longer bury him in my past, but call his name, celebrate his life and my new, totally unexpected paths. Death no longer burns my tongue.

∼ *Puente* ∼
Now What?

Where to begin? How to sort out the pieces? My child. How was I going to be a single parent? My home. My responsibility. A week later, everyone else had gone home. I wrote thank-you cards. So much paperwork to sign. Bills coming in. I needed a job.

I called Hamline and was put back in touch with Dr. Barbara. Within a week, I was lined up for a half-dozen interviews. Despite my conflict about teaching being the only thing I could do with my Spanish, I was exceedingly grateful for my teaching license. Forest Lake Senior High hired me. It was part-time. I would teach mornings and still be home with Gregory most of the day. That would pay some bills and keep me sane.

In September, I stood in front of my first class. My face disguised what my heart dared not feel in public. The departing teacher left me with one word: "Numbers." I would come to learn that referred to enrollment. No numbers, no job.

There was no textbook. There was Nancy, a helpful French teacher in the adjoining classroom. Nancy was recently divorced and I was three months widowed. We both liked Gordon Lightfoot music. We'd pour a glass of wine and listen. We cried together. We put on smiles and daily walked to the front of our classrooms, bringing our love of language to a room full of teenagers, all oblivious to our personal pain. There was no gain in looking back. At the end of each day, we sagged into each other's hug before locking up. Slowly, we healed. Nancy and I made it through the year.

In retrospect, teaching was a good match for me after all. Despite my trepidations, I discovered I could speak in front of a group of teenagers. I tapped into my love for language and culture and it carried me every day. I was convinced I was offering them one of life's treasures: bilingualism. Bilingualism took me to other countries, off the tourist beats and into experiences I'd never get as a white, monolingual midwesterner. No bias intended. I was determined to open their eyes to the world. Too bad it had to include conjugating verbs.

After two years in Forest Lake, I got a job closer to home in White Bear Lake. In the early days of 1980, while in the throes of singing *La Bamba*, putting up posters of Spain's *Alhambra*, and planning tacos for the White Bear Lake Spanish Club, I met Lorena. White Bear High School had foreign exchange programs, but it turned out she wasn't with one. My carefree days of salsa dancing, singing verb charts, and putting up *piñatas* ended when Lorena entered my classroom that afternoon.

16

Capítulo Dieciséis
Enter Lorena

"What do you mean, violence?" I asked Lorena out of my ignorance.

"There are a lot of kidnappings going on," she said, presenting a newspaper from her home city.

"The government is fighting the guerrillas and sometimes, people are kidnapped. Ransoms help fund the revolution." She turned the pages to the want ad section.

"See this here," she pointed at a small paragraph that looked like a job offer. "If you know the double meanings, you can figure out," she pointed to a date, "that this is when they want the money. The place to leave it is here," her finger moved to an address. "The amount is hidden in this information about salary," she concluded.

"Oh, my," was all I could respond. I vaguely listened to current news. I was a single mom raising a two-year-old and holding a full time job, for heaven's sake. Central America was miles and lifetimes away.

Until now. I looked into her dark, sparkling eyes and heard the strain in her voice. What was going on in Central America?

Most of the news the past few years centered on Nicaragua, not Guatemala. In 1979, Daniel Ortega had marched into Managua and overthrown the Somoza government. President Reagan called him a Leftist-Marxist rebel overlooking the fact this rag-tag group of Sandinista–revolutionaries had overthrown a forty-year-dictatorship dynasty. Reagan painted the remnants of Somoza's National Guard as "freedom fighters" trying to protect their country from this communist takeover whenever he approached Congress for more funding. The Sandinistas were a branch of an earlier revolution, led by Augusto C. Sandino, who challenged the U.S. Marines' occupation of his sovereign country in 1927. The Marines had been there since 1912 without invitation. Another piece of history not mentioned in our U.S. curriculum.

Lorena shut the newspaper and handed it to me. "Here," she said, "Your students can use this to read Spanish, if you like."

"But, Lorena, it looks like I need to understand a lot more than Spanish to comprehend this newspaper. Would you help me?"

She became my work-study. Besides designing bulletin boards and correcting papers, she educated me. She introduced me to her cousins, Ingrid and Fernando. I was delighted to have three native speakers in my life, but each story full of new vocabulary uncovered another dimension. My carefree memories of Mexico and Spain took a turn as Guatemala came into focus.

Lorena's newspapers included reports of *los desaparecidos*, the disappeared ones. Her hometown papers and mine covered very different perspectives quoting their own sources. Her letters from home related pivotal viewpoints. Knowing Spanish bypassed the need for a translator to further interpret what I read. Other countries, I discovered, had their points of view, including hard facts proving the U.S. wasn't so much the hero riding in to save the day, but a country of aggressive investors yearning to be wealthy. I could not un-know the facts she presented and return to ignorance. Lorena's evidence required that I change my world view.

~ *Puente* ~
Life Long Learning

There is no short, easy story. After completing sixteen years in the U.S. educational system, my ideas of history included the Walt Disney version of Pocahontas, turkey at Thanksgiving, Lewis and Clark accompanied by side-kick Sacajawea, Davy Crockett dying at the Alamo, beaten out by those Mexican guys, and Manifest Destiny, the belief that "we" had the right to forage from "sea to shining sea." It was told to me by my teachers as told by their teachers, without defining the "we." That was understood. We, the White People.

Some of the "we" joined the disenfranchised, invisible groups in history, and began to question that narrative. Now, Columbus day shows up on calendars as "Indigenous People's Day" in English and *Día de la Raza,* in Spanish. There is a story behind each label worth knowing. What is going on in Central America today has roots that were written in Columbus' first journals. He wrote: "...They would make fine servants...with 50 men, we could subjugate them all and make them do whatever we want."

Also absent from U.S. courses were Cortés and his slave-translator-lover, *La Malinche*, symbolic parents of the first *mestizo,* mixed-race baby boy, Martín. Symbolic only, as Gonzalo Guerrero, another Spaniard, was shipwrecked, captured, and taken as a slave before he worked his way up the Mayan ranks to warrior, married, and produced mixed-blood children.

Most early *mestizos,* however, were products of conquest and rape, creating generations of new names for racial color combinations. Reagan politics of the 1980s smacked of "little brown brother" diplomacy. In 2016, Trump elevated the rhetoric to "rapists, drug dealers and criminals" during his campaign and augmented his adjectives referring to Central Americans walking northward in the newsworthy "Caravans of invaders."

Lorena and her cousins are from well-educated, well-to-do families. They were able to fly their children to Minnesota in the 1980s. They returned to Guatemala to raise their families and follow their careers. Others at that time weren't so lucky. Today's Hondurans, El Salvadorans, and Guatemalans living amidst gangs, drugs and economic downturns are direct products of the 1980s. Or go back to 1954 and the U.S. overthrow of Guatemala's duly elected government. Or go back to the Aztecs. It depends on how much time and interest you have.

Since Lorena, my discoveries compound daily and will cease only when I no longer breathe. Such is life-long learning. I would like to say that these decades of attentiveness brought me great hope for the future. *Al contrario,* on the contrary. The philosopher George Santayana gave us, "If you don't learn from history, you are doomed to repeat it." We are not learning from history.

Section 3

Building a New Life - Literally

~ Puente ~
Belugas, Polar Bears, and the Backpacker

In between teaching at Forest Lake and White Bear Lake, I packed up four-year-old Gregory and accepted my parent's invitation to take the Canadian train trip to Churchill, Manitoba, located on Cape Merry, where we were guaranteed a long look at the tundra and a quick peek at polar bears. Once we arrived, we had less than a day to seek them out.

Stepping off the train, we headed directly toward the coast. Gregory and I ran along the rocky crags, looking for the best place to point our binoculars at the belugas playing in the surf. My mother walked along the sands with a train passenger from Arizona. They bumped into a bearded, back-packing man tenting on the beach and greeted him. Seems he and my mom's hiking companion had a mutual Arizona friend. The conversation went on to his teaching at Forest Lake Junior High School. No, he didn't know me, but . . .

. . . Mom called me over from my rocky perch anyway and introduced Robert Morgan, the man who would become my second husband.

JAN & GREG IN CHURCHILL, MANITOBA

Capítulo Diecisiete
The Move North

The same year Lorena moved back to Guatemala, I took my five-year old son, Gregory, north to embark on a new life with Robert. We moved into a 14' x 16' hut on forty acres and began building our home. That is a story for another day. I include this for context of my introduction to Camp Ripley, a National Guard training center and encampment, complete with its own military cemetery.

Out on our prairie patch, we enjoyed a large garden, chased away deer and bunnies, caught rain in barrels for bathing, and went to the front house each day to build. I previously envisioned an idyllic country life and got. . . unending sweaty work and bombings. Earth-shaking, glass shattering bombings. Every weekend, the National Guard practiced their war games. They did not stop at bedtime. I couldn't imagine how realtors sold properties within a twenty-mile radius. Surely they didn't show houses during weekend warrior maneuvers. Gregory wrote a letter of complaint, using his first grade penmanship, to then-Senator David Durenberger. The core message read: "Please stop the bombing by 8:00 p.m. That is my bedtime and I can't sleep." Durenberger agreed the camp should "be a better neighbor" and he appreciated Gregory's concerns.

When I say we were building a house, I mean chimney bricks, recycled windows, and backbreaking lifting. Robert and I, with occasional help from his brother, David, plodded along. The sporadic friend or hired carpenter gave me respite and hope. Do-it-yourself style was beyond slow and I wasn't a carpenter. Nine Inch Nails was a name of a hard rock band, not something I wanted to pound. I did pound nails, split kindling, hold up framed walls, sand and polyurethane thousands of board feet, but we weren't nearly finished. We were facing our second winter in the hut when. . .

I was literally called off the roof to be interviewed for a Spanish-teaching job. After a year of trying to be a carpenter and meld my family, I crawled down two extension ladders to take the superintendent's personal call. Carole, a Brainerd High School Spanish teacher, was planning a leave of absence the next fall to be home when her newly adopted baby was due to arrive. Would I like to come in for an interview?

¡Dios Mío! Oh, my God, yes!

THE WINDING ROAD TO TEACHING

Fall came, but her baby didn't. We kept building and waiting. Christmas passed and I still hadn't gotten the call to teach. We took Gregory out of second grade, got in our car, and headed to Mexico. Our first stop was Saltillo, no less! I introduced my little family to

Raúl and Lucio. They introduced me to their wives, Ilsa and Gloria. They placed their little toddlers on the floor in front of Gregory and off they went.

If we put multi-lingual kids in the same daycare, foreign language teachers would be out of business. Gregory, Raulito, Ilsa, and Gloria (they have this marvelous custom of naming daughters after mothers) played together seamlessly. My friendships with Raúl and Lucio were also seamless.

LUCIO, GLORIA & BABY GLORIA

We picked right up from our last visit in 1969.

A few days later, we waved our good-byes and promised to stay in touch. We were on our way across stretches of desert, through Durango and up to the continental divide in the Sierra Occidental mountains. I did not drive then and still refuse to do out-of-country driving. It was up to Robert to cling around the mountain curves between sheer bluffs and oncoming lumber trucks. In our tiny Horizon, we peered out the window at a Mack truck that didn't make the corner, lying on its side below, logs spilled out into the valley.

It was a relief to dip down the mountain slopes into Mazatlán and find Carnival in progress. There, Gregory saw his first big water, the Sea of Cortez. He stood in the foam of incoming waves,

RAÚL, GREG, ILSA, & ROBERT

looking out into eternity before we continued north along the coast to picturesque Álamos. There, among the whitewashed red and pink bougainvillea-draped colonial walls, we experienced Mexican "Easter" eggs. As we walked to the town center, these colorful eggs came flying at us from behind the corner building in the plaza. Before I could yell, "Duck and run!" to my startled family, I saw some teens sprinting toward us.

For a brief moment, I imagined we were being attacked due to another U.S. foreign policy posing an affront to Latin American issues. Before we could hit the sidewalk, one perpetrator veered off, splatted a colored egg on the head of another passerby, and took off down the street spewing a confetti trail behind him. Carnival? This was something an eight-year-old could really get into. I knew what Gregory was thinking when he pulled on my arm. There was a lady sitting by a stack of egg cartons on the curb. I handed him some *pesos*.

Álamos also provided us a free stay with two middle-aged ex-pats who had taken over a small *hacienda*. These two women were refurbishing the empty rooms with brightly colored paints, native pottery, and, with the help of Victor, reclaiming the overgrown gardens. With Carnival in full swing, the local hotel was full. After a short conversation in the plaza, they invited us to be their *hacienda* guests for two days. I don't remember their names, but their smiles. They were delighted to see Gregory splash about in their pool. Robert tried out his Spanish with the local barber and got a decent haircut. I asked a young girl where the post office was. She turned out to be the daughter of the postman and led me there. Cecilia and I became pen pals. Her dad would later send my dad stamps for their mutual foreign stamp collections. All that was still in our future.

GREG PLAYING WITH BABY GLORIA

Our immediate trajectory included stops at Guaymas where we camped in the sand dunes as the seaside villas were still under construction. We hoped to take the train tour through Copper Canyon, but were informed it had derailed. That ended our desire to tour. We headed to Gregory's grandparents in Apache Junction on the U.S. side. It was there we got the call.

It was not for me, but for Robert. His application for a rural mail carrier was accepted and he was to begin within the week. We left Arizona's deserts and got smacked by an Iowa ice blizzard on our return trip. The change of weather and life was abrupt. Robert got us safely home and took his little Datsun pickup on mail delivery routes. I, however, was still not a Brainerd teacher.

A JOB OR A CAREER?

My call did not come until a few weeks before school was out. My hoped-for semester seemed to have been condensed to a handful of days. But not so. Carole requested a year's leave to be home with her new daughter. My few weeks turned into a school year and a career—a career of promoting second language learning on a clearly monolingual island!

Inserting Spanish into an enclave of second- and third-generation Scandinavian immigrants still eating Swedish meatballs, playing hardanger fiddles and attending Sons of Norway meetings was a challenge. Immigrants tend to shed native languages in the quest to assimilate. Signing up to learn another language was a "foreign" concept—a frivolous elective, at best.

I bounded onto the scene as an energetic, naïve, cheery "foreign language" teacher, preaching the advantages of keeping your immigrant language or learning a second, maybe even a third, like in Europe. "Oh, the places you'll go" was my Dr. Suess mantra, but not so easy to convince administrators, counselors, parents, and finally, students to embark on

113

language learning adventures. My own journey had included the visionless advice to "only take two years" despite my apparent talent.

Language learning requires practice. Most parents promoted music and sports, which included hours of practice. Finally, the "two years" seemed to be accepted, but by junior year students wanted courses providing a good grade point average. Translation: An easy "A."

Remember the advice first given to me as a teacher? Numbers. What did a language teacher have to do to convince people that a second (or third) language created a richness in life, albeit not necessarily monetary? We sing, we dance, we act out verbs, offer Language Clubs and still have to speak to the Board of Education to promote our classes. When my year was finished, the enrollment had grown to include a full and a half-time position! Carole chose the half time, catapulting me into a full-time teacher.

I was on my way! That included taking over her annual trip to Mexico. I needed to rally student interest, sign them up, do fundraising, hold orientations, collect down-payments, and then be their guide/mother/teacher for ten days. Yet, my colleagues would ask me about my upcoming spring break "vacation."

The contract I agreed on included the junior high introductory class, travel between schools, and eating my lunch in the car. It meant helping with Spanish Club, co-coordinating Foreign Language week, and coordinating with the French and German teachers. Our motto was not to be competitors, but world language promoters. Cheerleaders for language!

About this time, I discovered Concordia Language Villages outside of Bemidji in northern Minnesota. There was a place called *Skogfjorden*, the Norwegian camp, and *Waldsee*, for Germans. I couldn't wait for the Spanish contingent to get organized and funded!

SPANISH CAMP AT THE NORWEGIAN VILLAGE

Ah, the Norwegians. They were busy promoting their language and culture in the form of a camp tucked into the northern Minnesota woods outside of Bemidji. Gerhard Haukebo, PhD, at Concordia College in the 1960s, came up with the idea that language learning is enhanced by cultural context. They gathered a small group of kiddos in the summer of 1961 just north of Alexandria, Minnesota and tried out immersion learning. The first permanent camp village to be built was the Norwegian *Skogfjorden* in 1969, followed by German Camp *Waldsee*, in 1978, French, *Lac du Bois* in 1988, and Spanish *Lago del Bosque* coming to life in 2000. I was reading the brochure in the mid-1980s.

It promised *tacos* and *paella*, the Mexican Hat dance and flamenco, soccer or crafts, all taught by native speakers representing a variety of Spanish-speaking countries. Concordia pursued the theory of living the language. This shouldn't be such a foreign idea. Think football camps, music camps, dance camps ... The foreign idea was to promote languages. Where do I sign?

I put out a call for interest, reserved transportation and collected their money. One

114

fall Friday evening, my students lugged their backpacks onto the bus headed north. I put on some Spanish music and we were off. *No inglés.*

My little group huddled around the Customs House with their authentic Concordia Camp passports and answered authentic border crossing questions, "*¿Cómo te llamas? ¿De dónde eres?* What is your name? Where are you from?" English books and music were contraband and quickly confiscated, before they pointed us to the *Banco* to exchange dollars to *pesos.* We unpacked in cozy Norsky cabins labeled Madrid, Sevilla, and Barcelona. This weekend's historical time frame was the 15th century.

From art projects constructing their own "knights in shining armor" out of cardboard boxes, to the full production of Isabella and Ferdinand reuniting Spain in Granada, we were immersed. At mealtime, the counselors pranced around the dining hall, chanting the names of foods and vocabulary of good manners. If you wanted something to eat, you had to speak Spanish. Now, there is a motivator. They learned to sing current pop songs and I learned methodology!

I blatantly stole ideas. I stepped away from the blackboard and walked into TPR, Total Physical Response. No more vocabulary lists of nouns with their friendly adjectives, but collections of items they had to recognize and touch before trying to speak. I loved it and so did the students. Or at least they were actively involved in their learning.

A main ingredient of language camp went beyond methods. It was the staff. The staff always included native speakers, mostly international college students from Concordia College in Moorhead, Minnesota. My high school students involved themselves personally if they were going to eat, dance or get a one-on-one conversation with a native speaker. No more one-to-thirty teacher-student ratio. Those energetic international students were great motivators, especially if they were cute. That gave me another idea.

~ *Puente* ~
Making Spanish Real

My crazy teacher fantasy was to fly all my students to Mexico, parachute them onto the geography below, and pick them up in a month. The second best option was flying students from Mexico in and having them stay here. Being the only mother duck with thirty or more ducklings following me and my accent around, I investigated exchange programs.

For the record, some teachers actually do attend Teacher's Conventions in the fall, as did I in the beginning years. It was in Minneapolis one October that I stopped at the University of Seattle's Inter-Cultural Exchange Program, ICEP, booth and met Bonnie Mortell. By the time I left for my next seminar, I had signed up to be a representative responsible for two students. She gave me a big three-ring binder outlining how to find and interview families, match them with student intro letters, deal with cultural shock, rules of conduct, general documentation forms, and government laws.

115

Capítulo Dieciocho
It Started with Polo

Polo was my first exchange student, coming in from Culiacán, Mexico, a city of over 200,000. He was coming to Brainerd, a town of under 15,000. In Culiacán, he dropped his bath towels on the floor, didn't have to make his bed, fix his snacks, nothing. . .because he had a maid. That did not make him spoiled, just untrained. It was his culture. This was the prototype of participants.

POLO, TROY & GREG AT ST. MATHIAS RACE

Bev and Jim stepped up to be my first host parents with their three children. Polo joined his new siblings in their woodland home south of town, off the highway, down the gravel road and into an acreage along the Mississippi River. There, Polo learned how to use the washing machine, warm up leftovers, and wield an ax. Splitting and stacking wood was a weekly chore.

Although not arriving with basic housekeeping skills, he was a model of good manners, attentive listening habits, and desire to experience this new life. The Mexican students participating in ICEP were from upper middle class families desiring global understanding and improved English for their futures. These kids were raised with the idea that they would be doing a school year abroad before college. The U.S. still has not embraced this enlightenment.

The students came with a variety of language skills and maturity levels. The youngest was 14 and the upper age was 18. It gets too complicated past that age, due to the risk of overstaying the visa and becoming an undocumented statistic. Their life in Mexico was extended-family centered, Catholic (in theory), socially active, with expansive beautiful homes, and *chicas*/maids (plural) that worked for them.

In the U.S., their homes were more modest, didn't include maids, families likely didn't attend church, and infrequently ate meals together. They unanimously agreed that our expectations for homework were lower than theirs and our classes easier. The program forbade driving, due to liability. Public transit in Brainerd included expensive taxis and mini-van buses requiring reservations. They ate their chicken, pizzas, and grilled cheese sandwiches with knives and forks. Potlucks got mixed reviews. Some couldn't stomach cold red Jell-O melting into hot tuna-macaroni casserole. When they went to Mexican restaurants, the food was unrecognizable from what *Abuela*/grandma made at home. The girls all gained weight. Boys looked to join soccer teams that were non-existent at that time.

Movies covertly export the nuances of our U.S. life. Incoming students exclaimed when they saw the schools actually did have lockers! They wanted to experience prom. Also, "just like in the movies", they saw people requesting paper or plastic at the grocery stores. In Mexico, reusable bags made of lawn chair type materials carry poundage without breakage. Countries wanting to emulate the U.S. life style without waste disposal services ended up with litter. In the case of plastic, the whole world has gained a plastic continent floating at sea! Think straws.

We could take the best practices from each culture, combine them, and . . .but no. That still isn't the precedent. My inner teeter-totter goes between optimism and cynicism. Each new student offered fresh insights to our culture's habits with their comments and, unwittingly, became the sole example for their entire country. They did break the stereo-types of Mexicans being poor, sarape-wearing burro riders. When I caught my students generalizing Mexican behavior due to Juan or Juanita, I put the mirror to their faces and asked if they wanted to be the standard by which all Mexicans judged us. Being the country's sole ambassador is a big responsibility, a thought that tourists should ponder.

Most adults wouldn't weather what these teens did. Gina constantly cried to me about the cats in her host family getting up on the table and sleeping in the beds. Patricia didn't want to live in a farm house. José wanted to play basketball but it was too difficult to get rides to practice. I weathered the bumps with them, trying to arrange the best expe-riences. Sometimes changes were made. Sometimes it was a growing up experience. Some-times the American dream turned sour.

For example, participating in the school's prom. Prom was a big dream to them. The special dress was like *Quinceñera*, fifteenth birthday time. The big dance, the after-prom parties. They had seen all these in the movies. On one such night, Gloria went to prom. Beautiful, until her date got drunk. She reasoned that it was safer to drive them home her-self, a forbidden act under the program and U.S. law. Prom night plus small town equals police "profiling" teen drivers. She was pulled over, didn't have a license, and ended up with a citation. Her drunk date was curled up in the backseat, oblivious to the transaction. Gloria and I went to court and got community service. She was mortified in two countries! We worked the soup kitchen and weathered the infraction. The local boy? Never heard from him! Now that was a crime.

One winter I was asked if all those little houses out on that great white expanse were where the poor people lived. They were fishing shacks on White Bear Lake. Some found living a half-hour from town in small country houses too isolated. Some found living in a town of 15,000 too tame. After 5:30 p.m., downtown stores closed and I was asked where all the people went, since that is the hour many Latin American streets begin to fill for the evening.

Some liked their country homes, basked in the quiet, took up fishing, or practiced long distance running on narrow dirt roads cutting through corn fields. One young man ran the New York Marathon and came in 113 out of 30,000 runners. Exchange programs are life changers.

The Corona Family: Baby Alejandro, Polo, Leopoldo, Teresita, Baby Teresa, Luis, Charlie The older boys came to Brainerd on exchanges.

Mexico City
A Night Out. . . of Teacher Mode!

ICEP had a two-prong operation, one for exchange students and the other for the participating teacher-counselors. I was invited to interview students and give orientations to the Mexican families, IN MEXICO! What a "big girl" moment! Teaching never honored me with all-expense-paid work trips to anywhere. Now I was going to Mexico City, Guadalajara, and Culiacán.

We were sent in pairs. That way we had a partner to set up interviews, do the recommendations, and take parents' questions about life in the U.S. Some brave parent would always raise a hand and ask us: "Are your schools safe? It is really safe to send our children to America?" At the time, there had only been a few school shootings, so we still said yes.

After one such day of work, my ICEP partner, Marian, and I headed out for some Mexico City nightlife. The concierge recommended the piano lounge at the Ritz Hotel. We glided through the revolving doors into the old-world ambience of dark wood, chandeliers, and soaring ceiling. The lights dimmed, gentlemen drifted past dressed in tuxes and the ladies clicked by in the highest heels they could tolerate. They sat at tables for two, clinking their crystal glasses and sending tiny paper requests with their waiters to the piano man for "Cielito Lindo," "Volveré," and "Guadalajara." Vintage Mexican comfort music. The genre changed when Marian stood up and walked over to the piano. She bent to whisper something into the pianist's ear. He patted the spot next to him on the bench.

What was she going to do? He slid over and swept his open hand over the keys. She sat down and took over! Her fingers danced over the keys from one end to the other. Then she opened her mouth and deep, rich notes came up from her solar plexus, filling the room. By the third song, he joined her in a duet and the patrons moved their chairs to get a better view. She ended by standing up, microphone to her mouth, other arm stretched out wide, swaying to the piano man's rendition of nothing less than the appropriate song, "Putting on the Ritz." She swayed, hit the high notes then swiveled into the finish. A Midwestern Spanish high school teacher gyrating at the Hotel Ritz in downtown Mexico City. She took a deep bow to the resounding applause and whistles of the crowd. She dipped again, placing a red-lipped kiss on the pianist's cheek and returned to our table as if she did this every night.

"Marian!" I exclaimed. "*Enhorabuena*, congrats! You're way out of teacher mode!"

"I've sung at family gatherings forever," she responded, before snapping her fingers to the waiter and giving a nod toward her empty glass.

He stood at attention, saluted, and grinned all the way to the table. "*Señora, lo que quiere, cortesía de la casa.*" Whatever you want. It's on the house.

Ah, what bliss! A night out of teacher mode!

CULTURAL LESSONS AND POLITICS COLLIDE

As much as I loved my room full of thirty-plus high school sophomores, juniors and seniors, I wondered what was beyond my standing there with a piece of chalk in my hand drawing verb charts on the blackboard.

True, I did more than brush chalk dust off my black pants. I arrived early and set their desks into mini-market stalls to practice vocabulary within a cultural context. We played Bingo with little prizes from Mexico. For prepositions, I ordered them to stand to the left, right, in front of, and behind their desks. I always ended with *debajo de* and crawled under my chair because I could fit. A few smarty-pants football players usually picked up their desks and put them over their heads, thus putting them "under," getting the last laugh.

I added live culture. I arranged for Susana di Palma and her then husband, Michael Hauser, to bring her flamenco and his guitar to class and school assemblies. She held up her castanets, explaining the smaller, higher pitched one in her right hand was the female voice and the larger, lower resounding pair in her left was the male. She sent the right hand into a rippling crescendo with her four fingers racing over the dangling castanets. Then a slow rum-pum, rum-pum methodically rapped from the lower bass voice. With a glimmer in her eye, she looked out over the class and explained, "Hear the female chattering on and on?" We nodded. "And can you make out her husband saying, 'Yes, dear. Yes, dear?'" So that's how it is.

Enrollment grew to two fulltime, but Carole wanted more family time. She left the Spanish Department and Edith was added. She brought her Spain accent and excellence in grammar. We joined forces and complemented each other's talents. I did the Concordia Camp weekends because, as she informed me, "I don't do sleeping bags." I love that about Edith. You know exactly where she stands.

She was a connoisseur of Spain's culinary delights. *Manchego* cheese, *sangria, aceitunas*/olives and *paella* came back into my life. When I got ill, she covered my classes. Other than the constant campaign for larger classroom spaces, funding, more staff, and administrative support for foreign languages, life was good.

AMITY AIDES: ANGELS, CRISTINA & FABIENNE WITH EDITH & JAN, 1997

But current events in Central America were creeping back into the news and my upper level lesson plans. Ever since Lorena's newspaper ads about kidnappings, I was unsettled. What the U.S. papers weren't saying was even more unsettling. What about the Sandinistas in Nicaragua, the Mayas in Guatemala, and the million dollars a day Reagan was feeding the El Salvadoran government? The debate topic of the year was Central America and, as the Spanish teacher, I was being asked questions.

Again, a phone call changed my course. There was an El Salvadoran man seeking sanctuary in Minnesota. He was invited to speak in Brainerd. The evasive current events landed in my lap.

Section 4

Seeking Sanctuary
in the 1980s

∼ *Puente* ∼
Rene Seeks Asylum

Rene Hurtado, fleeing El Salvador, asked for asylum in the U.S., right here in Minnesota. In the person of Rene, (an assumed name), the chance presented itself to get a first-hand account from an El Salvadoran who had been living these realities. In the photo accompanying the Minnetonka article, he appeared with a bandana covering his face. For the uninformed it made him look like a thief. The informed folks knew that, if he was recognized back home, his family could be harmed, even killed. The most popular form of terror involved the *desaparecidos*, the disappeared ones. The El Salvadoran government was behind the wheel of many dark-windowed cars roaming the streets of San Salvador. Each morning, bodies were scattered for those who dared go out, identify, and maybe claim them.

Before fleeing to the United States, Rene likely participated in some of his government's seedy practices. This was my impression then, but he is alive and I presume well, still living in Minnesota. I don't know what he has divulged since our meeting. I supposed he was either forced to participate in the El Salvadoran government's violent crackdown on rebels and then deserted or, as the Reagan administration purported of incoming Central Americans, came seeking "a better life." This is the difference between an asylum-seeking and economic refugee.

Ah, but asylum seekers had a slippery slope to climb. Since the U.S. was supporting the El Salvadoran government's actions, military advisors, and the School of the Americas, it was implicated, up to its eyeballs, in the very conditions forcing people to flee. That was an argument the Reagan administration did not want to see in court.

Then, as now, information trickled in. Then Rene was seeking asylum and sanctuary in Minnesota. A foreshadowing of the thousands of distressed detained at our southern border. Then, I was naïve, thinking that my country had the only story, the correct point of view, and the virtue not to commit atrocities. Now I have a different world view.

19

Capítulo Diecinueve
Translating Beyond the Words

"Jan, this is Connie. I have a few questions for you," she began. "Would you be interested in having Rene Hurtado speak to your high school Spanish classes?"

My mind raced over the few facts I had from an article about Rene. He was one of the first El Salvadorans to make headlines in Minnesota. The First Presbyterian Church in Minnetonka had taken him in, sort of a sanctuary situation, if you believed the government was buying the concept of sanctuary.

"When would he be here?" I hedged.

"Our Quaker group has invited him to speak at our next meeting. We are arranging a room at the college for a community event. If possible, we'd like him to go to an elementary school, just so they can hear some Spanish," she paused. "It might be in a week, depending on the transportation possibilities from the Cities."

Of course, the Quakers. Jim Corbett and his Quaker group were in Arizona courts due to their aiding refugees with food and housing. They resurrected the term "Sanctuary," perhaps from medieval England, when people hid out in churches, keeping out of the reach of the King. The idea of sanctuary goes back as far as the Greeks and even Clovis I, ruler of Gaul, in 511.

At the moment, Jim, John M. Fife III, a Presbyterian minister, and Ricardo Elford, a Catholic priest, had collided with the U.S. Immigration and Naturalization Service (INS) for transporting and protecting Central American refugees under the auspices of Sanctuary. If I transported Rene, could I be detained? I wasn't keen on being arrested.

"Connie," I hesitated, "Do you think there will be any trouble like they're having in Arizona? If I take him to my classes, do you expect any push back?"

"Guess that's up to you," she replied. "He can help with your lessons or you can have him tell his story. Might be a matter of comfort level for you both," she finished.

We both went silent. My students had studied Pablo Neruda's poem, *La United Fruit Company*, sung the "Who are the Terrorists" parody by Sabia, (a 1980s band falling under the South American revolutionary New Song genre), and done some political research for debate.

"Ok, when you have a date, let me know. I'll just take a day from verbs and he can speak to my upper level classes. They have some background and it's always good to talk to native speakers."

"That's my other question, Jan. Would you translate? We need someone for the Quaker meeting and the college forum. We could pay you, but not much. . ."

"This isn't about pay. This is about getting information out." (How many times I would say this in the decades to come!)

Before we hung up, we had planned the high school visit, the college venue, and I threw in an offer to take him to the elementary school and my home for an afternoon walk in the woods.

JANUARY 26, 1984

On this day, thousands of miles north of El Salvador's violence-ridden streets, the Quakers gathered. They pulled their chairs up around Connie and Steve's dining room table and waited for Rene to arrive. The doorbell rang.

Connie ushered him in, circling him around the table for introductions. I stood up and extended my hand. He loomed large in the newspaper articles, but was looking directly into my eyes. Me, the *Chaparrita*, the little one, at equal level.

"*Bienvenido a Minnesota*, welcome to Minnesota," I said, clasping his hand. His eyes brightened at the Spanish. Connie directed us to sit, me on his right as translator.

"*Me llamo Rene y soy de El Salvador*," he introduced himself. "My name is Rene and I am from El Salvador."

He slowly and deliberately spoke of his country as a peaceful place gone violent. He reaffirmed the accounts of the disappeared, the dead in the streets each morning, the overall fear. He had been accused of participating in killing and even of rape. He did not speak much of his personal involvement, but alluded to military maneuvers that went beyond his definition of service. He'd pause and let me translate.

"The orders given by El Salvadoran commanders were precisely to instill terror. When people fear for their lives and the lives of their children, they cower. They don't rebel. They are afraid to join unions or openly march in street protests. The government is not freely elected. The military is called upon to support regimes." He looked over at me, waiting for me to catch up.

Translating is a touchy business. Use of words. Choices. Words count. The use of "regime" over "administration;" the use of "rebel" or "freedom fighter;" the use of "communist subversive" to describe a Mayan *Quiché* Indian farming his cornfield *milpa*. Each word chosen carries weight, hints of your beliefs and revelations, implying things to those who know the history and culture. Translation is tricky. It includes context, tone of voice, vocabulary variances between country dialects, gestures, and body language.

Rene taught me the words for machine gun, handcuffs, and blindfold. Specialized vocabulary up until now meant medical or legal, not torture. He paraphrased, reworded, gestured, and drew pictures to help me. I listened to his tone of voice. Did he sound nervous or excited? How did he stand? Did he look up or at his feet? Did he sound confident yet fidget? My words and voice as the translator belong to the other. "*Yo soy de El Salvador*" translates to: "I am from El Salvador," not "He is." A good translator becomes invisible. Words of one language go in one ear and come out the mouth in another. I am a voice not allowed to show my bias.

I did the best I could and then went home to take care of my headache.

The Next Day

I picked up Rene and drove him out of our small town, down the backroads, and to my humble home on forty acres. I say humble because it measured 20' x 30' and the building inspector had thought I was describing my garage. My husband wasn't at home, so it fell to me to walk the woods trails and prairie with Rene, alone. I include the word "alone" because I carried around a speck of fear. I had read plenty about the behavior of the government soldiers. Had he really participated in civilian murders? Or rape?

His manner was quiet, his voice soft. We did not speak of his situation, past or present. I probably offered him tea and told him some stories of our building escapades. I found it difficult, not because of our language differences, but our lifestyles. I tried to put myself in his shoes and simply could not. I could not imagine being in another country, running away, depending on "the kindness of others," as Scarlet wistfully says in *Gone with the Wind*. I could not imagine someone ordering me to machete a child. I always try not to imagine rape. He may or may not have done any of these things that were graphically described in recent articles and books coming out of Central America. His presence here was a testimony to his beliefs. He did the dangerous thing: escape.

He was thousands of miles away from home in a forest with a stranger. He had to trust the Presbyterian Church's congregation. He had to trust the guy who drove him to Brainerd. He had to trust all of my students to take his story with respect. He had to trust that I would translate his words with intended strength and integrity. By the time we visited the elementary school, my personal doubts had turned to trust.

What a joy to see him sit on the floor surrounded by little children. Children that couldn't wait to repeat his funny sounding words in Spanish. Children who wanted to teach him some classroom vocabulary, pointing and saying: 'What's this?' He would then point to something else and ask: "*Cómo se dice?*" How do you say?" What a lovely game, learning language, a new secret code. What a lovely visit, seeing a roomful of monolingual, white kids chattering with a small, dark-skinned, Spanish-speaking, Central American man. What a lovely moment lacking judgment, accusations, fears. A moment of unbridled laughter and curiosity. A glimpse of humanity's potential.

20

Capítulo Veinte
First Congregational Church:
A Hotbed of Activists?

A GUATEMALAN PEASANT BEGS FOR CHANGE

The sun shone bright in a brilliant blue sky. Flowering crab trees were budding, leaves fluttered in the morning breeze. It was one of those days that lightens the heart and fills the lungs with hope. A Sunday morning in springtime.

Inside the church entry stood a woman dressed in a long colorful skirt, white embroidered blouse, and a black shawl. She humbly greeted each church member at the door with a slight bow of the head, a "*Por Dios*, for the love of God" and, instead of asking for a handout, presented a half-sheet of paper outlining the cycle producing hunger in her country. It was taped to a package of seeds for spring planting.

Behind her, a poster hung on the wall, showing cows eating their fill of grain along with a chart indicating the acreage needed to provide a pound of meat compared to how far the grain would go for human consumption. Another poster had magazine cut-outs of coffee, sugar, and bananas glued on a table with the question: "Who prepared your breakfast today?"

During the service, the congregation sang, "The Garden Song." "Inch by inch, row by row, gonna make my garden grow. . ." The children's sermon followed the journey from seed through rain and sun to harvest and table. During the service, this petite peasant woman explained the posters in slow, Spanish-accented English. At announcement time, "Garden Gleaning" was described. There would be a table in the narthex for all gardeners to bring in excess for others. It would be free for the taking, but a jar for donations would be available with the proceeds going to the soup kitchen.

That peasant woman was me. That presentation was my first public statement about Central America, starting with the hunger message. Unbeknownst to me, a couple from the Minnesota State UCC Church Council was in the congregation that day. Mardelle Bourdon came up to me after the service and exclaimed:

"Oh my goodness, girl, you were so real. I thought you were from Guatemala! Boy, do I have an idea for you!"

"I was born in Illinois and live here," I smiled at her, soaking in her praise.

"Your accent? The story you told about your family! You were so convincing!"

"I am a Spanish teacher and can fake accents, but the information is true," I assured her.

"I would like you to come to the annual UCC meeting with me in June and do this again. Would you?" she asked.

That was the moment my Guatemalan-self began a short stint of seminar and church visits around the area. Packing up my posters, buying more garden seeds, and dressing up was one way for me to take the message beyond my classrooms. The First Congregational Church allowed me the first platform. Rev. Steffen could have said no, but he said yes.

THE CHURCH BASEMENT BAZAAR FOR CENTRAL AMERICA

Church basement women have plays written about them. The vignettes capture the relationships, the laughter, the potlucks, and coffee after services. After my sojourn as a Guatemalan woman, the "church basement ladies" of the First Congregational Church's Women's Fellowship went into action.

Hunger was an issue that everyone could rally around, regardless of political affilia-tion. Church women are respon-sible for coffee hours, funerals, weddings, and bake sales. Instead of making pasties to raise money, like neighboring churches, the idea was hatched to do soup pack-ages. We live in a cold climate and packets of dried ingredients last for months. Motion passed.

That Saturday morning, I headed for the church basement and witnessed a swarm of women

JAN & MARDELLE AT DISPLAY TABLE

leaning over a children's swimming pool literally doing the "breast stroke." (no pun in-tended), swishing around pounds of beans and dried peas. There was an assembly line. Twenty to fifty pound bags of kidney beans, red beans and black beans were being cut open. Amounts were measured and poured into the pool. These legumes were measured into Ziploc bags with the corresponding concoction of herbs and spices before the paper with recipe and hunger facts was slipped in. *Voilá.* Soup packets to go. But go where? Sell-ing only to our own congregation was too confining. If we held a community event, maybe? The wheels of creativity churned.

RAISING AWARENESS THROUGH FOOD AND FUN

The hustle was on. Anyone have *realia* from Central American countries? A *sarape*? Well, that is not technically Central American, but bring it anyway. We could use those hunger posters with the cow. Who is willing to set up a hunger booth? We could make handouts with suggestions of how to save water, not use plastics so much, avoid Styrofoam coffee cups, environmental stuff...

The ideas flew around the meetings. Volunteers signed up to make posters, buy placemats, sit at information tables, and, the cherry-on-top, the Whitemans had an Old-Fashioned Photo Shop with outfits for dress-up. Why not?

"FIDEL"

We arranged a "fashion show" complete with the "players" in Latin America's story. Each model taking the walk down the aisle, up the steps to the altar, and back, wore a stereotypical outfit while the real history was being told. When a plantation worker "did the walk," for example, information was read including number of hours worked a day, conditions in the field, wages, health care, housing, and diet. In this way, their stories were told, including Castro. Yes, my husband had a large, full black beard, so we included Cuba's influence in the region.

The day came for the bazaar—a Saturday in November. If it were cold, all the better to bring in more people. An article was published in the paper. Ads were posted around town and sent out to dozens of churches.

The basement was adorned with booths dangling with crepe paper and *piñatas*. Hunger and current events information was laid out on tables next to authentic souvenirs for sale. The Photo Gallery was set for a photo of you "in Central America."

In the eating area, checkered tablecloths covered café style tables. A vase with a single flower and soup bowls sat on top of placemats printed with hunger facts. The smell of our steaming bean soup permeated

SHARON & CAROL

the room, setting stomachs growling. There were sides of rice and tortillas. I couldn't have been more pleased by the response of this church's people and their efforts to educate in such a major way. The detail, the hours, the care in every step overwhelmed me.

Time to open the doors! Remember the little kid rhyme where you hold your hands together and recite: "Here is the church, here is the steeple, open the doors and see all the people?" Well, I opened my hands and ... where were all the people?

A few trickled in. The afternoon wore on. Dribbles and drabs. The church ladies were not exhausted from running to serve the soup. Those that ate it loved it and bought a packet to go. My little family of three got our photo taken. A few pictures remain of

JAN, ROBERT, & GREG DRESSED UP

"Castro" in the "Latin American History Fashion walk" and one of Rev. LeDuc dressed as a military man with a rifle at the altar! That was a first and last. A few kids took a swing at the *piñata*.

We pulled down the crepe paper, washed the dishes, packed away the posters and hand-outs. Everything had been organized so well. Everyone had been so helpful. If it had been the Sons of Norway, would we have had a bigger turnout?

As we finished cleaning up, I moaned about having such a slim attendance. That is when I learned a thing about northern Minnesota culture. A man carrying out boxes yelled over his shoulder, "Didn't you know? Today is deer hunting opener! The guys are in deer stands and the 'hunting widows' are at the mall shopping!"

~ *Puente* ~
All Was Not Lost

All was not lost. The attendance was low but the seed was planted. A "Rice and Bean" dinner sponsored a sale of the unsold bean soup packets. We used up the placemats with the Hunger Myths at a soup and bread potluck. News from Central America filtered into UCC newsletters across the state. The Garden Gleaning project continues.

The hunger angle was safer than politics. I volunteered to write a monthly column combining hunger and environment. That door led into many rooms. A column on personal water conservation can include shorter showers and turning off the water when brushing teeth, or end up questioning designer waters in plastic bottles and the maldistribution of irrigation resources. Inspecting the tags on our clothes reveals a multitude of countries where workers can't buy enough food due to sweatshop wages. That involves hunger. Eventually, the subliminal messages become overt.

St. Luke's Presbyterian Church in Minnetonka had already surpassed mere words when they offered Rene sanctuary. Next, I heard about Yadira, another El Salvadoran refugee they were helping. She was only fifteen years old. She would be taken to Duluth. Could we provide supper at our church on the way?

Why was a fifteen-year-old girl fleeing her country? What was in Duluth? Was there a U.S. Sanctuary movement forming? Was this like the Underground Railroad of Civil War times, where different churches or individuals helped people along the way to freedom and safety? Canada accepted Central American refugees rejected by U.S. politics, a revealing political stand on their part.

21

Capítulo Veintiuno
Yadira and the Subversives:
Not a Central American Rock Band

Six of us sat around the table in the church basement that evening. Lilja, quiet-spoken activist in all manner of social justice issues, sat next to her husband, Jeff. Mary, former Peace Corps worker in Paraguay, was with her musician husband, Paul. My husband, Robert, was there with me, the Spanish teacher. Then in walked the driver from St. Luke's

with a diminutive teenaged girl following close behind. What in the world could she have done that ended her up here, at our table, so far from home?

ROBERT, JAN, YADIRA, MARK, LILJA, MARY & PAUL AT
FIRST CONGREGATIONAL CHURCH POTLUCK SUPPER (JEFF NOT PICTURED)

Yadira belonged to a Christian-based community. She had taught people how to read. Literacy work is an unspoken crime. It is not a law on the books. The ability to read is power. I doubt that any kindergarten teachers around here consider themselves to be subversives when they circle the kids up for reading Dr. Suess (who, by the way, wrote some very subversive stuff).

In Central America, catechists, folks with some religious background, took the only readily available book, the Bible, and read to small groups. Many hamlets did not have a regular priest or religiously trained leader, so community members took on the role. Since some people, especially the peasant populations or the Maya Indian villages, weren't literate, the Bible became the reading primer for those wanting to learn. This is double trouble for the powers-that-be.

This is how it worked. Let's say you are an illiterate plantation worker. It is time to vote for the next president. Your boss, owner of your housing, the company store where you buy things on credit, and the guy who decides if you have a job or not, comes around with election information that you cannot read. Looking over your shoulder with a friendly grin, he points to where you need to put your "X." Other times, that "X" signed an agreement to till the land for five years and then give it back. Sometimes it approved sending a percentage of your harvest to pay off the company store. You get the idea.

Teach that same worker how to read and there is a change. He doesn't want to sell his land, doesn't agree to the terms of employment, or maybe decides to organize a union. Now the government and oligarchy have readers protesting.

Remember, I said "double trouble" with literate citizens. The second punch of the one-two punch is religion. Catechists are Catholic by name and are reading Bible stories. The assembled listeners are people reaping the imbalance of global systems. Their chance of owning land, their own home, and getting away from the company store isn't always in the cards.

Into this scene walk such stories as David and Goliath, Moses and the Pharaoh, Jesus eating with the downtrodden and social outcasts. Now there are some subliminal messages, if you care to concentrate. David stood up to the Giant. Replace Giant with: oligarchy, corporations, multi-nationals, or even their foremen. Moses set the people free from bondage and headed for the promised lands. The Pharaoh (government) was not the hero. Jesus ate with "people like them," the workers, the peasants, not the Pharisees.

This is an extremely simplified way to introduce the whole Liberation Theology vs. Traditional Catholic Church movement. Liberation Theology is a fan of literacy.

What would it be like NOT to be able to read? If you weren't literate, everything you do would be altered. Driving a car, checking ingredients on a label, the door marked "push" or "pull." The beauty of literacy is that once you learn to read you can't turn it off. These words plastered everywhere educate and inform you. Without literacy, populations are easier to control.

Religion can be used to subdue people, en masse, or incite the same people into acts of rabble-rousing. Bible stories are a litany of kings, subjects, uprisings, freedom seeking, do-onto-others-as-you-would-have-them-do-unto-you revolutionaries. Yadira was labeled "catequist," which inferred dissemination of subversive ideas, in this case, via Bible stories. If I were living in Central America teaching what I taught, I would be on that list to be "disappeared." Teachers were found dismembered along the roads or hanging in front of their schools. People like Yadira were running for their lives.

Yadira was reading the Bible to groups and they were becoming literate in the stories and the alphabet. She had to go. I mean, far away. After another church basement supper, she was taken to Duluth where another church offered her refuge until the next step.

I believe she crossed over into Canada soon afterward. I didn't know about "*Proyecto Canadá*" until I became part of the Overground Railroad some months later, when Mardelle came up with another bright idea!

~ *Puente* ~
I Need a What?

Word came to me that there was an opening for a Spanish position at the Brainerd Community College (BCC). This coincided with a whisper inside my heart. Maybe this would be an opportunity to expand my queries. I applied for the job only to be told it required a Master's degree—a Master's degree that I did not have.

Again I looked to Barbara, my Hamline Spanish professor, for ideas. It turned out that Hamline had created something called a MALS degree (Masters of Arts in Liberal Studies), whereby students created their own itinerary, wrote a capstone thesis and received a Master's. They approved my design to study six weeks in Saltillo, take courses in Social Linguistics, Creative Writing, and a Reading Independent Study before going to Jubilee Partners for three months of volunteering with the Central American Overground Railroad.

22

Capítulo Veintidós
So Much to Learn

This was truly a personalized Master's program, including the independent study held over breakfast with Barbara at her home. With my professor still wrapped in her robe, we discussed a reading list, beginning with *Inevitable Revolutions* by Walter LeFeber and ending with my thesis. Patiently and quietly, she encouraged me to come to my own conclusions. I discovered the Central American oligarchies, the traditional Catholic Church, and the indigenous *campesinos*. The oligarchy was backed by the governments, the traditional church was challenged by Liberation Theology, and the workers joined unions and were called communists. That's it in an over-simplified nutshell. It was depressing. I bought a button that read, "One person can ~~only~~ do so much." I had to believe that or collapse into a dark abyss.

I was part of my country's collective ignorance and naivety. I was walking the periphery of unacceptable beliefs. My experiences exposed an ugliness in the United States that we collectively attributed to the basest of third world dictatorships. The sequestered documents that weren't publicized until decades later proved me correct, a fact that brought me no joy but deeper disgust. I hold a firm belief that members of Congress should be required to master at least two languages and be proficient in history.

Sadly, decades after my experience with the Overground Railroad, masses of Central Americans still forged their way toward our southern border. I believe this to be a direct result of 1954's CIA overthrow of Guatemala's duly elected president, Jacobo Arbenz, in favor of the stockholders in United Fruit Company's banana empire. The fallout of delivering our own hand-picked replacement, Carlos Castillo Armas, has upset Central America's quest for democracy and autonomy ever since. Don't take my word for it. Read *Bitter Fruits* by Schlesinger, Coatsworth, Kinzer, and Nuccio, which, according to Google, is readily available. Congress should read it with their morning coffee and bananas.

Dr. Barbara called Nobel Prize winner Pablo Neruda's *La United Fruit Company* poem to my attention. There, he aptly describes the division of Central America into strongholds of Coca-Cola, Anaconda and the United Fruit Company. He lists the dictators, either put in place or supported by the United States. In class, I'd read the poem aloud in Spanish, making the buzzing sounds of the "dictator flies" as they circled the sticky fruit and the dying bodies of the workers. Poetry, a concise, yet multi-level message. The indigenous workers falling into an abyss, a black hole of corporate land takeovers, a vortex of low wages and company stores, nameless victims of the world economic system falling into the garbage heap as the riches of their countries were exported northward. In Barbara's calm questioning voice, the poem's symbolism revealed itself. Pablo Neruda "nailed it" and now the poem has a sequel in the present.

In the poem, the metaphorical platters carried away the coffee, bananas, and sugar leaving the lands ravaged of their wealth and the abused worker falling into the rubbish. Since the writing of Neruda's poem, platters coming out of Central America not only float away with products but include people fleeing the abyss.

23

Capítulo Veintitrés
Coffee and Bananas

The news coming out of Central America was and is scarce, hitting mostly on the sensational. By 1980, the CIA coup d'état of 1954 was long forgotten, if it registered at all in the U.S. psyche. The slave-like working conditions of the banana plantations were not on the mind of northerners slicing this fruit on their cereal. Coffee drinkers weren't thinking about pickers broiling under the sun, charged a fine if they accidently broke off a branch while removing individual beans to fill their basket. Sugar was added to a plethora of products northerners consumed without thoughts of those folks hoisting produce from fields onto trucks. The cash crop overtook the foods once grown there, making self-sufficiency rare. Workers' wages were so low that sugar cane replaced food in the mouths of their children, staving off hunger while rotting their teeth.

These stories don't make headlines. The lid on my Pandora's box was lifting. The proverbial floodgate was open. Central American exchange students and church groups harboring refugees brought stories not touched by our main media. Personal accounts built a case against El Salvadoran and Guatemalan governments and their number one backer: The United States of America.

My rude awaking solidified at that kitchen table with Hamline professor Dr. Barbara. While reading *Inevitable Revolutions*, she took out a piece of paper and folded it in half. On one side she directed me to list the United States interests, on the other, Central American interests, and the "players" in each camp.

I drew two triangles and labeled the corners: Governments with military backing; Traditional Catholic Church, and finally, Oligarchs, with their lands and money. This represented the power and control. In fact, in 1984, fourteen families in El Salvador owned 60 percent of the land. Then I drew a second triangle, a mirror of opposites. Opposite the ruling governments were those factions rebelling against the stranglehold of status quo. Opposite the Vatican's Catholic practices emerged Liberation Theology, emphasis on the poor, and finally, the Workers, the union activists, the *campesinos*, removed from their lands, opposite the oligarchs that took their land, thus converting them into laborers.

Government/Military   Guerrilla/Rebel Fighters

Oligarchy   Traditional Catholic   Workers/Unions   Liberation Theology

Liberation Theology became a major factor in people's behavior so, begging forgiveness from academics, here is my much abbreviated definition:

"You don't have to wait until heaven for your reward. You are entitled to human rights now. This would include, but not be limited to: Food, shelter, and pursuit of some free time."

My equally short definition of the Traditional Catholic Church: "Accept your lot in life. Your reward is in heaven. You just wait and see."

Out of this fissure stepped Archbishop Oscar Romero. Originally of the Traditional persuasion, El Salvador's bloody quest moved him toward the poor. Conflicted and pushed to the edge by the violence being perpetrated against the community, he took to his pulpit on March 23, 1980, and delivered this message:

> I'd like to make an appeal in a special way to the men in the army. Brothers, each one of you is one of us. We are the same People. The farmers and peasants that you kill are your own brothers and sisters. When you hear the words of a man telling you to kill, think instead in the words of God, "Thou shalt not kill!" No soldier is obliged to obey an order contrary to the Law of God. In His name and in the name of our tormented people who have suffered so much, and whose laments cry out to heaven: I implore you! I beg you! I order you! Stop the repression!

The next day, on March 24th, he was gunned down when leaving mass at the Hospital of Divine Providence. The El Salvadoran government blamed the rebels. In 1993, the UN Commission for the Truth on El Salvador found politician, soldier, and extreme-right-winged death squad leader Roberto D'Aubuisson responsible for giving the orders. He had founded the White Warriors Union, a death squad made up of former military members, and had been trained at the International Police Academy in Washington, D.C., a noteworthy detail. D'Aubuisson's trail of death and damages filled El Salvador's collective memory.

D'Aubuisson formed the ARENA party and was elected El Salvador's President, despite his nickname, "Blowtorch Bob," referring to his favorite weapon of torture. He threw babies into the air for target practice. He was a graduate of the School of the Americas at Ft. Benning, a place of dubious curriculum preparing many graduates for futures as Latin

American dictators. Thousands of U.S. citizens protested annually, some getting prison time. One is a friend of mine. Stay tuned.

D'Aubuisson died in 1992, just a year before the Commission recognized him as a war criminal deserving punishment. Perhaps his death from esophageal cancer and bleeding ulcers was a direct result of all the vile hatred that rose from his burning innards through his throat into the universe. Just a mind/body/spirit karma thought.

Old news? Not so fast! Seriously. While googling Romero's quote, this popped up regarding his assassins:

Reuters/ Tony Gentile, October 24, 2018:

> "The order called for the arrest of Álvaro Rafael Saravia, a 78-year-old former soldier who has been a major suspect for years. His case was dismissed in 1993 after an amnesty law banned criminal trials connected to the Central American nation's bloody civil war. Some 75,000 people died in the conflict that lasted from 1980 to 1992. . .

D'Aubuisson gave that order but is not mentioned, likely due to his being dead. Yet here comes history back to bite us. My first reaction was goosebumps and "halleluiah finally" but close behind my second—Álvaro Rafael Saravia is just one of many minions, used and abused, following orders. Now who killed the nuns?

~ Puente ~
The Catholic Martyrs

Nine months after Archbishop Oscar Romero's untimely martyrdom, four Catholic missionaries made the news when they were raped and murdered by five members of the El Salvadoran National Guard. On December 2, 1980, Sisters Maura Clarke, Ita Ford, Ursuline Dorothy Kazel, and laywoman Jean Donovan were pulled from shallow graves. They had been working with Archbishop Romero and the poor, likely leading to their demise. The images of their bodies being rolled out on the grass got the attention of Catholics worldwide and gave fuel to those in the U.S. already working to bring awareness of the Central American atrocities. It also gave fuel to the fire pointing at El Salvador's government involvement.

24

Capítulo Veinticuatro
Who are the Terrorists?

Song sung by California group, SABIA, 1980s

"Well, I wanted to go to Nicaragua, (Nicaragua, Nicaragua),
the perfect place to end my vacation, in a revolutionary nation. . .
but when I got to Nicaragua, I found out that all the friction
was a U.S. funded Contra-diction. . . (CIA, CIA)"

The capacity to oppress was about to ramp up with the election of U.S. President Ronald Reagan (1981 – 1989). It was his "domino theory" belief that the Central American strife was due to communist infiltration that needed to be stopped before flowing over "our" borders. It is true that governments were being overthrown in that region, but for good reason, in my humble opinion. Take Reagan's poster child, Nicaragua, for example.

My synopsis:

In 1979, Daniel Ortega and his Sandinistas marched into Managua and overthrew Anastacio "Tachito" Somoza Debayle, third dictator in the family line covering forty years of squalor for the masses. The Somozas held the belief that Nicaragua was their personal *finca*, i.e. ranch, where "there are no homeless," pointing out the prevalence of good weather. Their workers were housed in warehouses with boxed-in cubbies for sleeping. In this way, the Somoza family amassed a fortune estimated at between $2 and $4 billion. (Brazilian newspaper, Gazeta Mercantil.)

When Daniel and his ragtag troops entered the capital, "Tachito" boarded a converted Curtiss C-46 and headed to Miami with the caskets of his father and brother (the two previous Somoza dictators), plus much of the Nicaragua's national treasury funds. President Jimmy Carter refused to harbor the Somozas, forcing them to continue on to Paraguay, where Anastacio was assassinated a year later. End of summary.

Yes, Mr. Reagan, there was a domino effect, not of communism but of oppressed people choosing revolution. Many of the Mayan Indians in Guatemala, the union workers in El Salvador, and the Hondurans who were hired to help with U.S. covert missions into Nicaragua, rose up in protest, only to be shot down.

During the 1980s, every day people disappeared into the backseats of cars with black tainted windows. The final estimated count was 75,000 civilians in El Salvador and 200,000 in Guatemala. Archbishop Oscar Romero's assassination in 1980 made him a martyr and, are you ready for this? On October 14, 2018, he was canonized. Yes, he is now Saint Oscar Romero. Every time I think I am writing about ancient, unrelated history, something like this surfaces. Another connecting dot, as valid as it is uncanny. Onward.

At the end of that decade, on November 16, 1989, to be precise, the world woke up to the news that six Jesuit priests, their housekeeper, and her daughter were murdered on the campus of José Simeón Cañas Central American University in San Salvador. The government figured these Liberation Theology priests were aligned with the poor, the struggling union workers, the disenfranchised, all considered subversive by the El Salvadoran government. In their eyes, Jesuits and their whole Liberation Theology thing were just plain cesspools of left-wing, communist, rebel doctrine.

The El Salvadoran government felt it had to do something about that radical element preaching human rights to the workers. Bananas, indigo, sugar, and the like were harvested by those living in hovels, without sanitation, running water, medical attention, you get the idea. I suppose if you consider Juanita running with a water jug on her head to the one spigot for two hundred people as "running water," I stand corrected. U.S. stockholders had a vested interest in not paying Juanita higher wages. That would mean lower dividends to them on their next statement.

Now, back to the scene of the crime. Soldiers entered the priests' residence, forced them into the garden, gunned them down, and left a placard that read, "FMLN (the rebel group) executed those who informed on it." However, it was the government that consistently murdered civilians for forming unions, trying to practice free speech, and even for teaching people how to read. The Reagan administration sent approximately $1 million a day to this regime. Notice, words do matter. Regime is a clue. I really need a stronger word, but it does not exist.

HOLY-MOLY, A PRIEST IN A TREE
(Father Roy and the School of the Americas' Torture Manual)

This highly visible crime was pulled off by an elite force of the Salvadoran Army known at the Atlacatl Battalion. That infamous military faction would be accused of many sanctioned atrocities when crimes of this era finally went before the Spanish court. Some perpetrators were brought to justice, nearly all blessed by their government at the time of the crime and sponsored by . . . the U.S. government. The U.S. wasn't keen on these facts coming to the light of day. This is where it gets dicey!

Atlacatl's soldiers were trained by the U.S.-backed School of the Americas, then located in Panama before its move to Fort Benning, Georgia. School of the Americas was already the target of U.S. protesters who knew stuff! People were rallying in their local cities, protesting in Washington D.C., and planning annual marches at Fort Benning.

Father Roy Bourgeois, Maryknoll priest and Vietnam Veteran, was their guiding light. He got wind of this training grounds exporting torture and questionable behavior to Latin America and literally stepped up. . . into a tree outside the Fort Benning base in protest. He founded the School of the Americas (SOA) Watch in 1990, organizing protests asking Congress to close it down. Across the U.S., citizens began to "cross the line" at Fort Benning, a trespass event that could get them arrested and often jailed.

Remember I mentioned having a friend involved? Her name is Mary. She protested by crossing the line at Ft. Benning and spent six months in the Pekin, Illinois, prison for that action. Long before that decision, Mary invited me to meet Father Roy over tea and freshly baked bars in her kitchen. The conversation left Mary and me both overwhelmed, yet encouraged. It encouraged us into actions. I chose Jubilee Partners and the Overground Railroad in 1989. She chose to cross the Ft. Benning line.

You would have to know this diminutive, thoughtful, soft-spoken woman to grasp the profoundness of this moment. She was known for opening her home to the international traveler, the poet, the activist, the neighbor, and putting out a pot of tea and tray of baked goods. Yet she risked going to prison. On May 23, 2001, Mary and 25 others, including her twin sister, were found guilty of trespassing by the Columbus Georgia District Court. The sentences ranged from thirty days to one year. She got six months. The oldest detainee was an 88-year-old nun.

The *Brainerd Dispatch* archives, July 17, 2001, contain Mary's statement before the judge and details of this moment. It was the day they locked her up. While incarcerated, a photo of Mary holding out a tray of steaming chocolate bars appeared in the September, 2001 issue of Minnesota Monthly with the article's caption: "Minnesotan Mother behind Bars," the perfect metaphor.

Despite nationwide protests and incarcerations, the school was never closed. It did get its name changed to WHINSEC (Western Hemisphere Institute for Security Cooperation) in 2000, in an effort to cleanse the image and divert attention from its reputation. Those who were involved during that historical period can be recognized by simply using the original name, SOA.

"So?"

In 2019, nearly two decades later, Trump contorted the profile of incoming Central American asylum seekers as terrorist, rapists, drug-dealers and thieves, if of nothing else, taking our "American" jobs. His rhetoric showcased a total absence of knowledge of the region and the United States economic, military and covert involvement. Foreign interference has wreaked havoc from the very first European encounter with the Americas and its indigenous cultures to present day ethnocentric and racist views. Study and reflection reveal that United States foreign policies produce the very migration to *El Norte* that is being vilified—a blind spot in our national psyche.

These migrations are fallout, "collateral damage," of multinational companies and their protectors' government policies. The fact that we use the term "collateral damage" for living, breathing people speaks volumes to our cultural attitude. After the Trump election, the U.S. came under a barrage of divisive, fear-mongering, ignorant tweets.

If you are on the other side of this opinion, I humbly ask you to do some homework. Read about supply and demand (think drugs); The U.S. aging population and need for immigrant workers (think funding Social Security); and check historical facts on who is coming to our borders (1980s U.S. policy in Central America). I arrived at my opinions via decades of small, yet insightful awakenings. As a professor, I encouraged students to have a minimum of three sources of divergent opinions. I encourage you to do the same.

Section 5

1980s Overground Railroad
Central America to Canada

~Puente ~
The Overground

Let's be clear on this. I am not old enough to have participated in the Underground Railroad of the Civil War. I'm talking about an Overground Railroad for Central American refugees in the 1980s. People were fleeing their homes in Nicaragua, Honduras, El Salvador, and Guatemala. It was an arduous and dangerous trip from their hamlets—hiking over mountains, crossing rivers, braving jungles—and that only got them to Mexico. In Mexico they tried to hide their accents, avoid Mexican police and military, traverse deserts, jump on moving trains, (look up The Beast) and make it to the U.S. border where they hoped to find rest and acceptance.

They did not find either. Sadly, it hasn't changed. In January 2019, the Trump administration demanded billions to erect a solid wall on a border measuring two thousand miles. He shut down the government to get his demand. His administration claimed that children separated from their parents for months were reunited, a separation that should never have happened in the first place. In 1989, as now, many immigrants turned themselves in, seeking asylum, but got detention followed by deportation.

In the 1980s, newspapers finally moved Central American news from short, back-page columns to front pages with photos. U.S. citizens returned from Central America with viewpoints that veered drastically from the official United Press International versions. Witness for Peace documented human rights abuses and sent accompaniers to stand with those threatened by death for their activities. Jim Corbett and the Quakers worked Sanctuary despite arrests. Locally, a group that would become The Brainerd Peacemakers was in its early stages of organizing protests.

The Peacemakers found a good use for Deer Hunting and Fishing Openers. Brainerd is the gateway to the north woods. They organized protests and held up placards along the northbound highways while the hunters and fisher people flowed into town. We got positive honks or not so friendly third fingers. Either way, we smiled back, knowing they were now aware of Central America's plight.

I joined the protesters. I wrote to my elected officials. I submitted Open Forum letters to the local newspaper. Yet I was unwilling to put myself and my twelve-year-old son on site in Central America. What could I do to reach these people personally?

25

Capítulo Veinticinco
Mardelle's Big Idea – Jubilee Partners

"Jan, if you are interested in volunteering, take a look at this. It's a list of United Church of Christ volunteer opportunities here and overseas. There is one in Georgia where you could speak Spanish and work with refugees." She handed it over.

"Jubilee Partners, Comer, Georgia: Intentional community working with Central American refugees. Gardening, cooking, office work, teaching English, translating for court appearances, organizing recreational activities. Volunteer for 6 – 12 months. Room and board plus $5.00/week stipend."

The $5.00/week wage didn't deter me, but committing for six months away from job and family gave me pause. I'd have to take a leave of absence, take Greg out of his Minnesota school and enroll him in Georgia. Georgia didn't have the best record on education. They still used corporal punishment, for heaven's sake.

In the end, I went for it. Jubilee approved my request for three months, not six. Hamline approved Jubilee as part of my Master's degree. District #181 approved my sabbatical. Greg and I flew out with no notion of what was next.

The first memory of our adventure was a tiny plane from Charlotte to Athens making its way blindly through thick, pea soup fog and bouncing turbulence. Greg's most vivid and embarrassing moment came when I turned white and threw up in the provided barf bag. My most embarrassing moment came when they insisted I deplane riding in their auxiliary wheelchair. I can only imagine my new employer's reaction when they wheeled me out.

LIFE AT THE K HOUSE

Our chauffeur, also named Greg, heretofore referred to as Gregorio, hoisted our two bags into the trunk of a very used car and wound us through the countryside to Comer. He turned off just outside of town and followed the long dirt lane lined with pecan trees and on to a large building with an A-line roof rising into the sky and touching the ground on the other end.

"This is the K House," he said, unloading our luggage. "The short term volunteers live here. It also houses the community kitchen and dining areas where all the gatherings are held."

He led us into the side door and up to the second floor. "This will be your room," he said showing us into a dorm-sized space. "Down the hall is the community bathroom. The showers are there. You put out a sign for 'male' or 'female' when you go in so everybody knows."

THE K HOUSE

We scanned the room, finding built-in desks along the wall with the window, two chairs and a ladder leading up to a sleeping loft.

"Dinner will be served in an hour, so that should give you some time to unpack. I'll come looking for you," Gregorio said, heading back down the hall.

"Let's get to it," I nodded to Greg, although my stomach had not settled. I still felt a tad weak as I hoisted my bag to the chair.

"Mom, look at this loft! It's like having a fort!" he said, finally giving me a hint to his impressions. I did not know how he would react to my new plan for our lives. It was something I was going to do and I was not leaving him back home. Regardless of what was ahead, it would be one of those "experiences of a lifetime."

It didn't take long to move in. I thought of the refugees, often traveling with, as they say, only the shirts on their backs. This arrangement may seem humble, but it included a roof, food and a job, albeit $5.00/week, all guaranteed. Many in the world would welcome such good fortune. I closed the dresser drawer and there was Gregorio, back to escort us to supper.

Folks were already lined up with plates in hand to go through a buffet-style arrangement. I didn't trust my stomach yet and opted out. Greg followed the leader and fit right in. When we sat, Gregorio made the introductions around our table. Jeanette, Kara, Tom, Jens, from Germany, and Tree, short for his last name, Roundtree. They were probably all in their twenties. This made me an elder at age thirty-six, along with having a twelve-year-old son. After supper we moved to the couches and went through brief personal introduction stories before work details were made for the next day.

ORIENTATION

The Jubilee Partners' community was divided into three population groups: The Partners, The Volunteers, and The Refugees. The Partners included founding members and those who went through the process for long-term participation. The Volunteers were vetted via applications and accepted for an average of six months. The Refugees, at this moment in history, were from Central America. They came through government channels headed on to Canada—a process referred to by participants as the Overground Railroad. At least, that was my pre-orientation understanding.

A thirty-something bespectacled strawberry blonde strode over to me with her hand extended. "Hi, I'm Terry, one of the Partners. I'm going to give you some of the background on this place and you can ask questions. Since the rest of this term's volunteers got here in January, we're going to do this informally over tea."

It was March. I was studying in Saltillo the first six weeks of the year as part of my Master's program, and was grateful that Jubilee accepted me for an abbreviated term of three months. Terry poured steaming water into our cups and tore open two tea bags.

"Volunteers live in the K House," Terry began. "K is for Koinonia, a Greek word meaning community. The name comes from the mother community, Koinonia, also located in Georgia. Koinonia was created in the 1950s with the idea that blacks and whites could live and work together." She described how Koinonia created a working farm where the races were integrated, a concept that didn't rest easy with the neighbors. "At that time, their combined living and work spaces were welcomed with machine guns and night attacks."

GROUP OF VOLUNTEERS

It hit me that I was now seated in the deep south, with a very different cosmology and history than northern Minnesota. "They not only survived, but thrived," Terry continued. "Habitat for Humanity and Jubilee are both sister communities to the mother group, Koinonia."

My thoughts wandered to my parents and their reaction when I told them I'd be living in an intentional community. Their minds went right to the 1960s "commune," a red flag term inferring hippies, LSD, long hair, sharing worldly goods, akin to socialism, and the iconic free love frenzy, a coined term equating rampant sex. I divide the word community into Com(e) and Unity, a much more fitting symbol for Jubilee's mission.

Terry's voice brought me back. "The Jubilee farm is divided into a refugee area with houses built by volunteers. There are garden plots for them, a small building of classrooms, and laundry space. It is a ten-minute walk between the Volunteer and Partner quarters which included the K House and homes for Partners, the long term people who have made a commitment to live here beyond a year. Don and Carol Mosley, among other original founders, moved from the mother community, Koinonia, intending to dedicate this project to refugee resettlement, regardless of country. Presently, the refugees are Central Americans."

At the end of orientation, I was signed up on the revolving kitchen-duty list and appointed to work in the office for Don Mosley. "Don isn't here right now," Terry pointed out, "but his correspondence and the paperwork for refugees has to be kept up. He should be back from his jail term in a few weeks." Jail term? What was that all about?

The jail term was being shared by another Partner, Max Rice. These two men intentionally had chosen NOT to pay the portion of their taxes funding war—a decision not lightly taken. When the day in court came, their statements were respectful protests and the judge was held to the rules of law, this time requiring he sentence Don and Max to prison time.

While we all awaited their return, I spent my mornings translating documents, creating a "Refugee Dictionary" and typing correspondence. Afternoons were spent gardening, visiting the refugees, cooling off in the swimming hole, and participating in non-competitive games, those that encouraged cooperation over clashes. There were plenty of opportunities to compete on the soccer field.

Greg's job was school and, when at Jubilee, being a kid. The Georgia school system offered Greg a curriculum he had covered two years earlier, as a fourth grader in Minnesota. I signed a waver stating they did not have permission to paddle him—probably a good thing, because he seemed lackadaisical, disinterested and always on the verge of sleep. They chose to put him in detention until they realized he was bored silly. They arranged for him to study with a ninth grade tutor in hopes of encouraging interest. This was not the only glitch.

One day he got off the bus and reported he had been in a fight. "What happened?" I began my inquest, wide-eyed and faint of heart.

"I was asked who won the Civil War," he stated blankly.

"And?" I prodded him on.

"I said the North won. The kid said I was lying and punched me."

On the upside, we had left our monolingual, solo-cultural, small town for a multi-country, multi-lingual, multi-cultural world. Greg waited for the bus with kids representing El Salvador, Vietnam, Guatemala, and several states in the U.S. His best friend, Savath, was a Hmong refugee, and Amy was his first Afro-American buddy. He did not give it a thought. I did.

~Puente ~
Riding the Overground

Sometimes you sign up for things and then find out what all is involved. I signed up for Jubilee and got the Overground Railroad.

Jubilee was a link, a stepping stone. Unbeknownst to me, there was a movement throughout the United States working on this whole crazy Central American crisis. I had so much to learn.

During my rare down time, I scoured the Jubilee library discovering a raft of books and videos complementing my Hamline studies. The "Walk in Peace" video showed their project of producing prosthetics for people who had been unfortunate enough to step on one of thousands of landmines planted in Nicaragua. Some books were compilations of refugee stories, replete with unimaginable atrocities committed by their countrymen. Jubilee was nonpartisan and ecumenical. I read the *Catholic Worker* newsletters, met Mennonite volunteers, followed Quaker actions, and wrote weekly updates to my congregation back home.

But. . . "Experience is the best teacher" and Jubilee was about to offer me that.

26

Capítulo Veintiséis
Want to Go to the Border?

It was time to go to the border and collect the next group of refugees held at The *Corralón* detention center outside of Harlingen, Texas. Did I want to go? Did I want to go!

A perk of living in community is the shared responsibility. Within minutes of my saying yes, a substitute was picked for my office job and the Rice family offered to take care of Greg until I returned. *Voilá*, I was on my way.

Terry, Don, and Gregorio were the designated drivers of the former school bus, now decorated "a la Guatemala chicken bus." *Año de Jubileo* was painted along both sides. The year of Jubilee in the Bible recalls a time when all debts were forgiven; everyone got a fresh start. How fitting for a bus picking up detainees at the Texas-Mexico border and freeing them to Jubilee Partners. Jubilee offered them English classes, cultural lessons, job interview role plays, Canadian court visits, and immigrant documentation.

GET ON THE BUS, GUS(TAVO)

Early that spring morning, I hugged my son good-bye, adjusted my backpack, and hoisted myself into the *Año de Jubileo* bus. Terry was in the driver's seat, taking the first three-hour driving shift. Tree and I were the two working volunteers. Don Mosley and Gregorio moved to the back of the bus where two bunks were curtained in. We headed out the driveway and turned toward Harlingen.

JUBILEE BUS

The miles slipped by the windows of our empty bus headed south. Every three hours, we stopped to stretch and rotate drivers. The Partners were veterans on these journeys. They patiently answered my queries about what we were going to see and do when we arrived. My questions revealed the depth of my ignorance.

150

One-thousand two-hundred eight miles later, the bus parked in front of a nondescript house in a quiet suburb of Harlingen. Richard and Ruth Anne Friesen, from Reba Place Church, Evanston, Illinois, greeted Terry warmly and showed us into the house they occupied while volunteering at the border. Tree and I unloaded our bags into the alcove off the living room. Ruth Anne introduced us to the kitchen and asked us to make iced tea and lemonade for the hot and thirsty volunteers.

The assembled included the Friesens, coordinators of *Proyecto Canadá* in Harlingen, our crew from Jubilee, some local volunteers, and the editor of the Catholic Maryknoll magazine, Moises Sandoval. He authored the most recent articles I had read about Central America. I couldn't believe I was in the same room with this guy—a "rock star" of the Maryknoll missioners, if one can say such a thing about a priest. I was aware of the Jesuit connection dating to the "discovery" of the Americas, but wouldn't learn until months later that the Fransiscan Sisters of Little Falls, just thirty miles from my home, were involved in sheltering refugees.

"How has it been going here?" Terry asked Ruth Anne when we were all settled in the living room. "Have things calmed down at all?"

"Sorry to say no," Ruth Anne looked at us. "The government has been ramping up deportations. There is about one 747-sized plane flying out of here every week, all refugees being sent back." She handed over the newspaper with a front page photo of the plane.

"Are they all going back to one country?" Gregorio asked. He had previously worked as a volunteer with Witness for Peace, documenting such activities.

"What we are seeing at the *Corralón*," Richard explained, "is a choice. The judges ask the detainee where they want to go. Many of them are picking countries other than their own. If they get off the airplane in their native country, they are likely to be jailed immediately."

"If they really fell under the U.N. definition of refugee," Ruth Anne continued, "having reasonable fear for their lives, then we are sending them back to a death sentence."

"That means more urgency in getting these people out of here," Don shook his head. "How are the interviews going?"

"From our daily visits to the nearby facilities, we might have twenty or thirty that can get permission to leave with you," Ruth Anne calculated. "That means we need to divide up tomorrow and cover as many places as possible."

"We'd like to visit the *Refugio Oscar Romero*, too," Terry added, "if there is time."

"Why don't you take Jan and Tree to the *Corralón* to watch the deportation hearings in the morning. The *Refugio* isn't too far from there," Ruth Anne suggested.

"They are having trouble with one of their neighbors out there," Richard grimaced. "The guy built a deer-hunting type of stand at the fence line between properties. The *Refugio* is only allowed a certain number of people on its premise for sleeping and eating and a few dozen more spots in a fenced off area. Standing room only. He sits up there with his binoculars and calls in the authorities to apprehend folks he sees walking through the desert. The

151

nuns keep close watch and get as many people inside the fences as they can before the INS shows up."

"Oh, my," I caught myself saying under my breath.

"People have different ways of looking at this," Don wisely observed. "There are people crossing properties every day. It is a trespassing issue, a litter issue, and an immigration issue."

"Unlike our *Refugio* neighbor, other residents around here leave water jugs in the desert," Ruth Anne added. "Texas churches collect food and clothing, just like up north. The Red Cross has some work-release programs. People sleep at the shelters if they have Red Cross approved jobs."

"That doesn't mean they are safe from the Immigration and Naturalization guys," Richard was quick to point out. "Once we get them permission, they are covered along the way to Canada."

"Are there more incidents of self-appointed militia acting as border guards?" Don inquired.

"They are not organized, but out there. When they find the water jugs, they empty them."

Tree and I made eye contact, but kept quiet. This was a time for the Overground Railroad veterans to review the situation and make plans. We surmised that churches were lined up along the return route, preparing potlucks and sack lunches for our busload. The refugees would stay at Jubilee for one to three months. The Canadian judge comes out to review cases and those accepted continue to other "safe houses" until they cross the northern border. There, they enter a year-long refugee resettlement plan including language classes, subsidized apartments and job training.

"Jan and Tree," Terry interrupted my thoughts, "how about you come with me to the *Corralón* tomorrow? Maybe we can visit the *Refugio* and see that guy's tree house."

"I'd be delighted!" I said with two thumbs up.

THE *CORRALÓN* – THE BIG CORRAL

The plan was to visit a few of the immigration court sessions, observe the process, and report our overall reaction. If possible, our groups would get permission to take twenty to thirty detainees, an INS immigration term synonymous with Canada's refugee label. Canada offered a refugee resettlement plan, the destination country for anyone getting on the Jubilee bus.

Tree, a slender man of medium height, and I, the smallest, were stuffed into the way back part of an old station wagon for the trek into the desert. We gazed over our tucked in knees out the back window at the dust trail following us down the hot, dry, desolate miles.

"There it is! Up ahead," Terry yelled to us over her shoulder. "There is the *Corralón* fence. You can see some of the big white tents on the right. They ran out of space in the buildings and, with these circus-sized tents, and I mean circus, there's room for five hundred more."

Tree and I squirmed around to follow her pointer finger. She continued, "They have added another batch of bunk beds in those tents. Problem is, the desert is hot in the day and cold at night, so tents aren't much shelter." She returned to her discussion with the others about divvying up duties.

Tree and I stared into the glare thrown down by the white hot sun. I could make out stick figures, dressed in blaze orange, walking along the steel fences topped with barbed wire. They were prisoners, escapees, as it were, from Central America's messy "covert" war. They morphed into "illegal aliens" when they stepped foot into the United States. I never cared for the term "alien," always expecting a green extraterrestrial. I don't believe anyone on the planet is illegal. Some just don't have politically approved papers for crossing man-made lines in the sand.

Outside our window, these orange-clad individuals became life-sized. Some were playing soccer, some strolled around the picnic tables, some sat quietly under no shade at all. A bell rang and they scattered to another area. Some were herded into a line entering the buildings.

"That is where they hold court," Terry informed us. "We will break into three groups to do our court visits. We'll monitor the proceedings for human rights issues. The treatment by the judge and officials. Is there a translator present? How many are being processed by the hour? What choices are they being given?" She finished clicking off our job description.

Terry parked the car and led us into the shade of the first building. "Wait here while I get clearance," she told us.

This place was so remote, so isolated. The fenced yards, the huge white circus-type tents, humanity milling around with no control over their lives. I'd go crazy locked up for one day! What does "locked up indefinitely" feel like? No information on family? Not understanding the language or how this culture's systems worked? Who do you trust?

"Let's go," Terry called out. "Jan, you'll be with me, and Tree, you go with the guys. We'll meet back here at noon."

And that is how I got into the Port Isabel's *El Corralón*, immigration's big holding pen.

IMMIGRATION COURT

We passed a line of orange jumpsuits on our way to the door. I glanced over to catch a glimpse of them glancing back. Timid. Humble. Orderly. Small of stature. Weathered skin. Dark-eyed. A slight woman, hands clasped in front of her belt, looked up. Our eyes met. These detainees, prisoners, refugees, immigrants, whatever you wish to call them, stood stoically.

Terry and I slid into two folding chairs in the last row and watched the guard guide them into the seats in front of the judge. It was a plain room, maybe measuring thirty feet square, with white walls. There was a large emblem for the United States of America placed behind the judge's table. A gavel rested there, waiting to call the court to order. A wilted United States flag hung limp to one side, perhaps ashamed to be part of these proceedings.

I heard the gavel smack the table and someone bellowed out for all to rise. A short, stout man dressed in a full, flowy black robe entered from a side door. A professionally dressed woman took her place in front of the bench. He handed her a list and called the place to order, followed by a simultaneous translation of how this was going to work. Terry folded her arms tight across her chest and slid down in her chair. I pulled myself up for a better view.

One by one the people in orange suits, all dwarfed by the guards in green, filed up to the man in black. He asked them their country of origin, if they had a lawyer, what was their plea, and whether they had any evidence to uphold the United Nations definition of refugee. That meant they had a well-founded fear of persecution for reasons of race, religion, nationality, political opinion, or membership in a particular social group. Really?

My mind raced, crashing around inside the confines of my head. Does this judge... do these guards... do the people in Harlingen have any idea of El Salvadoran government death squads? Of Guatemala's leaders ordering Mayan villages burned to the ground? How about the Christian-based community leaders "disappeared" for reading Bibles to the illiterate? Priests and nuns were being assassinated for helping the poor. I bit my lip.

Next up, two elderly people, arm-in-arm. Their facial topography implied Maya. Strong noses. High foreheads. Weatherworn, wrinkled, bronzed. If they were not in orange suits, I would expect identifiable native skirt, *corte*, for her, and striped pants for him. Here that heritage was stripped away, with all other individual, recognizable attributes.

The judge began: "What country?"

"Guatemala."

"Why did you leave?"

There was a pause. No answer. The translator went over to the bench and whispered something to the judge. He nodded. These people spoke *Kaqchikel*, one of twenty-two Mayan dialects. Spanish was their second, maybe third language.

The translator looked at the assembled and asked, "*¿Hay alguien que hable Kaqchikel?* Is there someone who speaks *Kaqchikel*?"

A volunteer stood up and was motioned to join them in front. The judge repeated his question.

"They left because their village was burned down. The men were forced into the church before it was torched and the women were told to gather in the plaza out front. Most of them were gunned down with the children, but this couple was working in their *milpa*. . . their field. They ran to the jungle."

"Who was responsible for the fire?"

"The government soldiers. . .they came in Jeeps and helicopters," the volunteer translated.

Tell them they have two weeks until their next hearing. They should get legal counsel. They need to verify dates of attack and any corroborating evidence regarding their claims." Heads down, they returned to their folding chairs.

I fidgeted. I wanted to stand up and yell. This is absurd! How are they going to find witnesses? What evidence? If you are running for your life, you don't stop and take pictures, for Christ's sake. I imagine they lived in the usual Mayan hut without electricity, a dirt floor, a center fire with a cooking *comal* for heating tortillas. They wouldn't even have a camera!

Furthermore, if these people were in their home country, they would likely be the most respected of their community just for being elders. What if these people were somebody's white grandparents? What if the shoe were on the other foot, as they say? Why, if the gold in California had been discovered a year earlier, it would have all gone to Mexico! Now that would put the shoe on the other foot. Maybe we would be cutting the lawns, climbing the ladders in fruit orchards, and doing dishes for our Mexican counterparts. California, New Mexico, Arizona, Texas, and Utah would still be Mexico's and they would be yelling at us to "go home Gringo!"

I felt steam rising from my chest. I looked over at Terry. Her jaw flexed, teeth clenched. My mind drifted to the 1970s Woody Allen flick, *Bananas*. In one scene, generals, touting their medal adorned chests, sit around a banquet table. In a balcony above, three musicians pull invisible bows over invisible strings. They sway to the silent serenade while the generals assume roles of exaggerated self-importance, ignoring facts, and creating their own rules.

The scene before me was a really bad movie, but I couldn't make it stop by getting up and walking out. Those assembled that day gave credence to the man with the gavel seated below the U.S. Seal of Justice. This was an other-worldly absurd agreement. The power bestowed by a seal and a gavel was felt, yet invisible. In this real-time movie, the black robe ruled over the orange jumpsuits. I tuned back into the action playing out before me. I shook my head, hoping to clear the clutter. All that did was clarify the injustice of this script.

These people did not understand English, the language used in the documents explaining their incarceration. They were to find lawyers. Where? With what money? From out here in the desert? I scanned the motley crew seated before this man with a robe pounding his gavel to bring the next orange jumpsuit to his bench.

One after another, they were given two weeks to come up with legal help for their next appearance. This was not a release from the *Corralón* to go find help, but to stand in line and wait for a phone. There was a list of immigration lawyers, services, and translators made available. A smattering of pro-bono immigration lawyers circulated in the halls. But even the local Spanish high school students were making money off the refugees' need for translation. How were these detainees to pay translators and lawyers? Their money was left with families in home countries, used along the way, given over to *coyotes*, those human smugglers promising safe passage across the Rio Grande, desert, or the treacherous mountains, and sometimes, the money was simply stolen. Really? You have got to be kidding me!

The next woman stepped up. She nearly disappeared inside the folds of her orange jumpsuit, cuffs rolled up around her ankles, and extra material poofing out around her belt.

By the third question, her shoulders gave a shudder. From our seats in the back, I could only imagine her emotionless face might be melting.

"Did you travel here alone?" the judge continued.

I heard a sniffle. Then a sob. She mumbled something about her *compañero en Cristo*, a term I heard used to reference a common-law marriage. They had been separated at the border. With that, her self-control gave way to weeping accented by hiccoughs and deep sighs.

The judge raised his hand to stop her story. The assembled held their communal breath. All eyes were on the scene unfolding in front of them, waiting. They had an idea of how things might go in their own countries when a "law-breaker" didn't cooperate.

The judge nodded at the translator and moved his hand. He pointed to a box of Kleenex and motioned for her to take it to the whimpering woman. A collective sigh swept through the room. Shoulders relaxed. A few people exchanged smiles.

For two more hours, the line of orange jumpsuit people filed in. They sat motionless on the folding chairs. Terry and I tried to remain inconspicuous, an impossibility considering our whiteness, her red hair, and our street clothes. More than once, I skimmed over the next entering line-up only to catch them looking expectantly back.

"They probably think we are some of the pro-bono immigration lawyers," Terry spoke quietly into my ear. "Sometimes the lawyers can get names while these folks are taken back to the barracks."

Another line of long faces, weary eyes, and slumped shoulders shuffled behind me. They were clothed and fed, but this was so wrong. Starting with our own government's foreign policy, the very cause of their leaving home, family and familiar foods, to this mock-up of a court room surrounded by circus tents in a desert. Worse yet, most U.S. citizens didn't have a clue this was happening on our soil and, if morality doesn't speak to this atrocity, then let's talk taxpayer money. Our very taxpayer money supported the violence that forced their exodus and now was blocking their escape to safety. I turned to look just as the last man in line came up behind our chairs.

"*¿Es usted abogada?* Are you a lawyer?" he whispered in passing.

"*Lo siento, pero no.* Sorry, I am not," I mouthed back. I was even more sorry I was not a fairy godmother. I would wave my magic wand and . . .

Where would I begin? The streets of Honduras? In the Guatemalan United Fruit Company's banana plantations? The ignorant halls of Congress in Washington, D.C.?

Reality came back with a pound of the judge's gavel. Court was adjourned for the day.

"Well," Terry sighed. "There you have it. There were translators, which is an improvement. No obvious human-rights violations, unless you consider the big picture," she put one hand over her heart while the other swept over the whole scene.

The guards came. The orange jumpsuits were herded back to holding pens. They were not free. They were separated from family, culture, language, and justice. That, in my opinion, was a human-rights violation.

THE CHOSEN ONES

It was 2:00 a.m. Harlingen, Texas, time. The faces in the living room belonged to Guatemalans, El Salvadorans, Hondurans, and the five of us from Jubilee. All leaning back on small clothing bundles, weary eyes closed, waiting. Some heads rested on folded arms, bodies curved around rolled-up sleeping bags and coolers scattered about the floor. Two people were late. We were anxious to be on our way and make the checkpoint before morning traffic and the heat of the Texas desert.

It was 4:00 a.m. when the stragglers finally arrived. People bent over to retrieve meager belongings and headed toward the bus that promised passage out of *El Valle*, The Valley, that one hundred-mile strip patrolled by the INS guards, their dogs, and helicopters. Many who have made it through Central American jungles, unfriendly terrain traversed by human smugglers, and even survived the occasional hurricane, are stopped and turned back here.

The bus idled, chugging exhaust into the cool, dark morning. We formed an irregular line from the porch to the driveway. The last to arrive were the first to board. Jaime and Imelda scooched sideways down the aisle and took seats toward the back. The entirety of their possessions fit into a brown grocery bag, wrapped several times around with twine. Imelda tucked this into the overhead compartment and slid in next to the window. She bunched her sweater into a ball and placed it on Jaime's shoulder until she found a comfortable spot. Her eyes closed. Last night she had slept among hundreds of other women in the Texas desert.

Edgar and Diego, two men in their twenties, grabbed the rail, sprang up the bus steps, and plopped themselves into the third seats from the front. They had met at the Harlingen Red Cross Shelter. They were fortunate in securing construction jobs for two weeks, reporting back nightly to the shelter. Their money was spent on a few items of clothing, a magazine, and some chocolates they now carried in small black satchels. They bounced in their seats and grinned, apparently finding them comfortable. After locating

157

the buttons and adjusting their seatbacks to the preferred angle, Edgar wiggled his curved pointer finger, summoning me over. With a wink and a grin he whispered into my ear, "Would you poleeeze brrring us two extra fluffy pillows? And, if not too much trrrouble, could we see a brrrreakfast menu?"

The next three men were traveling alone and found scattered seating. The shortest was weather worn, the wrinkles creasing his face disguising his true age. The youngest wore a T-shirt straining to fit over his bulging chest and biceps. The third wore an ironed, short-sleeved shirt tucked neatly into his trousers. His smooth skin fit snuggly over his high cheekbones and around a sleepy smile. His dress shoes and groomed hair were equally black and shiny. Terry took her place behind the wheel. Don and Gregorio crawled behind the curtains into the back bunks. Tree walked the aisle with pillows and I picked up the microphone, beginning my stint as unofficial bilingual stewardess on this Overground Railroad.

"*Damas y caballeros*, ladies and gentlemen," I began. "My name is Jan and I will be your stewardess this evening." I motioned for Tree to stand up. "And this is Tree. We will be serving you drinks, water that is, and trying to make this a comfortable journey. This bus goes straight through to a place called Jubilee Partners. We will stop every three hours to move about. We will be eating our meals at churches, prepared by their very best cooks. If you have questions in Spanish, don't ask Tree, ask me." I was on a roll.

Terry looked into the rear view mirror and saw smiling faces. "Before they get too comfortable," she began, "We have to prepare them for the checkpoint." I translated her explanation.

"For the first one hundred miles out from the border, there are checkpoints. We will be stopped."

This in itself would be terrifying having come from countries that regularly pulled people out of buses to smack them around or take them away, never to be seen again.

"Do not worry. They might board the bus and ask for your papers."

Good god, I realize as I am talking, this is exactly what happens in their home countries. If they don't have their *cédulas*, personal identification on them, they are fined or jailed. This cannot be reassuring news.

"Know that we have permission to be transporting you. Just show them your I.D., if they ask and it will be fine," Terry reiterated.

No sooner had I gotten that translated than Terry looked at me. "Tell them we'll be stopped in about ten minutes."

The dawn fog was heavy. Sometimes, vehicles could be seen pulling onto the highway shoulder, releasing crouched silhouettes into the desert. It was time for the refugees to get out their documents for the Immigration and Naturalization Service inspection. How many times had they done this on buses back home? How many times did they witness someone taken off? Beaten? Disappeared? Our passengers went from peaceful rest to tense alertness. Hands clutched their papers. The bus slowed. The fog surrounded our windows, clogging the view of the officers and suspending us in time.

Fifteen miles an hour. Ten miles an hour. Everyone was sitting up straight, wide-eyed, trusting. Terry pulled over and stopped. She turned on the interior lights, illuminating the contents... a load of brown-skinned people. An official stepped aboard, looked down the aisle and tipped his hat. I wondered how those cowering in the dark behind me were doing.

What if I were in their country, having the military board my bus, look at my papers, and not understand what was happening. Add the dark night, the language barrier, the threats they carried in their very recent memories... they had come so far. Some had been traveling for months.

The INS officer looked back at Terry. His face softened and he waved us on without looking at a single document!

He stepped down off bus. Terry pulled slowly into traffic. I could hear them breathing again.

PASSED THE CHECK POINT

Buses are not the best place to get a good night's sleep. Buses full of refugees coming from detention centers and heading again into the complete unknown only makes it worse. They were physically and emotionally exhausted. I did not know what hid behind their closed eyelids. That would come when I translated their stories back at Jubilee for the Canadian judge.

It seemed like every time they nodded off, I had to wake them for our next driver rotation. No one complained. I could only imagine their previous travels, according to accounts I had read. At least here they had pillows, church basement ladies and . . . a stewardess!

Sometimes we stopped at parks for lunch. Without needing to be asked, they pitched in. The guys carried the containers of food to the picnic tables and the women unpacked them. Someone always stepped up to pump fresh water while others set the tables. They repacked, recycled, and boarded the bus for *siesta* time.

When the meals were served in local church basements, I not only translated words, but identified foods and got culinary insights from their perspective.

"I'm not so sure about this purple food," Dominga confided, passing by the dessert table. "And what are the white things stuck inside?"

"It's Jell-O with miniature marshmallows," I explained, realizing its total lack of value outside of tradition.

"Am I really supposed to put that on my plate by the hot food?" she asked. "Won't it all melt together?"

"Well, yes," I admitted. "It will make everything else taste sweet. You might want to come back for it."

"I get to come back? For more?" she looked at me in surprise.

"Until the food is all gone you can," I gave her a gentle jab.

Her son, René, was listening. "Are you saying I can try a little of everything, see if I like it and come back for more?"

"As long as everyone has gone through the line once." He looked at me. "But, come to think of it, I don't remember anyone ever going hungry at a church potluck," I said, putting a dollop of hot, mashed potatoes just out of range of the red cranberry Jell-O-salad.

Potlucks and church basement ladies. The food and the cooks were foreign to them, but the main ingredients were smiles. The sun shed light through the stained glass windows, casting long shadows behind the refugees filing out to reboard the bus. Behind them, women in stained, white aprons waved good-bye. Farewell. Fare well.

~Puente ~
Back at Jubilee

After several days of highway living, we pulled into the parking area by the K House. The Jubilee community was waiting. The refugees looked out their bus windows into smiling faces. Baggage was unloaded, introductions made, and housing assigned. Just like that, our bus community dissolved into yet another phase of the journey.

The houses were comfortable cabin-sized buildings with kitchen, bath, living, and sleeping spaces. The refugees did not have a lot to unpack. Jubilee ran a thrift shop where most needs could be purchased for twenty-five cents. Soon their lodgings took on personal touches of wild flowers in vases and daily sweepings.

Food shelves donated a portion of what was available for menus. Atlanta often sent unmarked tin cans, which we used for special events, affectionately called, "Shiner Suppers." One volunteer, Joe, was especially good at concocting full meals from these unidentified shiny containers. New recipes morphed with the opening of each new can. Perhaps the very first casseroles were invented from unidentified cans that turned out to be mushroom soup and string beans. Just a thought.

The path between the Volunteers' residence and the refugee housing wound through a Georgia woods, arching branches above and red soil below. At a strolling pace, it took about ten minutes between locations, giving time and space between the two populations. English classes were held every weekday morning and an Ecumenical bilingual service on Sundays. Field trips were planned into Athens, where scavenger hunts were educational opportunities to use maps, English skills, and buses. Those were the days of pay phones. Each refugee was given a quarter to call home if they got lost. A few days of acclimation to Jubilee life and it was time to get serious.

27

Capítulo Veintisiete
A Walk in the Woods

Samir deeply inhaled Georgia's spring breeze. It was early evening as we sauntered together along the path between our respective village sites.

"*¡Qué increíble estar al aire libre, respirando la primavera!*" he sighed.

"Yes, it is incredible to be outdoors, breathing in the springtime air," I agreed, aware that his meaning likely went much deeper than mine. He was incarcerated at *El Corralón* for a month before he got on the bus to come here.

"Samir, what was it like in detention?" I cautiously asked.

"They make you wear that orange suit so that you can be seen if you try to run away," he began. "As if you could jump over those tall fences! I'm not used to so many people!" he continued. "Noisy all the time."

Here we were, walking through a woods, quiet except for the last chirps of night birds and our footsteps on the red earth.

Samir took another deep breath and went on. "It was nice that they gave us soccer balls so we could have games, but it was so hot out there in the desert! People who slept in those tents had it worse than those inside the building. It seemed to always be too hot or too cold." He paused before continuing.

"What I really found difficult was only having fourteen minutes to eat. There were hundreds of us being fed in shifts. We got pushed through the line, off to a table, ate and got out. Fourteen minutes! In my country, the meal of the day can last an hour," he recalled with a sad smile.

That image filled us both with our own private memories of long lunches, time with friends and family, some leisure before returning to our daily to-do. Suddenly he stopped, put a finger to his lips, and a cupped hand to his ear.

"Did you hear that?" he asked me. My overactive imagination went directly to some jungle scene where the military was getting closer to the folks hunkered down behind a boulder.

"What?" I whispered back, holding my breath.

"That bird? Is it an owl?"

I exhaled, let go of the image of impending capture, and listened.

"There, there it is again," he whispered.

"Yes, it's an owl. I don't know my owls here in Georgia and wouldn't know how to translate the species if I did," I confessed.

"In my country," he spoke slowly, "owls are an omen. Sometimes it means someone you love has died or is about to die. Sometimes the shamans have an owl hovering around, a special energy or spirit animal. Either way, it is a very strong presence. Listen, there it is again."

This owl's call sounded more like a lullaby. Not a warning "Whooo, whoooo," but a "cooooo," soft and gentle. Or, maybe that is just the way I heard it standing beside Samir, upturned face outlined in the emerging moonlight, eyes closed, taking in some peace that he hadn't known in months.

I closed my eyes to get a better listen. The buzz of bugs. A breeze tickling the budding leaves. A flutter of wings. The owl took flight. Samir would be safe tonight.

JOE & SAMIR

THE INTERVIEWS

All the reading I had done did not prepare me for flesh and blood accounts of Central America's horror. Hearing their stories, retyping them and retelling them to the Canadian judge who came out from Atlanta, didn't make it any less harsh.

This time Samir sat across from me in my capacity as the translator, preparing him for his audience with the authorities.

"What happened that made you decide you had to flee your country?" was the usual first interview question. Here are glimpses of some Jubilee refugee stories:

SAMIR:

"I was a mechanic in the military, fixing their bigger trucks, some the size of semi-trailers. They were moved around a lot throughout countryside and into the mountains. They kept breaking down. One time, I decided to look inside to see what they were hauling. They were torture chambers! Mobile torture chambers so they could pick up people, interrogate them, and drop them or their corpses along any road. I didn't want to have anything to do with that, but I was enlisted. It wasn't a job I could just quit.

"Then, I got a chance to run. I went away into the jungle, but they caught me and put me into the back of that same truck I had been servicing. They had these chains inside and locked me up by the wrists and hoisted me to the ceiling. Then they let go and you fall, maybe breaking some bones or get some internal bleeding. They preferred internal injuries because they are not visible. They thought they had killed me and threw me on the back of a truck with other bodies. It was a bumpy road and I bounced off. Some country people, *gente del campo*, found me and took me in.

"When I was better, I knew I had to get out of the country. I left a wife and child back there. They probably believe that I am dead. It is too dangerous to try and contact them. The army might try to hurt them. So, I just kept running. It took me months to get through Mexico. I had to stop and take odd jobs. Then, I got caught in Hurricane Gilbert by Monterrey. Monterrey isn't even on the coast! I found a big box and crawled in until the rains quit. When I got to Texas, I turned myself in and they put me right into the *Corralón*. They said I needed a lawyer. Then you people came and brought me here."

DOMINGA AND RENÉ:

"I came with my son, René. I wanted to protect him, or at least be a witness to what happened, in case they tried to kill him. I was working on a plantation. Long hours. Not enough money. René was thirteen and thought he would help by working on a bus. Boys ride along and collect the fares. They stand by the drivers or walk through the bus getting the money. Once a month or so, the soldiers would come through town and just grab boys and take them away. If they 'look old enough', or tall enough, they are taken. Sometimes, we got word that soldiers were coming, so we kept our boys home from school. If someone saw soldiers coming, children were told to hide.

"One day, we weren't so lucky. They took my son off the bus. I didn't know what had happened. He just disappeared. A few months later, he came home with a friend. They had both run away from the military. He told me how they had been thrown into deep wells of cold water to show them what would happen if they did not obey. They did other horrible things to 'toughen them up,' I guess. They were given uniforms and guns and ordered to do terrible things.

"They finally couldn't stand it anymore. One night they were told to do 'mop up'— to clean up after a raid. Kill anyone still moving. They saw a soldier throw a baby in the air and spike it with his bayonet. Another soldier just cut a pregnant woman open and took her baby out. They told me awful things.

"My son and his friend stayed further and further back, then ran and ran. When they got to my house, we decided to leave immediately for my brother's. Right away, we knew he had to leave. I thought I would go with him as far as the Mexican border, to make sure he made it. When we got there, I just kept right on going. By then I was probably a target, too.

"We worked our way through Mexico with odd jobs. I made and sold tortillas sometimes. René washed cars. We earned a little, then caught a bus further. Or just walked. It took about six months to get to Texas. We figured we'd turn ourselves in and tell them our story.

"That is when they locked us up. We were separated. They put me on the women's side of the center and René in the man's side. We didn't know that then. We lost track of each other. By the grace of God, someone recognized him and knew where I was. They arranged for us to meet at a meal time. What a joy to see his face again. We knew that the other was ok. Then, when I got interviewed, I could tell them where my son was. That's how we were together when Jubilee people showed up. I feel very lucky we are together."

José:

"I left my country with my family because of the threats. My family and I lived in a Christian-based community, had a good life and good friends. My three children were all doing well in school. My sons are nearly teenagers, the age when the army starts looking for them. My daughter is sixteen. My wife and I participated in the Bible classes, so I think that is what got us in trouble. The owners of the companies and the government don't seem too happy about people reading. Illiteracy helps them make the rules and, if you can't read, what can you say? They began threatening people that attended our meetings. I was a *catequist*, meaning I went to various villages and led discussion groups using the Bible. One night when I got back from my meeting, the soldiers came. Maybe they followed me, I don't know.

"They kicked the door down and burst into our kitchen. I told my daughter to run to the back room and lock herself in. They tried to take one of my sons, but I stopped them. They beat me up, then left the house. I knew they would be back for my sons. They are about the age they like. And many girls my daughter's age have been raped. We didn't want to take the chance. We just had to go. The best option seemed to be *El Norte*. The North.

"My wife's brother was already living in Pennsylvania. We called him and told him what had happened. He is a member of a church there that said they would help us. They would support and sponsor us. I don't know how that worked, but I guess they contacted Jubilee. We did not end up in detention, like most of the people here now. We did get information about *Proyecto Canadá*, so we thought that was our best option."

Imelda and Jaime:

"Jaime left first. He was publishing an underground student newspaper and attending *manifestaciones*, protests. I told him to be careful because the police were taking pictures and finding out where people lived. That was too visible. He wasn't too worried until the soldiers broke into the student offices and trashed everything. They started to watch him and he didn't want them to discover his newspaper work. Then the work and all of his friends would be in danger. He said he'd notify me when he got somewhere safe.

"It wasn't too long after that I started being followed. I suppose, since they couldn't find him, they thought he'd be in touch with me. I lived in an apartment in the city with my sister while going to school. I didn't want to think I was in any trouble because I wasn't doing anything. The problem was being associated with him. We decided he shouldn't call or write. That way I wouldn't know anything.

"That didn't matter. One night, before I got home, someone broke into our apartment and tore things up. There wasn't anything to find, but I was scared. I didn't want my sister to be in danger. That would be next. I couldn't stay. I packed a few things and left for my parents' place in the country. From there I got word to Jaime and he told me he was in the U.S. Maybe I could get to the border and he would meet me.

"Luckily, he had been sponsored by a church and got help. They sent someone with him to find me. When I arrived, it had been arranged for us to go to Jubilee."

The interviews continued. There were Edgar, a student, and Diego, a business man. There were nine-year-old Myrna and her family, escaping after her grandparents were hung in their front yard tree as a warning to the village. This was a normal means of spreading fear to get cooperation. I translated a litany of stories that mirrored the ones I read about in my studies.

There were other refugees before them and more to come after they were processed. If their stories were approved by the Canadian judge from Atlanta, they would be put on buses to points north. One after another, they came into the library study. Don asked the questions. I interpreted and took notes. Then we wrote up reports and added them to the immigration papers and Canadian forms. The files included physical examinations, mental health assessments, and any documentation in the form of photos, letters, or newspaper articles, any proof that what they were telling was true.

How, I wondered, could anyone make this trek and preserve documentation? There were not pictures of René being pulled off the bus or José being beaten in his kitchen. Eye witnesses were thousands of miles away and in fear for their own lives just for being associated with those that fled. Myrna's family did not stop to take pictures when they cut the ropes and lowered her grandparents' bodies to the ground.

They were just two out of 70,000 civilians estimated to have been killed in El Salvador's war. I sat there with my little bilingual Amsco dictionary and shook my head. The authors didn't include the words I needed to describe these brutal stories. This was beyond words.

INTERVIEW DICTIONARY

Bob Flickenger worked in the Jubilee office connecting *Proyecto Canadá* with qualified program candidates. He was in daily contact with the border, prepared interviews, and communicated with the Canadian Consulate for their visits. As I eased into my role as translator, his expertise was literally life changing. Had I mistranslated vital information regarding the refugee's location, associates, torture, philosophies, career, you name it, their acceptance or rejection in the program could be affected by my mistakes.

My textbook vocabulary did not include machine gun, blindfold, brass knuckles, ambush, shrapnel, rifle butt, and bullet wounds. I found out that *capucha* meant a rubber hood used in torture. Up until these interviews, I had not needed "beheaded" but could figure out *colgado por los gordos*, hung by the thumbs. *Hogar* means hearth or home, but add "a" in front and you get *ahogar* to drown, suffocate, or choke. Context and good listening was imperative, but maybe the most important attribute was being humble and admitting I did not know something. If I did not understand, I asked them to repeat or describe. Even the most experienced translators need to verify idioms, taking into consideration social class and educational levels.

Add to that the regional differences. *Sapo* was not a frog but a Honduran term for informant. *Oreja* was not an ear but a spy. *Violar* wasn't just to violate, but rape. In Mexico, the police detected Central Americans trying to pass as natives by using the word *pisto*, meaning money to the refugees and hard liquor in Mexican slang. In the movie *El Norte*, the Guatemalan peasant hopes to blend in by practicing his Mexican accent and adding *chinga* to his vocabulary. This very strong yet common curse has a deep history and peppers the Mexican vernacular, separating them from other Latinos.

I began writing "refugee related" words in my notebook and took them to Bob. The list grew so I put them in alphabetical order. Bob became interested in this as a long-term tool and added his most frequently used interview terminology. Perhaps our little project would be helpful for the next volunteer. For the time being, it helped me.

~ *Puente* ~
Intentional Community Activities

JUBILEE GAMES

Cooperation was a community concept. Only in soccer did competition overrule this intentional focus. At least once a week, alternative group games were presented with the goal of working together. One cooperative game used a full-sized parachute. Everyone circled up and it was my job to call out colors of pants or short sleeved shirts or tennis shoes. People matching the category raced to the opposite side under the chute while the group heaved the billowing cloth into the air. I called out everything in Spanish and English, covertly teaching language to both linguistic sides.

Another game required cooperation to form a "living maze" with moving runways for the person who was "it" and the one fleeing. Six lines were made by outstretched arms

166

creating corridors. The leader called out "right" or "left," directing the entire group to shift lanes, throwing off the two runners in the giant, ever-changing labyrinth. We cheered, yelled, and gales of laughter brought tears.

Laughter and tears are two sides of the same coin. These games were no accident. They were an intentional part of the healing process. Post-traumatic stress wasn't a buzz term yet. People who hid in pits dug and covered by trapdoors when troops swarmed in, qualify for the diagnosis. They didn't have to be shot at to develop PTSD. Living with the "maybes" produced the same symptoms. Maybe today the troops will come through town. Maybe this time at the market, I will be asked for my ID. Maybe today my son will be forcibly recruited.

Jubilee was designed as a healing place of gardens, walking paths, swimming hole, and yes, these games. The refugees worked side by side growing their vegetables. They stumbled over English lessons together, laughing or grimacing at their attempts. They were dropped in the streets of Athens to practice their lessons through shopping and map searches. On field trips, they encountered grocery stores that gave them headaches.

Next time you shop, stand in the cereal aisle and simply scan the length of floor to ceiling boxes. If not overwhelmed, consider the number of choices you make when eating out. Salad? Which dressing? Potato? What type? How do you like your steak? You get the idea. We are rote participants in our culture, unaware of our habits unless others point them out. To the refugees, this was total sensory overload.

Jubilee coordinated each day for a transition into a new culture while acknowledging the refugees' turbulent past. What they brought with them was a lesson for us, as well.

GREG WITH THE CRUZ FAMILY
FROM EL SALVADOR

Capítulo Veintiocho
Mi Amiga, Dominga

Evenings at Jubilee often included gatherings of the refugee and volunteer communities for music, games or home-grown entertainment. One night we presented a variety of skits portraying community members. I chose to parody Dominga, a slight, spry *compesina* woman with a dry sense of humor and mischievous grin. She had a saying for everything and everyone.

"*¡Qué sueñes con los angelitos, y qué sean guapos!*" she would call out, when bidding us good-night. "May you dream with the angels and may they be handsome!" That gave me an idea.

"Bruce," I approached the tallest and a most handsome man indeed, "Would you work with me?" I asked, slipping back into my shy high school jitters.

"What's up?" he answered with enough interest to bolster my hopes.

"I need a guy to play opposite me at skit night. I thought we could cook up something about Dominga. Are you in?" I hesitated and looked way up at him. In a heartbeat, he said yes!

We met that afternoon and threw some scenes together. Dominga, flitting around the tables at meal time, the fairy godmother waving her magic words over everyone, sprinkling good cheer. Dominga, face screwed up, pronouncing her new vocabulary in English. Dominga, watching her son play soccer. And the finale, Dominga, saying good-night, the whole reason for the skit, and my favorite part.

That evening, one after another, we took the stage. We sang together in Spanish and English. Some played guitar. A trio of Latinos mimicked how we *gringos* looked trying to dance the salsa. We could laugh at that. Then it was our turn to pay homage to Dominga. She laughed during my representation of her English lessons and yelling at her son playing soccer. Would she still be laughing when Bruce showed up?

He walked on stage and stopped by the hassock that I would stand on to put me up to his level. I jumped up, looked dreamily into his eyes, bent toward his ear and purred "*Voy a soñar con los 'angelitos guapos' y tú eres el mío.* I am going to dream of handsome angels and you are mine," I ended emphatically with a possessive squeeze. The audience let out a roar. I peeked over at Dominga.

She raised her eyebrows over her wide eyes. Her jaw tightened and flexed. Oh no.

She lowered her chin to touch her shoulder and looked at us, knitting her eyebrows into a Frida Kahlo uni-brow. Slowly she got out of her chair and headed straight for the stage. In three giant steps, she raced past me and threw her arms around an astounded Bruce. She gazed up into his face, then back at me. "*No señorita. No es tuyo, es mío,*" breaking into giggles. "No, missy. He is not yours, he is mine."

BONDING OVER A BABY BLANKET

It was our quiet times together, however, that I most cherished. Dominga and I sometimes met after English classes to sit on the lawn and just be. On one such afternoon we talked about Josie, one of the Partners, who was expecting a baby within the month. Surely we could think of something to do for the new arrival.

"Maybe the baby could use a blanket," she said, sifting through ideas. "It would be nice to make something ourselves, no?"

"Excellent!" I blurted out. "I can crochet. I could make an afghan. I've done that before and, since it is for a baby, it won't have to be that big. I'd have time to finish before its born," I clapped her on the back.

Dominga made a dubious face and tilted her head toward mine. She didn't have money, but my $5.00/week allowance was being subsidized by my checkbook from home. "Let's go to the store in Comer and get some yarn. You pick the colors and help me roll it into balls. What do you think?" I looked at her for some enthusiasm.

"I can go with you?" she asked surprised.

"I think it's okay for you to leave the property. I'll ask. There might be a legal documentation thing, some identification in case anyone asks." I leaned in and whispered, "Just don't tell anyone what we are doing!"

So it was that we began our clandestine project. We had the habit of meeting after lunch, so no one suspected. We spread a blanket on a back field, out of sight of the others, and began work. Dominga wound the yarn into balls and I moved the crochet hook through its paces.

"*Sabes*, Dominga, do you know that I never spend times like this at home with my women friends?" I mused. "This is so nice, to sit, to talk. At home I feel so busy. We run our kids to sports, to lessons. We have jobs and come home to 'women's work' until we drop." I realized my tone had shifted from whimsical to complaint to whining. I stopped.

"Juanita," she looked over at me, "Juanita, I lived in a hut with a tin roof. In El Salvador I worked all the time in the fields. Field work is hard, physically hard. Women were always busy there, too. We didn't get time off the harvest for sick kids or drunken husbands." She stopped.

"Juanita," she struggled. "Juanita, in El Salvador my husband became a drunk. First he used his money for drink, then he lost his job and began hitting me. Lots of women get hit, beaten up." My crochet hook stopped. My tirade of first world problems echoed back at me.

"But what do you do?" she resumed, piercing her eyes into mine. "One night he came home and put a knife to my throat. That is just too much." She looked down at her hands in her lap. "By the time René came home with his buddy after the awful massacre, I was afraid for them, yes. I also knew that we could not stay with my husband. Nothing was safe. We could not stay," she slowly repeated, "we could not stay."

I had read accounts of lives like Dominga's. Reading the words doesn't mean understanding. She lived in a *choza*, a small hut with a center fire ring for cooking. I lived in a small house with a wood cook stove, yes, but also a gas stove, running water, electricity, not to mention forty acres. Teaching at the local high school could be grueling but not back-breaking. My comparisons bounced back and forth as the Georgia breeze blew over our moment together.

There we were, "happy as clams," an idiom worth pondering but not translating. I wasn't up to explaining and reverted to *contentas* to describe us. I smiled and reached for another ball of yarn.

"Do you think the next row should be the lavender?" I asked her. She handed me a cream colored ball. "I think this would better bring out the lavender, if you use it first," she suggested.

I held the colors up together. "Yup, you're right," I agreed. "I like the contrast."

She began unwinding another skein. I reflected on the two of us, such different lives, sitting on that blanket spread on the newly sprouting Georgia spring grass, helping each other create an afghan for a baby yet to be born.

Contrast is good. It brings out the highlights. And so it was for Dominga and me.

Dominga & Jan

29

Capítulo Veintinueve
Final Preparations
The Judge, the Doctor, and the Zoo

The three months were intended to put time and distance between the present and the demons still residing in their nightmares. Ironically, their worst nightmares were the exact horror stories, the "bad enough ones" to be "good enough" to be chosen by the Canadian consulate for acceptance into Canada's refugee program.

After the Canadian judge did the interview and election process, the chosen went to Atlanta for physical exams. If they passed without any rare diseases, their documents were issued. I was grateful to have the opportunity to accompany a group going to Atlanta for physicals, followed by a picnic at the Atlanta zoo. After seeing the doctors and waiting for results, there was a sigh of relief to be out of the clinic and on our way to see the animals!

René loved the gorillas. Dominga looked for her *angelito guapo* among the crowds. Jaime walked hand-in-hand with his now fiancé, Imelda. Our business in Atlanta was finished. They were a step closer to Canada. It was time to go to the park and relax. Time to celebrate. We put our blankets on the ground and pulled out the basket of foods prepared by that morning's volunteers. The sun shone in a blue sky. There were kids running everywhere!

It was late May and Atlanta's end-of-school field trips had unloaded every elementary kid in town right at our feet. The kids raced around trees, over the green grasses, passed us yelling and chasing each other. It was difficult to hear ourselves think. I was on the cusp of getting irritated by the ruckus when María, mother of three, leaned over grinning. "Isn't it lovely to see all of these children running around free, without a worry?"

At that moment, six Army helicopters, blades chopping the air, swooped over the tree line behind us. María's face went white. She swallowed her breath as she ducked down to the picnic blanket. The copters passed. She looked up sheepishly, "Habit" she stated, breathing out again. She cast her eyes over the hillside full of children giggling and playing.

"Look at that," she said astounded. "Not one child ran to take cover under a bush."

Pupusa Farewell Feast

Dominga models her new glasses on *Pupusa* Day

It was a custom for the El Salvadoran refugees to prepare a parting meal for the entire community. *Pupusas. Pupusas* are a national dish, or at least one of their favorites. I went into the kitchen that day and watched the women prepare the dough and chop the vegetables. In walked Dominga, back from her eye appointment. She burst through the door, "I can see again!" The women cheered and hugged her before she tied a red, full-bodied apron around her slender waist. She held out her arms and looked down at it. "The little flowers aren't blurry!" She took off her new glasses and put them on again to check the difference.

A door opened at the back of the K House and six of the El Salvadoran men walked in. "Dominga," I said, "Look at this," and I headed toward José, his two sons, and the four young men, Edgar, Diego, Pacheco, and René.

"*Oye, amigos*," I began. "Listen up, friends. We have need for some big strong men," hoping to bait them with compliments.

"*¿Sí?*" answered José taking the lead. "What do you need?"

"*Vengan conmigo*, come with me," I gestured, and they followed me to the kitchen where large rounds of mozzarella cheese topped the center table.

"It would be helpful to have these cut into smaller chunks so they can be grated," I explained.

Edgar looked at Diego and then at me. "*Pero*, but men don't work in the kitchen," he protested with a grin. "That's women's work."

I tilted my head and waved my finger at him. "*Pero, nada, señor*, men eat and it is the perfect day to help with the big *Pupusa* Feast," I continued while corralling them around the table.

Cutting knives, graters, and a platter were ready to go. I carefully handed the long knives to José, Pacheco, and Diego. Diego took his and made a big show of looking it over, testing the blade with his finger and flexing his macho biceps before taking the first cut. José, who was used to helping his wife, gave me a sympathetic smile, then handed the graters to his sons. They all went to work.

"Did you see that, Dominga?" I asked when I returned to the kitchen counter window. "Those guys agreed to working in the kitchen."

"I'm glad I have my new glasses or I never would have believed my eyes!" she laughed.

The women continued their chatter over their *pupusa* production, putting fingers full of chopped meats and cheeses inside the dough held in the palm of their hands. They made the dough into a ball around the filling and patted them together like tortillas with fat little bellies. The kitchen resounded with the pat-pat-patting heard in the streets of their homelands. Then the sizzle of *pupusas* hitting the hot griddle and the aroma of meats and cheeses melding together.

It was Imelda's turn to go to the cheese table to refill another bowl for the cooks. Her eyes went wide in surprise when she spotted Jaime, her fiancé, cutting away with the other men.

"¿*Y, ésto?* And, this? You cut the cheese?" she said in English. Jeanette, one of the U.S. volunteers, let out a giggle. "What is so funny?" Imelda asked.

"You asked if he cut the cheese," she gig-gled again. "'Cut the cheese' has another mean-ing in English and it is something men do a lot!" Her giggles were now out of control.

Imelda looked at me, confused. "What? Have I said something wrong?"

"No, Imelda, your English was perfect. But I am not going to translate. I'm going to let Jeanette explain this one herself," I said, looking over my shoulder at Jeanette on my way to the kitchen to taste my first-ever *pupusa*.

MEN CUTTING CHEESE

173

30

Capítulo Treinta
Off to Canada

For three months they practiced their verbs and repeated their English sentences. They learned which cereal they preferred from the grocery aisle. They packed their Jubilee Thrift Store clothes into their Jubilee Thrift Store suitcases. They had lived a protected life inside the acreage of the farm, working in the gardens, walking the red earthen paths, jumping off the rope swing into the pond, and playing community-building games.

WILL, JOSIE, REFUGEE FAMILY, GREG, & JAN

The interviews were done and the Canadian judge deemed them eligible for the Canadian Refugee resettlement program. Documents received official seals. Churches between Georgia and the northern border were preparing for their stay until the day came to cross over. We had eaten our last *pupusas* together, played the last game of soccer, and even welcomed a baby into the community. I hugged them all, saving Dominga for the last.

"Dominga, I really don't have the words. You taught me so much. You are the heroine, the strong woman. Such faith and grit," I looked down so the tears wouldn't show so much.

"Juanita," she whispered. "life is a long journey. There are always fears, doubts, and questions."

We embraced and the tears let themselves loose.

She pulled away from our hug to take a look at me. I stared into her warm eyes.

"I have a question, Juanita."

"Yes, Dominga?" What would she ask? To date, I had not found the words to prepare her for a place of forests not jungles, corn fields not banana plantations, black bears not jaguars, pizzas not *pupusas*, peace not war.

"What do you want to know, Dominga?"

She paused, held my hands and whispered, "Tell me about snow."

ODE TO DOMINGA

I squeezed your weatherworn hand,
just a few years older than mine.
So you—You are the woman whose crops were burned!
You are the one whose son ran from the Army!

You have cast away the woven cloth of your people
to take on the thrift shop clothes of mine!
You, whose eyes somehow still laugh,
Whose illiterate hands are so wise.

You—You look at me with the trust of a small child.
You hold on and earnestly ask:
"What will it be like in Canada?"

I pause... ponder a moment,
Inhale deeply and try to describe: SNOW.

Juanita

JOSIE & BABY ELI USING OUR AFGHAN

MAYRA & BABY VANESA

MARILU

175

~ *Puente* ~
My Time to Leave

A few weeks later, it was my turn to leave. I knew my departure date before I even arrived. I arranged for my son to be with me. How different than Dominga and her son. They were headed north and so were we. She would experience cultural shock and so would I. I wondered what it would be like to stay. I reflected on how I had choices, when so many do not.

Staying would mean using my Spanish every day. Others play golf, knit, buy collectibles for their shelves, but my hobby is Spanish. At Jubilee, it allowed me to be useful during a political struggle that I abhorred. I felt helpful in a time of crisis. Spanish linked me to the refugees. It served a worthy purpose.

At home I would again teach verb tenses and meet the occasional native language speaker. Someone once coined the phrase, "Life is so damn daily." That is how home felt. Living in an intentional community was inspiring. Something new every day, even if sometimes I missed my own autonomy or comfort zones. The work with the Central Americans more than made up for those twinges.

At home I felt disconnected and overwhelmed. At Jubilee I was surrounded by people from all over the world. Yes, volunteers came from other countries, people also concerned about our U.S. policies and the harm to Central Americans. The Jubilee people were living their beliefs. Every day was about action, however quiet. The self-sufficiency of gardens, the architecture of their buildings, matching our talents in work assignments, the emphasis on community, not individual social ladder climbing. Yes, but . . .

My life is a series of "yes, buts." Could I have stayed through the summer? Yes, but. . . my family lived in the north. We have our cabin, the lake, my soul.

Could I stay for a year? Yes, but. . . I would have to extend my sabbatical or quit my job.

Could Greg stay and live with me? Yes, but. . . the Georgia educational system had nearly extinguished his desire to attend school.

Decisions are not made in a vacuum. When I changed directions to go to Jubilee, others had to change, too. That is not a bad thing, just different. I had my three months at Jubilee with my son and now it was time to resume life in the north.

North to a job that waited, a never-done house building project that waited, my parents who waited. One day Terry would visit us. Vicki would come and stay over. Pacheco would end up in Sanctuary with the Fransiscan Sisters in Little Falls before crossing into Canada. Brian would walk across America and stop by. The people who walked through Jubilee opened me to a flow of Americans, North and Central, living out lives so vastly different than mine.

The refugees flowing with the Overground Railroad made choices to leave their countries to save their lives. The volunteers made choices to leave their communities to intentionally help the movement of refugees. The Mennonites, Quakers, students on college interims, professional volunteers traveling all over the United States, getting room and board for their labor—regular people stepped up to confront an intolerable situation.

Leaving Jubilee meant going back to being a cheerleader for culture and language instead of living it every day. Leaving Jubilee meant departing from people that understood my concerns for Central America, homelessness, the death penalty, hunger issues and simple human compassion. Or was it "Jubilandia" as some called it? A place where our fantasies of utopia covered over the pain that ran through every vein? If so, it was still good to be in a place where, in theory and in practice, we worked together for common goals.

Greg and I got on a plane and left Georgia thousands of feet below. We taxied into Minneapolis and were driven back to our forty acres south of Brainerd. Our daily chores returned. Robert, my do-it-yourselfer husband, still hammered away on the house. Firewood still had to be split. A new teacher inhabited my classroom and I lost a rung in seniority. Culture shock happens even when it's your own.

Thankfully, I had a supportive community of like-minded people in my northern woods. That fall, women from First Congregational Church took up my idea of knitting and crocheting scarves, hats, and mittens for "my" Jubilee refugees facing their first winter in Canada. The women gifted me thirty matching sets, made with the type of love only church women on a mission can muster! I photographed my couch covered in warm, colorful yarn projects, packaged them and added personal notes.

> *"Querida* Dominga,
> I hope this gets to you before the first snow.
> *Abrazos*—Hugs"
> Juanita

Section 6

Cultural Exchanges
Just Call me *"Profe"*

∼ *Puente* ∼
Me? An Adjunct?

In 1992, on the 500th anniversary of Columbus landing in the Caribbean and my 40th *primavera*/springtime on this planet, I put on my black robe and tasseled cap to walk the Hamline grounds a second time. I took my diploma back to Brainerd Community College and had an informal chat with the Dean. When I left, he reached out and shook my hand. "You're hired." I didn't realize I was being interviewed. Would this require changes in my methodology? No more singing silly verb songs? "Professor" felt stiff. "Profe" implied respectful camaraderie.

I was led to a large room with five adjunct desks, one phone, and no file drawers. Then on to the library, where I was introduced to Liliana Hennis, the only other Spanish *profesora* on campus. I forfeited my big high school classroom, tenure, and incremental raises for academic creativity and flexible scheduling. Fortunately, I never went into teaching for the glitz or money.

JAN WITH HAMLINE PROFESSOR DR. BARBARA AT JAN'S GRADUATION

31

Capítulo Treinta y uno
Latin American Exchange Teachers

I was not pleased when I heard the knock on my office door. With three short days of workshop to prep for the beginning of classes, already chuck full of multiple administratively mandated meetings, I did not have time for another thing. I took a deep breath.

"Yes, come in," I said in my professional, hide-my-true-feelings voice.

"Hello. Do you have a few minutes?" came the question from a woman with the air of wanting to sell me something.

"Yes, but only a few," emphasis on the last word of my cordial lie. "But I already have my textbooks ordered."

"This isn't about textbooks," she smiled back at me. "This is about an AFS-American Field Service, International Teacher Exchange program. We have teachers from Latin America who need placements."

Was she talking about bonafide, licensed teachers? Not teenager exchanges nor the Amity Teacher-aides, those college-age students heading into an assortment of professions willing to work in a foreign language classroom? Was AFS talking qualified, native speaker professionals? Really? Liliana wasn't in yet and I was "only" the adjunct, but I motioned her to the extra chair anyway. "Please, take a seat."

I don't know which of us was more surprised. In less than fifteen minutes, I had agreed to be a host teacher. I perused a half dozen resumes including family letters, photos, and a personal essay outlining future plans. I choose a young woman from Argentina. That AFS rep and I shook hands before she left with the promise to send necessary paperwork.

"Who was that?" asked Liliana, my colleague and office mate, as she walked in.

"You'll never guess what I just did," I bubbled, then remembered she was the tenured professor in this department of two.

"Well, what is it? Something more on the grant we are writing to get Mixed Blood Theater up here again?" she guessed.

"No, bigger yet. That lady you just passed leaving our office is from AFS-International. They have a program like AMITY," recalling that Liliana was once herself an AMITY aide, the very way she ended up in Minnesota.

"Go on," she said, nodding.

"The AFS program offers language teachers to come and be part of U.S. schools at no charge! Well, almost. The host school offers a hot lunch ticket and finds a host family. They are required to attend the host instructor's classes, help with any clubs, attend field trips, team-teach. They are pronunciation role-models, tutors, you name it." I looked over to read her facial expressions.

"The school doesn't have to pay a salary? Only lunches?" She was liking that.

"That is what I understand." I handed her the information packet left by the rep.

She asked me more questions as she flipped through the pages.

"You're going to find the host family?"

"I think I can find someone from church. That is an already-been-approved bunch of people in my book. They were often my host family prospects when I worked with ICEP."

"And where will the lunch money come from?" she asked, always attentive to budgets.

"I thought we could ask the International Travel committee or the college president. He says he supports international studies and culture. Let's give him a chance to prove it. Estimate lunches at $6.00 for around 150 days is nothing to ask to have another Spanish *profe* here!" I waited while she did the math in her head.

"How do we decide who we want to have work with us? We are already squished into this little office. We work great together, but what if someone new. . .?" her question trailed off.

"It's a good thing we do work well together," I put on a positive spin, "because I already asked about one prospect. Her name is Rocio from," I paused for effect, "ARGENTINA." I looked at her.

Liliana's serious face broke into a radiant smile. "Argentina? What part?"

"Resistencia. I never heard of it before an hour ago. You?"

"I lived in Rosario, about an eight-hour drive from there."

Rocio

Liliana had not returned to Argentina since her college days. She had met and married a Minnesotan, and had three kids before the divorce. Her private life was hidden behind hints of a difficult childhood, Argentina's Dirty War, and personal detours. I didn't ask. She didn't tell.

"Do you have any data on this Rocio person?" she returned to her line of questioning.

"Here is her personal introductory letter, resumé, and transcripts," I said passing them over.

"I'll read them later, but now I'll make a few calls to dig up some money."

Thus began a parade of AFS Exchange teachers through the halls and lives of Central Lakes Community College. They came from Argentina, Chile, Mexico, and Spain. They had different personalities, accents, and vocabulary words, all adding sparkle to our curriculum. They helped organize Spanish Club events, worked the Festival Latino, gave community-wide presentations, corrected papers, and covered conversation practices.

LILIANA, DARIO & JAN

Liliana and AFS teacher Dario, also Argentinian, began an outreach language program in Long Prairie for the Jennie O turkey factory personnel. We initiated cultural communication outreach using the intercultural simulation game, Bafa-Bafa, for administrators, faculty, law enforcement, and the Fransiscan Sisters, in their cultural preparation for two novices arriving from Saltillo, (back in my life again)!

I was awarded a grant to host Mixed Blood Theater's production of *Minnecanos*, Juan Acosta, Mexican artist and muralist, and wrapped it up with photographer Dick Bancroft and his Latin American photo exhibit. The infusion of Rocio, Dario, Irma, Juan Pablo, Ana, and Luisa brought life to our students and our program. Their enthusiasm moved Liliana and me to greater visions. When our dreams stretched beyond our energy levels, the AFS teachers stepped in and ran with it.

On their end, all enjoyed carving pumpkins, chopping down and decorating Christmas trees, seeing snow for the first time, and learning how to speak Minnesotan, ya betcha. The Argentines might not have eaten enough beef here, but they didn't perish from marshmallows suspended in their Jell-O, either.

~ *Puente* ~
On to Central America

It wasn't until five years after waving good-bye to the Jubilee refugees heading north that I deemed it feasible for me to head south. The news and U.S. travel advisory restrictions did not encourage tourists to make Central America their vacation destination. Ever since Jim died, I was determined to remain alive until my son reached the age of maturity. I knew that wasn't in my hands, but I could make decisions favoring that outcome.

Around this time, an Augsburg College Global Education flyer broke through my fears. Pamphlets from their International Travel department ended up on my desk, informing me of study venues offering college credit. As a teacher, continuing education credits were required. I was especially interested in those options that got me out of cloistered meetings in windowless rooms during summer break.

Augsburg's ads read like a savory menu to me. "*Cuernavaca*: The Role of Women in Mexico," "*Chiapas*: The Zapatistas and NAFTA," "*Guatemala*: Peace Accords and Refugee Resettlement,", or maybe, "*Nicaragua*: Sandinistas and Literacy" would be good. You get the gist. The trips attracted activists and concerned citizens from around the nation. They focused on "giving a voice to the voiceless" with emphasis on presenting varied groups with opposing points of view. The agenda was not to have an agenda. Our own critical thinking was expected to formulate conclusions. Our homework: Return to our communities and share what we learned.

My first study trip into Central America was titled: "Guatemala & Nicaragua: Conflict Resolution & Indigenous Issues," sponsored by the Political Science Department of St. Mary's University, San Antonio, Texas and organized by their Professor Larry Hufford. The seminar's goal: ". . . to expose participants to the reality of poverty and injustice in Central America, to examine the root causes of those conditions and the role of the United States foreign policy, and to encourage reflection on the role and responsibility of people of faith in working for social and political change, not only in the Third World but also in our own society." Whew! Not the glitzy, tourist rendezvous sought by springbreakers, but exactly what I wanted. On my own, I would never be able to make these sorts of connections.

For me, it was the perfect way to go from my book learning directly to the main countries of my interest. Guatemala was 52 percent Mayan and Nicaragua's revolution was the center of a U.S. covert war (think Iran-Contra, Sandinistas) reaching into all the areas of 1980s violence. If I could see these places in person, I would gain the post-war insights into their continued immigration to the U.S. What were the homes, communities, and schools like now? Were the peace process and reconciliation efforts working or just another pretty myth?

32

Capítulo Treinta y dos
Travel with Augsburg Global Study – 1994

CALIXTA AT IXIMCHÉ

Our Augsburg student travel van left the din of Guatemala City's early morning traffic and climbed into the surrounding hill country enroute to Iximché, a lesser known Mayan ruin. Fidel, our trip leader, stood in the front of the bus clinging to the overhead bar with one hand and holding a microphone to his mouth with the other.

"Today," he informed us, "we'll be stopping to pick up Calixta Gabriel Xiquin, a Mayan priestess, who will take us through Iximché, a sacred Mayan ruin. It was once the capital of the Kaqchikel Maya kingdom from 1470 to 1524. Presently, it is a favored place for healing rituals. Calixta will lead us in such a ceremony at the Mayan altar within Iximché still used for that purpose. To be respectful, there will be no photos taken."

CALIXTA (CENTER) & HER SISTERS

I had never heard of Iximché before, but was familiar with codices, the Mayan creation story, and scattered beliefs in shamanism held by the twenty-plus Mayan linguistic groups. Outside the bus window, the images I had seen in books of Maya clothing jumped out of the page and onto the pedestrians along the highway. I watched the women balancing turquoise and white plastic water jugs on their heads. Some wore folded head clothes to soften the load. As we got into the village, all were wearing traditional *traje*, Mayan clothing. When we slowed to circle the plaza, it was like a parade of colorful fireworks sparking before my eyes.

The women's blouses, called *huipiles,* were works of art from their own back-strap looms. The zig-zagged patterns were a riot of bright yellows, rich reds, royal purples, and sky blues. It is said that when a woman's head slips through the slit of the *huipil*, it symbolizes the center of the universe and the female's core role in life. Their long, striped *cortes-* skirts wrapped around them and were held into place by a cloth belt, also hand-woven. In

185

this village, the skirt was black with purple stripes held at the waist with a rainbow-colored belt, tied and draping to their knees. Each village wears a specific color and pattern that identifies them with that area.

I was once told that the early Spaniards mandated this arrangement so as to better know which group of Mayas belonged where. I cannot validate that, but can verify it worked very well during the recent violent years that were finally labeled genocide by the world court. In the 1980s, the Guatemalan government was suspicious of anyone traveling outside of their village area. Wearing regionally specific *trajes* made "outsiders" easily visible.

Those traveling outside their villages were considered, at the very least, *catechists* teaching reading or, at worst, communist subversives recruiting guerrilla fighters. Mayan men took to wearing western clothing and speaking Spanish to fit in. Women stayed traditional, carrying on their languages and cultures.

I recalled these things as I gazed out the window at these women taking the hands of their toddlers to cross the bustling street, baby bundled in their back shawl. I noticed men wearing wrapped turbans or western straw-brimmed hats. Older men sat on benches in the center's park, leaning into their walking sticks, watching passers-by who had places to go.

A young man, stooped beneath his load of firewood held on his head by his strapped *mecapal*, trudged up a cobblestone street. Our van slowed to a stop at the lights. A boy ran between the cars with a limp rag and spray bottle, offering to wash windshields. Our driver gave him a few *quetzal* coins to NOT wash our windows!

A gaggle of young girls in matching plaid skirts and white-bloused school uniforms stepped off the curb into the crosswalk. There was a taller business man in his refined suit, a shorter sun-burned man in weather-worn gray trousers, and finally, a well-coiffured thirty-ish woman with starkly painted eyebrows, red lips, smart dress, and very high heels who staccato-ed her way across the pavement. We eased back into traffic. Fidel tapped the microphone.

"We will be stopping for Calixta and her sisters in just a few blocks. Calixta is very well known in these parts as a shamaness and will be doing a healing for one of her sisters. You are invited to participate at any level you feel comfortable."

Was this, like in my classroom videos, going to involve killing a chicken? I reasoned that joining in a healing ritual could do me no harm. I was grateful to have the honor of being invited.

The bus door cranked open and first Calixta and then her sisters stepped aboard. They clasped the shiny pole and steadied their legs as the bus moved away from the curb. They were dressed in full Mayan traditional *traje*. They spoke to Fidel in a Mayan dialect, so I wasn't able to eavesdrop.

I began to imagine Calixta's life. She was probably from one of the small Mayan villages. I wondered if her house had a tin laminate roof, keeping sun and rain off a large room with hammocks hung on pegs during the daytime and stretched across the room at night. Maybe there was a dirt floor with a center cook fire or one of the new-fangled appropriate-technology brick stoves. Maybe even a new appropriate-technology composting latrine out back. Did she carry water on her head or have a spigot in her yard? Maybe a *pila* washboard for washing clothes, and some chickens underfoot. Some of my ideas came from a life-sized diorama on display last year at the Science Museum of Minnesota. I was deep into my stereotypes when Fidel clicked on the microphone and turned to face us.

"I would like to introduce you to Calixta and her sisters," he began. The women nodded their heads and smiled. "We are going directly to the Mayan ruins of Iximché, a place pre-dating the Spaniards. Calixta will walk us through the remaining pyramids, tell us some history of the area, and finally, set up for a healing ritual at the far end, by the jungle. Again, we are all invited to participate or to simply observe."

I continued my suppositions about their lives until the van pulled into the parking lot and we gathered the things we'd need for the next few hours. For me, that included my water bottle, camera, granola bars, and Kleenexes tucked into my small backpack. For Calixta, it required several helpers. Her bundles would reveal their contents later.

We followed her over the short grasses, along paths, past low pyramid platforms and rock walls that delineated former buildings. She spoke of her people, the ancestors. Fidel translated her Spanish into English for the group. Once again, I was pleased not to have to depend on his services. Occasionally, I'd walk beside her and ask my own questions.

The ruins butted up against the jungle, as Fidel had indicated. Up ahead, large rocks and a pile of ruins sat at the edge of the woods. When we got to their base, Calixta dropped her bundles. We followed suit and neared the rocks between several towering trees. We could now make out the melted candle wax, decaying flowers, fluttering streamers, and circular burn scars on the rocks and in the dirt. This was their altar.

Calixta began to unpack. Several of us were instructed to take a bag of what looked like volcanic rock the size of small barbeque coals and place them in a large circle. They were flat on one side and rounded on top. We began the circle, putting the flat surface to the earth. About half way around, she came running over. "No, no, not that way," she cautioned. "That would be very bad."

We halted and looked at each other.

"See the shape of these coals?" she pointed to a flat side. "That side must go up." To us, flat seemed a logical surface to put down.

"The rounded side brings in the bad spirits," she continued. "The flat side allows the good spirits to enter. The good spirits heal."

That set us quickly flipping all the pieces we had circled into the correct position. When we finished, she came to inspect. We were relieved to receive her approval.

Other items pulled from her bundles included a large bouquet of sage, handfuls of small, skinny colorful candles, copal incense, matches, and some small, sample-sized bottles

187

of *aguardiente*, the local firewater. She motioned for us to stand behind her and be silent.

Calixta straightened herself to her full five-foot height. She faced north and raised her hands into the air, calling out to the ancestors in Quiché before going to Spanish and then, surprise . . . English. She invoked the trees, the jungle animals, the wind, the sun as she turned to the south, east, and west. We turned with her, following her lead. We bent on one knee toward each cardinal direction, listening to her prayers. She called out to Mother Earth, the universe, peace, health, love, and our integral part in creation. She raised her voice to the living and the dead, the animal spirits and plant life, professing our connectedness, past and present. Then she knelt on both knees, bowed down to the earth, and kissed it. We too, knelt and kissed the planet.

She led us over to the piney coal ring, now properly prepared, and motioned for us to gather around it. Calixta took a match and lit one, then another. She handed out more matches and indicated we should help. When all little coals were smoldering, we stood back in the circle and watched her take a large bouquet of sage and dip it into the embers. It lit. She blew out the flames and let the smoke rise from its dry leaves.

With this, she slowly walked behind us, lifting and lowering the sage, wafting the smoke over and around us with her free hand, repeating something in Quiché. I recognized the sage as a cleansing, a *limpieza*, practiced by shamans.

Next, she pulled out her collection of multi-colored candles and placed them in groups. "Green is for foliage," she laid those in one pile. "Blue is for sky and water, red is for blood, black is for death, gold is for sun, white is for. . ." she continued down the line. Again, her chanting rose up in Quiché.

It was such a different sound. A lullaby. Some clicking. A rhythmic mantra. She took a candle from each color and tossed it into the fire circle, accompanied by more prayers. Red coals sputtered into low flames with each addition of candle wax. Now it was our turn.

"Kneel down facing the fire," she instructed us. "Think of something in your personal life. Do you need guidance? Is there pain? Joy? What is on your heart today?"

She opened a bottle of *aguardiente* and sprinkled it on a handful of sage. She faced the fire and sprinkled some of this alcohol directly on the coals. Flames erupted and crackled into the air. She dipped the sage into the flash of flames, let it burn a moment, and then snuffed it out. Reaching for the now blackened end of the sage, she crushed it into ashes and smudged our foreheads. She walked among us, all kneeling there, rubbing sage ashes into our hair, on our faces, any exposed skin on our necks and arms. Her other hand moved the tied sage bunch around our heads, over our chests, across our backs, down our legs, and touched our feet before moving on. As she finished each one of us, she whispered, "Now pray for your loved ones, your ancestors, your grandmothers and grandfathers. Name their names."

Photo images of my great-grandparents paraded across my mind. Susan, Stephen,

William, Amanda. Then my grandparents, Nellie, Floyd, Edith, and Ford. Then my generation. Brother Steven. Greg's dad, Jim. Their faces came to me and then vanished into the sage smoke.

When Calixta finished her rounds, she returned to the piles of colored candles. "Now take the candles. With each one, make a prayer and then toss it into the fire. Pray for your Mother Earth, for all of its children, plants, and animals. Pray for all creation. Pray for yourselves." She picked up a slender, pink, five-inch candle and rolled it between her thumb and pointer finger, closing her eyes and mumbling what I supposed to be her prayer. Next she laid the candle in the fire and the flames rose at the touch of wax.

I took a candle for my cabin and all the critters there. I took a candle for eagles and herons and chickadees. I took a candle for world leaders making decisions over all living things. Each of us silently took candles, paused with closed eyes, then walked to the now flaming fire and watched our prayers flare up, then melt, smoke sending our messages into the heavens. When all the candles were gone, Calixta called one of her sisters into our circle and placed her by the fire.

Calixta swirled her hands around the rising smoke and swept it over her sister, starting with her head. Wisps of our combined prayers rose around her sister, as she stood with eyes closed. Then, Calixta dipped into one of her bags and pulled out the eggs.

I had seen eggs used before to calm a baby with colic. There is a belief that the eggs take in the bad, ill, or disruptive energies. In the case of the baby, after passing the egg around and over the baby's body, the mother took the egg to a clay bowl in the patio and broke it open to release the bad energy. I was directed to look into the bowl and witness a large dark spot in the yolk, the blackness that was the baby's colic, now removed and released. I report that the baby was fine after that.

So here were the eggs again. Calixta took several eggs from her bag and walked to her sisters, still by the fire. When she passed the eggs around their heads and bodies, she continued to sweep smoke over them with her free hand. When she had gone from head to foot, she held the egg with both hands before throwing it into the fire. She followed this by tossing in full, fresh lemons. The eggs popped and the lemons exploded.

Clouds were gathering behind us, like angry jungle beasts coming to the edge of our clearing. Calixta got a fresh bag of candles and continued to hold them up, chant, pray, and place them into the ever-growing fire. It stayed within the confines of the rocks, but the flames now warmed us and provided some light in the encroaching dusk. More prayers. An hour passed. Our faces glowed with each additional candle.

The winds started to pick up. They blew through the once bustling streets of Iximché. Our group melded into centuries worth of humans who passed this way, raising up prayers from the pyramids below. Another gust bent the flames toward the three Mayan women engulfed in sacred smoke. Palm branches quivered above. Air passed through jungle thickets creating a faint moaning, or perhaps it was a distant howl whispered from the lips of an ancient jaguar god. Was that Calixta with us or one of her Mayan ancestors?

Calixta again turned to the four cardinal directions, then took a branch and swept through the fire until it died into wisps of occasional smoke puffs. She emptied the rest of the *aguardiente* into the dying flames. Sizzling fire sparks jumped into the air and sputtered out.

In silence, we picked up our bags and followed the three women, passed the stone altar, the blowing ribbons, the quiet remains of well-worn streets dotted with 15th century Mayan temples, to the van waiting to return us to our hotel in Quetzaltenango.

The snap of the van doors closed behind Calixta and her sisters. We settled into our seats, returning our gazes out the windows over the night falling on Iximché. A streak of lightning burst through the dark, outlining the pyramid profiles. A clap of thunder. The rains came.

***

That evening at our debriefing meeting, Fidel gave us a glimpse into Calixta's life story. After all my imaginings about their likely lack of much public education, their hauling water and wood, their role as women in a chauvinistic culture, I was unprepared.

"Calixta," Fidel began, "is an activist for Mayan rights. She has a Master's degree from the University of Guatemala City. As you noted in the ritual, she spoke English, *Quiché*, and Spanish. She also gets along in several other Mayan dialects. Her work with the Maya involves her in the local peace processes. Due to her activism, she came to the attention of a group representing the Maya and was invited to go to the United States. Calixta spoke before the U.S. Congress on behalf of indigenous rights and the atrocities committed here during the 1980s war." He paused. "She and many Mayan business women wear the traditional *traje* as a statement of their culture and solidarity with each other. What once targeted them for atrocities is now a badge of courage and community."

Once again, I had fallen into the dark pit of stereotypes. Again, I stood corrected.

ON TO LA ISLA – A LAND-TAKEOVER

Around the rim of Guatemala City, the landscape drops into a series of ravines. They fall away from the hilltops at steep angles into creek beds or flat, dry, narrow strips of land. On that Sunday morning, our van headed to one such geographical area referred to as *La Isla* – The Island, a land island jutting up among the deeply carved ravines.

La Isla was reached by crossing a land bridge linking a hillside at the periphery of the city to a land outcropping on the opposite side of a large ravine. The road was rough, pock-marked with fist-sized sharp rocks, divots left by their removal, and gravel added to designate this stretch as a passage for vehicles. The driver slowed to spare his tires from puncture. The van bounced and occasionally lurched to miss a pothole.

190

The slow pace gave us time to take in the scene outside our windows. Low lying adobe buildings were all that was left of the city's sprawl. Faded turquoise or white paint clung to the chipping cement walls. Footpaths led off the road in myriad directions. Riding the spine of this steep ravine gave us a vista out over the logged-off mountains and down the gulley's eroded, debris covered slopes. White plastic bags floated on air currents and piles of blue garbage sacks lay ripped open, spilling their guts into roadside heaps attended to by circling vultures.

A bevy of wooden, shack-sized structures came into view on a neighboring ravine parallel to our path. Fidel took the microphone as the van signaled our turn toward the narrow, connecting land bridge.

"We are about to enter the area now known as *La Isla*," he informed us. "This is one of many land parcels around Guatemala where people moved after being displaced by the violence of the war. They came together and did a take-over. If the land has an owner, this would be called squatting. This particular community is on public lands, but their land takeover is being disputed by a local politician. I'll let them tell their story."

The van came to a stop at a locked gate. We pulled off the road and piled out into the hot sun. Fidel led us around the blocked entry and onto a rutted path that best served foot traffic, although it was their main road. We followed him along a stretch of shelters constructed of weather-worn planks, tin-*lamina* roofs, and cut-out window holes, as we made our way to the first destination, their church.

It was a sturdier, oblong, cinder-block building, also with window openings. Fidel put his finger to his lips to quiet our entrance through the wooden doors. Church was already in session. The wooden benches and extra folding chairs were filled and our arrival caused a momentary disruption as people shuffled around to make room. Despite the cross breeze through the glassless windows, it was stifling. I scooted onto the end of a bench.

Women wearing native Mayan dress with babies swaddled in their back shawls sat next to women in western skirts and blouses. Men wore gray or brown trousers with short-sleeved shirts. The pastor wore vestments, like those of a Catholic priest, despite being Lutheran. The young woman next to me modestly covered herself with a shawl while nursing her baby. A group of young people sat up front. I decided this was the choir when they stood up and led the singing. There were no musical instruments. I picked up a Xeroxed pamphlet from the bench and found the hymn number. I could follow the words but not the Guatemalan tune. Other songs were memorized, so I concentrated on deciphering melodies and hummed along.

The pastor rose and stood before us. In a clear, directed voice, he left no question about what he perceived was the case before this congregation. I took out my journal and hastily scribbled down key points for our discussion later.

"This community has suffered violence and displacement. We need to organize, to come together to meet our needs in this lifetime, not the next. We have rights, human rights." He went on, "There is rift between the rich and the poor. There is great inequality between those working in the *maquiladoras,* these multi-national company sweatshops, barely paying minimum wages. They do not have safety standards. People are being harmed by non-living wages and injuries." I wondered how many people in this congregation were walking across the land bridge for *maquila* work on the other side. His words were textbook examples of the workers and oligarchy.

"In the past, the military. . ." my ears perked up, "the military probably used this very land for their dirty work." He hesitated before bringing the point home. "Right here on this land, we have found bodies. When we dug foundations for this church, there were human remains. We must remember the atrocities of the military on the *campesino,* on our own families. The very reasons we had to leave our homes and come here. This is why we are united today in obtaining this land. They have tried to burn us off. They are trying to prove we can't stay here."

He inhaled deeply. This man was total Liberation Theology. I wondered if the message was revamped for our benefit. Or was this minister always so direct?

After church, he joined us and introduced our group to some of the community leaders. One of the elders stepped forward and explained:

"The land we are living on was public land when we arrived. Over the past few years, we have built these humble homes you see around you, our *covachas.* You will visit these next. We inquired about this land, but the government did not answer our requests for a place to live. It was impossible to stay in our towns with the constant military and guerrilla attacks. We were neither, but each group accused us of being on their enemy's side. We had to leave our homes and villages to survive. When our numbers grew here, some politicians took notice."

He paused, looked at our group and then resumed. "One in particular claimed that we were on his land. There is no record of this. He has no deed to this property. He is powerful, however, and tried many ways to get us off. We don't have proof it was him, but some people started a fire at the bottom of the ravine that swept up the hillside to our community here on top. There were injuries, but we put the fire out. In that way, he tried to frighten us, even kill us. He wants to build condos."

There was a communal groan before he continued. "Other politicians have their own fears, as the pastor mentioned. We found human remains while building here. It is our belief that this was the site of one of the clandestine military cemeteries. There are secret spots where they used to dump the bodies of their victims, sometimes by the hundreds. It would not be good for the government to have this come to light." He stopped and let that sink in.

"But, we are here. We are fighting his claim in the courts. We believe we can win and we are saving our money to buy this land. Land is the key to everything. We aren't squatters. We want to be landowners with signed papers. We have no home to go back to and the government has not acknowledged our plight. We built our *covachas* of planks and tin. We planted corn and beans. We plan to stay," he concluded, making eye contact with each one of us.

With that, Fidel split us into small groups to take the walking tour and see for ourselves. Since I could speak Spanish, Fidel introduced me to my own private guide, Amérigo, and sent us off together. Amérigo was a young man, maybe in his late twenties or early thirties. It was nearly impossible to guess ages. We stepped toward each other and he reached out to shake my hand.

"*Me llamo Amérigo,*" he offered his hand.

"Me llamo Jan," I accepted and gave a squeeze.

"Would you like to see my house?" he offered. Just like that, I was on my way to fulfill a long-time desire to see inside these homes, these lives. He extended one arm in the direction of his property and we were off.

The huts were built with poles, recycled tin, and thin, probably 1" by 6" planks, haphazardly nailed in place. Some were constructed with the use of a level and others not so much. Sometimes ropes were strung between poles around the house, designating a sort of yard. Beans and squash vines grew along some lines, providing a sense of privacy and property.

The paths between the buildings were slick with mud. It was the rainy season. We stepped over puddles and slid along foot trails. It was gooey, sticking to my shoes and splattering my legs. How did they manage to walk, let alone work, on these steep inclines? I read once that El Salvadoran peasant farmers tied themselves to bushes while farming so they wouldn't slide down the steep and slippery slopes. I knew Guatemala had horrific mudslides, especially with the jungles being clear cut. Only corn stalks seemed to be holding this soil in place.

We continued on. Amérigo greeted everyone who passed, often by name. There was a whiff and confirming oink that identified pigs as one of the animals behind these fences. Clucking was prevalent and the occasional dog rounded out the animal population.

"This," he pointed to a spigot rising out of a 4' x 4' chunk of cement, "is where we get our water." Presently, an elderly woman with her deeply wrinkled, bronze face held the typical white and turquoise plastic pitcher under the stream of water being pumped by a small girl.

"*Es tu nieta,* is that your granddaughter?" I asked, wondering if I was being too forward.

"Oh yes," she said, wrinkles breaking around a toothless grin. "She helps me three times a day, morning, noon, and night." The little girl looked at me from under her furrowed brows.

I went to my knees to be at her level. "*¿Cuántos años tienes?*" I asked her.

"*Cinco,*" she said, holding up five fingers, just like kiddos at home. I held my fingers up one at a time, counting them out in Spanish. She joined in.

"We have some teenage girls working as teachers," Amérigo said, smiling at the little girl. "We scrape together what we can to pay them. There is a small building with some benches for a school. The girls have finished the sixth grade, but we have a problem with the government. They refuse to acknowledge them, so we get no credit recognition. Without accreditation, our children aren't allowed to go on in the government upper levels. Right now, we only offer three grades. It is difficult to attract teachers when the pay is so low and irregular."

By now the *abuela* and her granddaughter had filled their pitchers. I asked Amérigo in a whisper if it was alright to ask them permission to take a photo. He said yes and they said yes. I was sorry I didn't have a way to get them a copy. I could only say thanks and move along.

A block down, we stopped at a crooked gate leaning precariously from one hinge. He took one end, lifted it, and motioned me to pass through.

"*Esta es mi casa*," he announced, "and that is my wife and baby at the door."

MAYAN GRANDMOTHER WITH GRANDDAUGHTER

She shyly bent her head before sending her eyes from my head to my toes. He motioned for her to join us around back. A long lean-to drooped out behind the house. Underneath was the traditional *pila*, scrub board. Water was scooped from a bucket onto the soap sprinkled washboard with one hand, then both hands were employed in mashing the clothes over the washboard ridges. A second sink was filled for the rinse. Around the brim, several ceramic dishes rested inside of each other on a stack of plates. Two turquoise and white pitchers, like those the *abuela* carried, rested on a board propped up as a shelf. Gray water drained into a bucket and went to the vegetable garden. Here, running water meant you ran to the community spigot, one for several hundred people.

Amérigo had a tidy, well-organized yard area. The lean-to also provided shelter for a shoulder high stack of firewood. Another lean-to in the back shaded a small pig and several ducks. A cinnamon colored hen pecked for ground bugs and a majestic rooster strutted toward a small garden plot with corn, beans, and squash. One lone, scraggly tree rose out of the center, bearing a small fruit, unidentifiable by me.

Before I had time to see the inside of their house, the van honked our five-minute warning. "That was quick," Amérigo said. "There is so much I wanted to ask you."

We headed back into the street, talking as fast as we could. While he questioned me about my job, home, and family, I noticed a sales stand, built of fresh cut lumber, a slanted roof, and front counter. I peered past the vendor to her shelves. Her inventory included a smattering of chocolates, gum, pop, candles, bars of soap, and other minor essentials. "It is really helpful to have this new store," Amérigo noted. "We don't have to find a ride all the way to town if we just need a little something."

We passed another woman entrepreneur sitting by her vegetable stand. "She is a good gardener and has a plot behind her house," Amérigo pointed out. "Some of us work the *maquilas* and don't have as much time to weed," he laughed. "I don't make much money, but enough to buy a few fresh carrots or lettuce to go with my tortillas. It is good to have businesses here."

At that, he got serious. "The work at the *maquilas,* the sweatshops, isn't all that good but they say we should be happy to have a job. Like the pastor said, they don't have many safety regulations, if any. Leaning over a sewing machine or a factory line is hard on the body. Ten to twelve hours is normal. They pay the minimum wage, 15 *quetzales* a day."

"Just a minute," I interrupted. "I got an exchange of 5.9 *quetzales* per $1.00, so that is less than $5.00 a day. We were told that a family of three requires 25Q a day to feed themselves. And you say your day is ten to twelve hours." I decide not to tell him that the U.S. workday is calculated at eight hours and the minimum wage is per hour.

Up ahead the van waited. I was the last to arrive. No time for flowery gratitude. I offered my hand shake and gave a tight squeeze with my *mil gracias.* I pulled two Minnesota postcards out of my backpack, offering him a view of a cross-country skier deep in a snowy woods and a canoe floating down river. Even if I had time, I doubted I could explain the cold winters nor the expanse of the Mississippi.

I stepped into the van, turned, and waved. From my seat, I watched him head back down the mud-rutted road to his *casita* with his wife, his baby, the piglet, a rooster, and ducks.

Me, I was headed to Quetzaltenango, where I would purchase a Mayan skirt for 40 *quetzales*, not dollars, but *quetzals.* That's just under three days' wages for Amérigo and half an hour for me.

So this is how it is. We are two humans set up in a world economy based on inequity and maldistribution of goods and services. I, too, built my house. I hammered, sawed, and did cement work, but I didn't get run off by soldiers. I had a job that included vacation, health, and retirement benefits. His baby is his retirement plan.

The bus bounced down the road and turned onto the highway. The driver picked up speed. The countryside blurred. I scanned the fields, trying to imagine the scene about a decade or two ago. The clandestine revolution that crept into their villages, the government soldiers rounding up citizens and gunning them down in the plazas. Amérigo was probably five or six years old at that time.

I shut my eyes. It was simply impossible for me to relate. No one in the bus was talking. We had a lot of things to think about.

Capítulo Treinta y tres
Pagans Among the Presbyterians – 1996

Jesus Loves Me

"Cristo me ama bien lo sé	*Coro:*	Cristo me ama,
Su palabra me hace ver		Cristo me ama,
Que los niños son de Aquel		Cristo me ama,
Quien es nuestro Amigo fiel.		La Biblia dice así."

SINGING IN A CINDERBLOCK CHURCH

The tune was familiar but the words were only understood by two of the six Minnesotans sitting under the palm-leafed roof in the open air. Under its shade, the congregation of twenty-some Guatemalans sang at the top of their myriad note ranges. This cacophony had become familiar to the guests of Reverend Jorge, a local Presbyterian minister, and now, our guide.

The Minnesotans wiped sweat from their brows and fanned themselves with the song sheets despite the shade. It was July in the countryside bordering the southern coast of Guatemala. The entourage was the first guest exchange exploring a connection between a Presbytery of the north with this one in the south. My friend and Spanish teacher colleague, Edith, was the connector.

Her Brainerd Presbyterian church was in the embryotic stages of setting up a Sister Church relationship. Letters between the powers-that-be needed translation. This correspondence filtered through Edith's capable talents and she became the go-to person. At the time, she did not realize it would be a lifetime volunteer position.

Until that summer, I had always thought of Edith as the Spaniard side of our collegiate relationship. She came to us with Spain's vocabulary and accent, due to her years living in Ávila. She had, however, North Dakota roots, and that is where our superintendent found her right before fall classes were to commence. By then I was frantic to have help and relieved when the contract was signed, formally making us colleagues.

Despite my supposition that Spain was her preference, she surprised me by getting involved in Central American issues, my personal bailiwick. When the translated letters included an invitation for a small contingency to go to Guatemala, she approached me.

After a chat, the idea grew beyond the relationship-building church visits to include a few extra days for our own personal endeavors. We contacted my former Guatemalan student-aide and life-changer, Lorena Miranda, and Father Greg, of New Ulm roots, at his parish in San Lucas Tolimán, to inquire about potential visits.

The Guatemalan Presbyterians met us at Guatemala City's international airport with a pickup and two cars, one with all blackened windows. The pickup had a homemade frame made of pipes braced in back, but was presently without canvas. In theory, six to eight standing men could fit in there, clinging to the framework on takeoff. I was more concerned about the car with blacked out windows, most recently a sign of government sponsored death squads. Edith, Gary, Marion, Maxine, Cathy, and I were distributed between vehicles with Marilis, the only Guatemalan woman, getting a front seat in the truck.

Manuel, Pastor Jorge, and Pastor David were our appointed drivers. I was put in the backseat of the black-windowed car. I was dubious about black windows, but these were Presbyterian cars now, so in I went. The drivers took a moment to discuss their route out of the capital and agreed to keep each other within mirror sights. They had no desire to call attention to this group of *gringos*.

Our drivers edged us into the busy streets and Marion stuck her new VHS camera out the window. She began her narration of downtown buildings blurring by, darting taxis, and, once out of the city center, log-filled semi-trucks and the occasional donkey-drawn cart. Three lanes went to two, then one with narrow shoulders. Jorge mentioned something about stopping for gas. At that moment I heard a police siren. He glanced into his rearview mirror and let go a phrase I didn't comprehend, but understood from the tone that he was not happy. He pulled over.

So did the cop with his flashing lights. I looked over at my non-Spanish-speaking companions and shrugged. We were squeezed into the back seat, likely over the legal limit of occupants for this car. We were foreigners. There were these blackened windows. My information from Central American refugees left no doubt that any police or military was not to be trusted. I peeked over my shoulder to see where the policeman was. Jorge took his eyes off the rear view mirror and rolled down his window.

El Señor Policia leaned in and surveyed the contents of the car. I felt like an egg in a carton being checked for cracks. There was no way Jorge was speeding. There were too many speed bumps. Did Manuel see us getting pulled over? Where was he?

The conversation between Jorge and *Señor Policia* was too fast for me. The Minnesota bunch in back stayed quiet. Was it something about the windows? I don't know if we really had to be stopped or if it was an excuse. The policeman implied he was checking to see if we were alright. Now that we knew we weren't being detained, we were much better, *gracias*.

Back on the highway, Jorge shook his head and apologized for the welcoming committee. Up ahead, Manuel had pulled over to wait for us. I could see Marion with her new movie camera hanging out the window. It was time to tell her not to take any photos of police or military.

"What are you getting?" I asked her, just in case.

"Everything," she grinned. Edith added, "She has had it rolling since we got in the car. There should be a lot of blurry footage of semis and palm trees flying by," she chuckled. Then she turned to me and added in Spanish, "At least I am speaking Spanish so when she shows this, no one will know what I was saying!"

SEMANARIO SAN FELIPE

It might look close on the map, but the estimated 113-mile drive west of the capital took approximately four hours. We arrived in time for supper at the *Semanario San Felipe*, a collection of office buildings, classrooms, and guest dorms. Hunkered under our umbrellas, we walked through the evening rain along the groomed paths, through the towering red *Heliconia* flowers, and entered the cafeteria. All except for Marion. She swooped her camera from groomed gardens, to brick paving stones to tops of soggy coconut palms, all to the surround-sound of the jungle drizzle. Inside the cafeteria, she zoomed in on the plates, getting close-ups of the chicken, black beans and plantains. Several seminarians bent their heads low over their suppers when she cast her sights in their direction. It seemed that no one wanted to be the star of her travelogue.

After supper, Marion made her way back to our rooms, swaying her video from side to side giving a continuous monologue. To watch this documentary later was dizzying. She continued her filming as we moved in. Edith and I could hear her mumbling.

"This is Maxine sitting on her bed. This is my bed with my stuff. Over here we have the bathroom. It has a shower." At this, Cathy stepped into the bathroom and took the shower curtain in her hand.

"And this is the shower curtain," Cathy said with a serious face right before breaking into laughter.

Next door, Edith and I were changing into our pajamas. Edith yelled out, "You better warn us if you're coming in here. This is a church function you know."

It was true. We were here to visit as many neighborhood Presbyterian churches as possible. We brought Sunday school materials and gifts from Minnesota churches to distribute. We carried messages to the sister congregations to translate. We would sing their songs and be ambassadors of goodwill. The seminary was our pivot point to a flock of humble and struggling area churches. The Biblical definition of: "Wherever there are two or more gathered in my name," summarized the days to come.

A PAGAN'S SACRIFICE

From our Sunday service under the palm fronds to the cinder-block church with actual pews, we were welcomed as dignitaries. Our arrival was anticipated and the church ladies were busy peeling hot tortillas off the *comal* grills heating on a variety of stoves.

WOMAN COOKING OVER OPEN FIRE IN PRESBYTERIAN CHURCH KITCHEN

These stoves ran the gamut from open fires on dirt floors to block stoves with pipes, the "appropriate technology" design. I was interested in the new-fangled cement block model and more recent, smaller solar stoves. The heavy, non-movable prototype got the fire off the floor and into a tinder box. Being enclosed, it warmed the bricks and radiated heat back to the pots over time, thus cutting back on firewood consumption. The pipe carried the smoke out of the room, often the only room that constituted their entire house. The taller stoves also prevented toddlers from tripping into the flames.

Perhaps more impressive than the stove evolution was the generosity of the *gente humilde*, a term for people of lesser means. They always offered us a welcoming meal regardless of their scarce resources. There was a drawback to welcome meals for us northerners. Despite the cooks and their ingredient options, Moctezuma's revenge, the plague of tourist tummies, lurked inside of each chicken and rice dish, or worse, the fruit drinks prepared from dubious water sources. They weren't trying to poison us, but didn't realize our inherent weakness. Northern digestive systems aren't prepared for southern bacteria.

199

Maxine and Marion were preemptive. They chose to take their doctor's diarrhea prevention pills seriously, buying and consuming their product beginning a week before the trip. With their stomachs thus iron-coated, they plunged forward into each culinary offering. Not so for Gary. During one such church potluck, he went white, I mean more white than normal, and collapsed on his way to the table with his full plate. The flutter of church ladies to his side was impressive, but cut off the air flow. When I assured them he was not dead, I got help to ease him to a spot where he could get some space and regroup. He would need a deep breath of fresh air for his trip to the church outhouse.

It's time to mention that, along with the appropriate technology block stoves there were appropriate technology dry-composting toilets. Outhouses ran the spectrum—from a hole in the ground surrounded by a hanging sheet, to indoor toilets surrounded by beautiful tiles. The common denominator for travelers is toilet paper. We were warned to carry along our own roll. What type of bathroom you got was a toss-up.

Gary was better by morning, but then Edith came to me. "I don't think I can make it today," she confided. "Do you think you could translate for the service tonight?"

I had watched her in action and picked up the vocabulary used in their services, including her endearing introduction of me as their token pagan.

"Will they mind that I am not Presbyterian?" I asked her with a mischievous grin.

"It will be alright. They seem to like it when I tell them you're our personal pagan." She managed to smile at me before heading to the privy out back. She was in luck. It was a nice one, clean, raised up on cement blocks, and included a wood door.

That evening's *Culto*, church service, was at Marion and Maxine's sister church, so they were inside practicing their presentation. Outside, people were arriving in old Datsun pickups filled with up to ten standing passengers. Others walked on narrow paths carved by generations of foot traffic through cornfields and jungle vegetation. Pastor David greeted them by name.

Gary walked in, improved but on wobbly legs. I hoped to see Edith, but she was a no show. Cathy, Marion, and Maxine were monolingual. It was up to me. I was confident, but hadn't considered the one thing that could do me in.

Since this was Maxine and Marion's church, they sat up front with the elders. Gary sat behind with Cathy. The women taking their seats wore an assortment of house dresses and the girls, a variety of skirts and blouses, often part of their school uniforms. Men and boys wore *Ladino*/western trousers and cotton, short-sleeved shirts. The kids ran over to tall, photo-taking Gary, jumping up and down to get into his pictures. When a young man sat at the Casio keyboard and began a song, people rose to their feet.

This church was a visible upgrade, perhaps due to income, but also number of years in existence. There was a decorative, slatted altar railing on the platform, a step up from the main church floor. The floor was not dirt, but finished clay bricks held in place with mortar. There was a fresh bouquet on the altar and above it, hanging on the wall, a large ceramic Bible, open, with verses painted in black on both pages. "*Jesús dice: Yo soy el Camino y la Verdad y la Vida.* I am the Way, the Truth, and the Life."

The music stopped and the minister motioned for me to join him. In front of God and everyone I introduced myself: "*Yo soy una pagana entre presbiterianos, según mi amiga, Edith.* I am a pagan among Presbyterians." I made a sad, apologetic face. I heard chuckles and noticed their smiles. "*Pertenezco a la Iglesia Unida de Cristo.* I belong to the United Church of Christ," I added, hoping to reassure them that I did belong somewhere. This is Marion. . ." I finished off the introductions of our crew.

They clapped and the service began with me whispering translation for my little group into English. After the welcoming hymn, Pastor David motioned for Maxine and Marion to step up for their special program, a symbolic outreach for their new sister congregation. I introduced the two and their song, "I am the Church," a children's ditty with hand signs. Maxine led the impromptu English lesson by singing loudly and over exaggerating her gestures. She raised her soprano voice and threw out her arms in a wide circle when she hit the stanza, "We are the church together." Despite the language barrier, they got the message.

Everything went smoothly and intercultural relations were on the rise. I thought my job was coming to an end when the pastor announced . . . Communion. Standing in front of this crowd, there was no way to avoid communion. This wasn't a matter of theology but of my stomach. The sacraments. The bread wouldn't be a problem, but the "blood of the lamb shed for you" could be. It was highly doubtful this place was serving wine.

The pastor motioned for Marion and Maxine to take places of honor at the altar rail while I stood by the pews and ushered people from their seats to go forward. Maybe I could avoid this altogether in the hubbub of all this moving around. But no, he called me up to be among the honored guests. He held up the bread, broke it, and offered us the first pieces. We ate.

He took a pitcher of something dark, maybe grape juice, and poured it into small paper cups. Larger than communion cups, maybe the four-ounce size. He filled them half full. If this juice was made with water, I could be in trouble. I'm thinking this could bring me to my knees, most likely in front of the porcelain god.

I looked over at Marion and Maxine, oblivious to my dilemma in their state of Cipro-anti-diarrhea medicated bliss. They picked up their paper cups, pinky fingers aloft, and drank it like a shot of tequila.

I looked down into my cup, sure that this potion meant no harm and would do no good. I told Jesus this one was for Him. I swallowed it down.

Church ended with another discord of musical notes completely disguising any melody. The benediction was pronounced. We were guided to the door where my English-speaking companions grinned widely, bobbing their heads in pseudo-comprehension, shaking the hands of the departing congregants filing back to their pickups and home trails. I returned to my room, climbed in bed, and waited.

Next day, Edith resumed her translation duties. I didn't notice if her appetite had returned or not. Gary was back to his jubilant, energetic self. Cathy and the two Cipro girls were doing fine.

Me? I was in the fetal position under my covers, reliving the moment I accepted the paper cup filled with the *sangre de cristo* shed for me. Clearly, that dark, grape juicy concoction had been made from unbaptized water.

IGLESIA PUERTA DEL CIELO

CONGREGATION OUTSIDE OF PUERTA DEL CIELO CHURCH

I love the name of that church. Heaven's Door. And I loved the fact it was in Retalhuleu. That is where Lorena lived. Lorena, that teenaged exchange student from 1982 with her newspaper telling me of kidnappings and general Guatemalan malaise. That Lorena. It took fourteen years, but here I was, finally in her country.

On Saturday, July 13th, the Guatemalan Presbytery took us to the *Instituto Arana Osario* and led us down the hallway into a classroom. Inside, along the front blackboards, four marimbas were lined up next to a bass leaning in the corner. Our grinning hosts motioned for us to find a pupil's desk and take a seat.

One of the elders cleared his throat, and with great pomp, began, "*Damas y caballeros,* ladies and gentlemen. We have the great honor of bringing you the *Instituto's* marimba band and ensemble." His arm swept out over us and his hand unfolded, pointing toward the door. In marched a parade of young men dressed in black pants and white shirts.

The first walked to the corner and claimed the bass. The next batch divided into groups, picking up their mallets and taking positions behind the marimbas. Another teenager sat at his drum set. The last man took a baton and was introduced as the director. All mallets were poised. Then his baton went down in a swoosh. A torrent of lively notes saturated the room.

Their hands blurred. The short mallets ricocheted off the wooden keys in a flurry of sound. One player, then the next, then all of them bounced their sticks across the double keyboards in syncopated rhythms traditional to Guatemala. It occurred to me that my next action might not be appropriate, but music requires movement. I turned to one of the hosts and reached out my hand, inviting him to dance with me. To my delight, he accepted, and up we went.

The reaction was immediate. The Guatemalans standing close by scooted the desks out of our way, enlarging the dance area. Perhaps my Minnesotan colleagues were shocked. They were not Southern Baptists, for heaven's sake, so dancing wasn't prohibited. Maybe it's a north country heritage thing. Even at dynamic musical events, entire audiences politely sit mute, hands folded in their laps with nary a toe tapping. Was that a sigh of relief when another pastor cut in to finish the dance? Not sure.

At the final stanza, I raised my arm, guiding my partner to allow me a pass under and we took a bow. When I raised my head up to thank him, there, behind him, with a radiant grin, clapping her approval, stood Lorena. Lorena! My Lorena! I let out a squeal and ran into her open arms. Next stop? Lorena's home in Retaluleu!

LORENA AND LUDWIG

I believe our eyes were sweating by the time Lorena guided us into their living room. The house tour included an entry patio with walls covered in green mosses and the occasional darting salamander. To the side was a washroom with shower and washtub *pila*. Jimena, their three-year-old daughter, was the lucky one. She was sitting naked inside one of the tubs full of cool water, splashing about while Leslie, the house helper, wrung out their wash on the scrub board. Diego, their five-year-old, was off with daddy, Ludwig.

Lorena left us and returned with an oscillating fan and glasses of cold lemonade. We looked at a photograph album while moving our upper bodies to stay in front of the fan. That, and lying on top of my sheets and watching a gecko circle the ceiling light are my memories of that day.

The next morning we got the town tour. Lorena drove us to the Public *Pila*. I call them Guatemalan laundromats, but they serve as so much more. They are another example of appropriate technology. To get the women out of the rivers on laundry day, these stand up wash basins are built around the edges of what I can best describe as an above ground swimming pool. Except you do not swim there.

This compilation of basins around the pool allows women to stand up, scoop out clean water, wash their clothes on the washboard, and rinse sudsy water down a drain.

This is superb. Now the women aren't on their knees, hitting their clothes against rocks, sending soap and pollution downstream. The basins also corral toddlers, who can sit and splash in the water without floating away.

Ah, but the first world response is often . . . why not get them all Maytag washing machines? Besides the logistics of plumbing, electricity, mechanical breakdowns, and up-front expenses, these *pilas* uphold culture. This is the chance for indigenous women to socialize. They come in from their villages with laundry loads on their heads, sometimes walking, sometimes ride-sharing in trucks, plunking down their bundles, and shooing their kids off to play.

This is a difficult idea to those of us in our private, tidy laundry rooms with washer, dryer, cabinets, detergents, fabric softeners, Clorox, static cling products, ironing board, iron, folding counter. . . Your laundry area might measure the same as their entire house. Point being, *pilas* aren't right or wrong, good or bad, but appropriate.

JAN TRANSLATES WASHING INSTRUCTIONS AT COMMUNITY PILA

At the market I discovered something that was not appropriate, at least not to Lorena's Christian beliefs. We passed a host of banana options, neatly stacked red tomatoes, a rainbow of Guatemalan weaves, and turned a corner into an area of wood carved masks, walking sticks, and over there . . . a shop filled with all sized statues of *MAXIMÓN*.

I ran to the stall. "Edith, look at this!" I yelled back at her. "*Maximón*! Do you know about him?" I asked, panting.

Maximón is a premier example, the absolute definition of synchronicity, the blending of two things to a recognizable yet different product. The Latin American version of Catholicism is another perfect example of synchronicity. Spain's forced Catholic conversion, mixed with a plethora of indigenous religious beliefs that did not die, but morphed into a unique religious blend, recognizable, but not the same.

Maximón is such a mixture. He is either a Catholic Saint referred to as *San Simón*, in memory of a priest who declined to give up smoking, drinking, and womanizing, getting him ejected, or more respectfully put, excommunicated by the Pope. Or he's a Mayan grandfather, god of tobacco, virility, and fertility, in that order. It is generally agreed that he is an icon of good and evil "incarnate" in the wooden statues that depict him wearing a black hat, black moustache, black suit, cigarette dangling from his carved lips, and bottle of liquor clutched in his carved hand. He can be found enshrined in *Santiago de Atitlán*, surrounded by cartons of cigarettes, bottles of alcohol, and wrapped in colorful, flowing scarves, all offerings given with petitions made for minor to major miracles.

"Here he is, Edith! Just like in my textbook. This guy is taken out at Easter time for the Holy Week parades. He's like a trickster-god. You might want to give him a cigar, just to be safe," I suggested before walking over to pick up a smaller version that would be perfect for my office desk.

At this moment, Lorena rounded the corner with her two little kiddos in tow. Before I could share my excitement with her, she swooped in and swiped the figure out of my hand as if he were on fire.

"Oh, Jan, you must not even touch him," she gasped in horror. "He is evil," she pronounced, quickly placing him back amongst his buddies and then wiping her hands of the contamination. "You should not even utter his name," she continued. "I would not want you to bring him back into my house and you do not want him in your suitcase on the way home," she finished emphatically.

I glanced at Edith and peeked back at the little statue, overshadowed by his life-sized peers. Clearly I was in over my head. She left no room for my argument that *Maximón* would make a good prop for my classes. This syncretic moment resulted, not in acceptance of the new but in a strong revulsion to the mix.

I wistfully examined the now unattainable collection of black hatted, mustachioed, cigarette smoking mannequins. Out of respect, it was not an option to take this effigy into Lorena's home. Jimena and Diego tugged on Lorena to move on to the promised *Dulcería* section to buy some candies. Edith shrugged. I swallowed my disappointment, turned my back on *Maximón* and . . . then stopped.

Would I be safe from *Maximón*'s dark side and not be disrespectful of Lorena if I . . . snapped a photo?

Perhaps I tempted the gods. I took my chances. I raised my camera and captured an image of this Catholic/Mayan god-devil, miracle making, spell-casting, saint of a sinner for my Latin American Studies class.

Even as I write this, Lorena's warning returns so strongly that I am undecided if I should include his photo for you to see!

The Rubber Plantation

Ludwig was and still is one of the fortunate ones. He is not one of the rubber workers, going into the plantation under the burning sun with his special knife to slice the trees and make the white liquid latex flow into containers. He is an executive, traveling the country and beyond. He does know about the hard labor side of the plantation, and that day took us into the forest with a foreman and gave us lessons in rubber tapping.

He held the knife in my hand and slowly sliced a curved cut into the tree's bark. The foreman adjusted the catch container. The latex began to bleed out of the inner tree and drip, rather like maple trees and sap. This liquid was transferred to large holding tanks before going through a chemical processor. That area reminded me of a winery or brewery.

Somehow all of this becomes rubber and a sluff-off by-product. The residue ends up as fertilizer in the fields. The rubber is hung in sheets to dry and packaged for export.

JAN & JIMENA TAP A RUBBER TREE

"So, Ludwig," I asked at the end of the tour, "where does most of this rubber go and what do they make out of it?"

"To the United States," he hesitated before leaning in to whisper, "for condoms."

Father Greg and San Lucas Tolimán

The distance between Retaluleu and San Lucas is 109 kilometers, but again times are more meaningful. Ludwig converted our delivery to Father Greg's parish into a family road trip. He packed us with Diego, Jimena, and Lorena into their vehicle for the two-and-a-half-hour drive to the infamous *Lago Atitlán*, a lake surrounded by many Mayan villages and many horror stories from the 1980s' years of violence.

Father Greg was one of only a few priests who stayed put during the massacres. Father Stan Rother, of Oklahoma, had served the neighboring village of Santiago Atitlán. He was murdered on July 28, 1981. Records show that he was one of ten priests killed in Guatemala that year. Father Greg continued his work among the Maya, including building homes, schools, a medical center, an orphanage, reforestation, water projects, and coffee production. Edith and I signed up to translate letters for children with U.S. sponsors.

Ludwig parked the car by the parish and we hopped out. Father Greg wasn't there at the moment, so we took this time to walk the town streets. Unlike Retaluleu and its *Ladino*, mixed race, population, these streets were a photograph album of Maya Indians

JAN & LORENA IN SAN LUCAS

in their traditional dress. And, at five-foot height, I was looking down at the women, unless they were carrying baskets on their heads. Lorena and I strolled among our peers, admiring their woven clothes and their strong necks, balancing laundry in plastic buckets on their way downhill to the lakeshore.

Atitlán is a Nahuatl word meaning "place of water." The lake fills a crater surrounded by three volcanoes—Atitlán, San Pedro, and Tolimán. This large beautiful lake has an afternoon wind with its own name, *Xocomil*, a *Kaqchickel* Mayan word meaning, "the wind that carried away sin." Edith and I would learn about this strong breeze later in the week when we boarded a large, wooden, paint-chipped boat without life preservers, headed to *Panajachel* for a day of textile shopping.

But today we walked in the uneven streets past wood-slatted huts, lopsided gates, clucking hens and men carrying large digging hoes over their shoulders. They wore traditional weaves, sometimes pants under kilt-like skirts, long sleeved shirts and straw hats. One such man greeted us when we returned to the church yard, only he was carrying a machete.

In this case, there was no call for alarm. This diminutive elder was hunched over a patch of green stems, the Guatemalan equivalent of lawn grass, deftly swinging the machete back and forth. This wasn't the first time we saw mowing done in this fashion. Considering the sparse clumps of offending plants, it made more sense than a riding mower. With one hand on his lower back, he straightened up and approached us.

"*¿En qué les puedo servir?*" he asked.

"You can help us find Father Greg," I answered. "We are signed up to work here for a few days. He's expecting us."

With that he disappeared into what we would learn was the Mother House. While he was gone, Ludwig organized us for a few group photos in front of this towering Colonial era church. Behind us, women were scurrying inside and out of this history-filled structure. Then we saw him. Father Greg looked even taller than his six-foot-some frame next to the bent, shuffling gardener. Unlike his bronze counterpart, he was starkly white, a "you-are-going-to-get-a-sunburn" white. He wore a thin halo of hair, also turning white. His traditional Mayan shirt hung loose over his tan trousers. He strode over to us and reached out his hand.

"*Bienvenidos*, welcome," he boomed with an ear-to-ear grin while pumping our hands up and down.

So, this was Father Greg. The man from New Ulm, Minnesota. A town of German heritage complete with Oktoberfest and brats. He chose this life, including protecting these people throughout the Mayan genocide perpetrated by the Guatemalan government. Lorena and Ludwig never spoke of those times. I didn't ask them. They had not heard of this man, a protector of so many in their own country.

I'm not good at *despedidas*, good-byes, but it was time. Edith and I turned to them, gave out hugs and *gracias por todo*, thanks for everything, before they climbed back into

their car and were waved down the road. Edith and I picked up our suitcases and followed *Padre Gregorio*, as he was called in the parish, to our accommodations. The *Casa Madre* included bedrooms for volunteers, a kitchen, living room, and a door that led out back to a patio between buildings. That is where we met other volunteers and were invited to join them for lunch.

It was a smaller than usual meal, they explained, as preparations were going on for a wedding that night. Were we interested in attending?

LORENA'S FAMILY IN SAN LUCAS

"Edith, did you hear that?" I whispered under my breath. "We are going to see a real Mayan wedding ceremony! This is beyond great," I finished, thinking about my Latin American Cultures class and all the real-life stories I was gleaning for lectures.

The traffic to the church and in the *Casa Madre* increased throughout the afternoon. Tables were set up for the supper to follow the ceremony. Streamers were strung, swaying in the breezes over the patio. Flowers were put on the altar and some of the church pews. Like home, the church women were scurrying around the kitchen. Unlike home, they were assembling hundreds of *tamales*. I made a mental note to only drink out of sealed bottles, no more punch or unbaptized liquids for me.

Dusk came and so did the people. First a trickle of villagers, all in their best Mayan traditional head-wraps, hand-woven skirts, and brightly embroidered blouses. Their outfits identified them as members of this community or others around the lake. We watched from the front door of the *Casa Madre*. The trickle swelled to a flow in evening's darkness. We stepped off the porch and filed in behind a trio of young Mayan women whose eyes sparkled in the glow of the stringed bulbs, now turning on with nightfall.

We sat in the back pew, the better to watch everything. "Edith," I gave her a nudge, "look at the statues of saints on the ledges around the walls. They are all wearing Mayan shirts!"

I don't remember if there was music or what made us all stand up, but we followed what everyone else was doing. We were out of our knowledge range both in the sense of culture and religion. We were both "pagans" in a Catholic setting and had no idea how the indigenous ritual would play out.

From the back narthex, it was difficult to see the groom by the altar. He was tall compared to his father and mother, standing at his side. They were cut of the traditional local cloth but he wore western clothes, a full-fledged business suit complete with tie. Only his facial features gave away his heritage.

A shuffling of feet drew all eyes to the main door of the church. A bustling clutter of women entered. How would we tell which one was the bride with everyone dressed in their identical traditional clothing? Would we even see her cloistered within this crowd?

The great doors closed. The women parted like the Red Sea and there she was. The bride emerged, wrapped in traditional *corte*, a full-length skirt, the brightly-embroidered huipil-blouse, fingers gripping a bouquet of flowers. But it wasn't the bouquet that gave away her identity.

She was easily a head taller than all her entourage. She had light brown hair under the crown of woven ribbons. She was of larger build, not the bone structure of these people. Why, she could have been Minnesotan!

And, she was.

Later that evening, we learned she once volunteered here, met her future husband, and was back for one of two ceremonies, one in Minnesota and this one on his home turf.

It was impossible to see and hear the service from our back seats, but we got a good look when they exited past our pew. The groom took his bride's hand, then his mother's. The bride took

SAN LUCAS GROOM & MINNESOTA BRIDE

his hand and then her father-in-law's. With the newly married couple in the center, they processed down the aisle, his parents looking almost frail in the shadow of their much larger, western-dressed son and his Mayan bedecked Minnesota wife. The congregation clustered behind the departing family like city folk boarding a metro. All personal space vanished at the door, where the surge bottlenecked before pouring out into the courtyard.

There, the night erupted into multi-lingual chatter from the mouths of global volunteers, local Mayan dialects and Spanish, the unifying tongue. It was a metamorphosis of melding cultures, a mosaic of colors, languages, clothing, traditions, and of course, foods! Edith and I happily helped ourselves to the *tamales* and observed from the shadows. The tamale-piled platters kept appearing and their corn husks soon filled once empty barrels. *Barriga llena, corazón contento*-full belly, contented heart.

Edith and I ended our evening early. Back in our room, we listened to the sounds of merry-making across the yard until the wee hours. After crawling under my covers, the events of the day replayed themselves until I dozed off. Partaking in such an integrated wedding was as unexpected as it was surprising. It was not to be my last surprise from this couple.

A year later I attended a weekend study on Central America, presented in St. Paul by anthropologist Nancy Black. I signed up for break-out topics and was excited to go.

I entered the meeting area, arranged my notebook and water bottle, and surveyed my surroundings. The professor seemed to be on the *hora latina* schedule, so we began to introduce ourselves to each other and share our interests while we waited.

When the door opened, my jaw dropped. In walked our professor, books cascading from his arms. I stared. I blinked. It was none other than the... groom... from San Lucas Tolimán, business suit, Master's degree, and all!

Section 7

The Infamous North American Elections of 2000

~ *Puente* ~
The Back Story

The year was 2000. Tensions were brewing on both sides of the U.S./Mexican border in the form of elections. To the north, Al Gore was the democratic candidate, opposing George W. Bush, son of President George H. W. Bush. To the south, there were three candidates, one for each major political party. Francisco Labastida Ochoa represented PRI, Vicente Fox Quesada was with PAN, and Cuahtémoc Cárdenas Solózano was the PRD man. In reality, Mexico had only one ruling party. Since its inception in 1929, PRI, the *Partido Revolucionario Institucional* a.k.a the Institutional Revolutionary Party, had won every single time.

This system of "electing" a president even had a name. It was referred to as *dedismo*, from the word *dedo* i.e. finger. The pointer finger, that is. Each PRI president appointed (pointed to) a successor who shadowed him for his six-year term. In Mexico, that is the limit. One six-year term, unlike our two four-year arrangement. Elections came up, candidates made the rounds, handed out T-shirts, tacos, and promises. "You vote for me and we'll put electricity in your village" was common. It worked. This practice went from clandestine to blatant.

Meanwhile, the U.S. election was in gear, with immigration rhetoric ramping up to a froth. The system was clearly broken. The Central American civil wars of the 1980s resulted in tentative Peace Accords in the 1990s. These fragile pieces of paper did not stop the pain of massacres, land takeovers, distrust, and growing economic inequity. Guatemalans still lived in refugee camps along their border with Mexico. El Salvadorans festered in the *barrios* of California's largest cities. The U.S. deserted their military use of Honduras as an air force base to launch attacks against the Nicaraguan Sandinistas, abandoning support of that country's economy.

Central America was ravaged, literally in flames. Village churches full of their male inhabitants had been torched. Peasant farmers displaced by multi-national plantations used scorch-n-burn agriculture to open new lands higher on the volcanic mountains. Hundreds of widows and orphans were without sustainable livelihoods. When hope ran out, they dreamt of *El Norte*. With babies and old clothes bundled on their backs, they abandoned homes, favorite foods, familiar surroundings and fled. Borders are imaginary lines across the planet when it comes to seeking survival. Immigration issues joined the pile of grievances aired during the 2000 campaign on both sides of the border.

Mexico's situation was exacerbated by an overall disgust toward fraud and corruption accumulated over seventy-one years of same-party rule. Would PRI win again with bribes of electricity and tortillas? Would the oligarchy continue to stand over their workers in the voting booths, indicating where the illiterate should put their thumb print? If Vicente Fox broke the monopoly of power, would there be a peaceful transition between parties?

Mexico had no experience with changes of administration. This part of their "democracy" had never been tested.

Meanwhile, in the United States, George Bush garnered millions of campaign dollars from wealthy Texas Republicans and his father's one-time presidential cronies. Yes, I said cronies. Words matter. This can mean: followers, colleagues, or accomplices. There were some of each. Was the U.S. turning toward dynasties instead of free and fair elections?

Perhaps the Bush family's experience of living in a border state would bring understanding to the immigration issues. Add Jeb Bush, brother of George W., Florida's new governor as of 1999. He spoke Spanish and was married to a Mexican-American, Columba Garnica Gallo. Would that have any influence on immigration issues getting air-time in the U.S.? Spoiler alert. Florida was to become the pivotal card in deciding the U.S. Presidential election result. Stay tuned.

All this was swirling around in my head when another Augsburg educational brochure came across my desk. I was impressed by my earlier Augsburg trip to Guatemala and Nicaragua. They had provided access to the Guatemalan Vice President speaking on peasant land takeovers and, that same afternoon, put us in the displaced protester's organizing tent in the plaza below the Vice President's window. Augsburg offered the antithesis to normal.

This trip offered an overview of Mexico's election issues, political parties, and the opportunity to participate as official observers if we chose. This could be an historical overthrow. Would it be peaceful? Would the election results be accepted? Stories of fraud were legendary. In the last election, ballot boxes were found floating down rivers. Electrical black-outs mysteriously deleted computer tallies. If that happened this year, it wouldn't be pretty.

Even former President Jimmy Carter, the most renowned election observer on the globe, was packing his suitcase. He was in the forefront of gathering observers to be present in Mexico for this round. If a country got his stamp of approval, likely the world would recognize the outcome. The chance that PRI would commit acts of fraud was pretty high, so he and a multitude of world volunteers were making their travel plans. This was too good to miss.

34

Capítulo Treinta y cuatro
Stationed in Cuernavaca

I flew into Mexico City, took the Morelos Bus to Cuernavaca, and caught a taxi to *Calle Preciados* street where Augsburg had its Center for Global Education. People from around the United States were arriving and getting room assignments. We got the usual orientation about not drinking the water, composting our leftovers, and safety tips. After that they handed out the week's schedule. Each carefully planned day included meetings exposing us to varied points of view important to comprehending the sides involved in this election.

Tuesday, June 27
- Visit State Congress for a panel with representatives of the various political parties
- Meeting with political analyst, Salvador Guzman, for political overview
- Optional video: "A Place Called Chiapas"

Wednesday, June 28
- Meeting with Alberto Arroyo, Citizen Advisor to the Federal Electoral Institute (IFE)
- Roundtable discussion: Areli Carreón and Miguel Rodríguez, founders of grassroots environmental organization, "Guardians of the Trees"
- Economist, Leopoldo Ferreiro, the current economic situation in Mexico

Thursday, June 29
- Tour of Xochicalco archaeological site. Pyramids, ball court, museum.
- Meet Don Félix Serdán, honorary Zapatista, activist and survivor of the 1910 Mexican Revolution. Visit his house and organic garden project

Friday, June 30
- Juan Cintrón, international business consultant.
- Rafael Álvarez from the Miguel Agustín Pro Human Rights organization.
- Visit Base Christian Community of San Antón

Saturday, July 1
- Municipal Democracy Programs at the Center for Encounters and Dialogue
- Preparation and Training for Election Observers

Sunday, July 2* ELECTION DAY**
- 8:00 a.m. to 6 p.m. Election observers to their posts. Unofficial observers have optional trip to Tepotzlán or street duties.

Now, into Cuernavaca's streets.

My roommate, Janice, was a reporter/photographer from the *Milwaukee Journal* in Wisconsin. We unpacked and were antsy to hit the streets. Since I knew my way around Cuernavaca, I was to guide. She took out an array of high-end cameras and then clicked open her briefcase. It was full, I mean totally full of film. Maybe a hundred rolls. She stuffed some into her pockets, her small backpack, and her camera case.

"Let's start in the plaza," I recommended. "There is always action in the park in front of the Government building, even without elections."

We left the Augsburg House and traveled along *Preciados* street to the new *Ayuntamiento 2000* bridge spanning the ravine leading to the city center. Every block was decorated with something related to the election. In the window of a small bar, a magazine cut-out of one candidate's head was glued upside down in a drawing of a bowl of *pozole* soup. Banners with the faces of competing candidates fluttered over the streets like sheets drying in the wind. Below them whitewashed walls were covered with freshly painted icons depicting the three political parties and life-sized political graffiti cartoons. The PRD

STREETS FILLED WITH POLITICAL BANNERS

used yellow and black. PAN used blue and white, the same colors as their patron saint, the *Virgen de Guadalupe*. The PRI used the red, green, and white of the Mexican flag. For the illiterate citizen, colors were the recognizable voting clue.

We followed Obregón street south a few blocks when it hit us. Music! Loud thumping music. We followed it to its source. The plaza! A generous amount of bass was being shared by a band leaning into their microphones from the flat back of a semi-trailer truck.

The lyrics were mostly obliterated by the screeching sound system, but it was drawing a crowd. Janice and I flowed over with the masses to check out the show.

The PAN banners, strung between the plaza's palms, slapped the sky, making it difficult to see the candidate's image. Between flaps, I deciphered a few words.

"This guy wants to be the governor here in Morelos," I yelled out over the din. "I guess this is his day to own the plaza. He's on all the banners and posters."

Janice held a camera over her head and started clicking. I, on the other hand, held my little point-n-shoot model covertly in my palm, snapping only if I was sure the intended subject was unaware. I was taught to ask people's permission. There was a definite different code of conduct for journalists going on here.

"How do you know what you are getting?" I asked, confused by her unbridled clicking.

"I don't," she answered. "I take as many as I can and, when I get back to Milwaukee, I'll know what I have. Remember my briefcase? The newspaper provides the film and I shoot."

"Maybe you can get that group over there," I suggested, pointing to six men wearing rubber masks in the image of Vicente Fox. They looked like Halloween gone bad.

The song ended, oh glory be, and a tall, well-groomed man strode onto the stage. He brought the microphone to his lips and welcomed the crowd. I don't know how much was my Spanish ability or how much was the sound system, but I missed a lot. People crowded in, pinning our camera arms to our sides.

"Let's get out of here," Janice nodded to a crack opening between some of the bystanders. "I don't want my camera this close to folks." I don't know if she was concerned about the camera's getting broken or stolen, but I turned and began a litany of "pardon me" until I broke loose on the other side.

"Whew," I exhaled, then turned to see if she was behind me.

"Hang on, Jan," she motioned to me, bobbing above the crowd. "I think that is the candidate climbing up the steps to the podium." The crowd erupted in whistles, cheers, and applause. That's when I noticed his helpers. They were recognizable by the T-shirts they wore. The ones with his face on the front. The ones they were beginning to throw by the scores out into the uplifted arms of the milling mob.

Really? T-shirts couldn't really be enough to buy votes, could they? It didn't hurt to give out clothing, I supposed. Cuernavaca was not and is not a backwash village looking for tortilla handouts and a town well. Yet here we were in a T-shirt shower. But wait. Where was Janice?

I stretched to my tiptoes in an attempt to search the vicinity. She was by far the tallest and should stand out. A convertible decorated with yellow and black streamers honked its way around the square, throwing out opposition T-shirts. Was that her dashing behind the car with a handful of other hopefuls? It was! She reached out for a flying T-shirt. I saw her just miss it as they both fell into the street. I pushed through the crowd. Several passersby rushed to her side. I grabbed her camera. Others helped her to the curb, where she took a seat.

"Janice," I gasped, "Are you alright?" I offered her one hand and put the other under her elbow to help her rise to her feet.

"Can you stand?" I continued, already racing to images of her foot in a cast. This was only our first day, for heaven's sake.

"I think the only thing I broke was the camera. I landed on it." She patted her shoulder feeling for the strap. "Whoa! Where is it?"

At that point, I realized I had dashed for her camera before reaching out to help her. What was that all about? Total strangers reached out to give her aid and all I registered was saving her camera from theft.

"I have it right here," I said, holding it up. "Looks like the lens is smashed and . . ."

She slowly stretched out to her full height, dusted herself off, and tried to put weight on her right ankle. "It's okay but not perfect," she reported. "I think our little photo shoot is over for the day."

We left the hubbub and retraced our steps to Bridge 2000. I peered over the railing and squinted down into the precipice below. A small ribbon of creek meandered at the bottom, still cutting crags into the landscape. Some footpaths, a goat, rock piles, and some tin that might be someone's roof. The breeze blew little swirls of sand up into my face. Then she did it.

She took the camera strap off of her shoulder, lowered her arm, and then swung it like a big league pitcher, flinging the broken camera up over the rail and into the cavern below. I watched in disbelief as the camera whirled its way to a smashing finale. I glanced over at her, dumbfounded.

"What was that all about? You just threw that camera over the edge and . . ." I was speechless.

"It's like this, Jan. It is way easier to ditch this camera and say it was stolen than to write an insurance report claiming I ran into the street after a flying T-shirt, fell, and broke it. What is more believable?" she finished.

So that is how it works outside of my world. What is believable?

The story we tell until it becomes our truth or what "really" happened?

A 1910 Zapatista Environmentalist

The days filled with visits to people on all sides of Mexico's current reality. We met in their homes and discussed neighborhood organizing. We rode into the mountains where railroad tracks were removed and environmentalists advocated for bike trails. We gathered with a Christian-based group in front of a crucifix believed to have been involved in a miracle. The miracle to me was their generosity in the face of their poverty. The recent

DON FELIX - OLDEST LIVING ZAPATISTA IN 2000

rains had washed mudslides down the slopes of the ravines destroying hovels, homes to those living in an even lower economic bracket. Under the miracle cross, they placed a dozen plastic bags filled with food and blankets to take to their less fortunate neighbors.

I especially enjoyed meeting the world's "oldest living Zapatista," Félix Serdán. The more recent Zapatistas of the 1994 NAFTA uprising in Chiapas were named after the original revolutionary, Emiliano Zapata. Félix was but a lad when his parents rode with Emiliano, the hero, giving him the honorary recognition of this unofficial title.

He was leaning on a crooked cane, accompanied by his loyal short-haired black pup when we saw him creak his way toward us. His craggy nose stuck out from under a worn, straw hat. A wispy white moustache sprouted under his nostrils. Under that, two dried, cracked lips formed a smile and a fuzzy white beard bobbed when he spoke. He eased his way into a wobbly white plastic chair and filled us with stories, not of the past, but of the future.

Félix Serdán pointed his cane to his compost pile next to a large garden. It was a community garden he helped create to demonstrate how people in the *barrio* could supplement their diets with healthy choices for themselves and the land. He nodded to a cement block building behind his humble house. "That's a dry latrine," he continued, keeping his cane poised in its direction. "Twelve people can use it every day and it composts the waste. It separates the liquids from the solids and the latter is used in the fields. We must recycle and take care of our piece of the planet."

Even though I expected to hear some personal tales of his parents' ride with the Mexican hero, Emiliano Zapata, Félix Serdán and his projects were truly revolutionary.

ELECTION DAY, JULY 2

All the visits were over. Those choosing to be official Mexican Election observers were trained and sent off to their twelve-hour shifts. They wore official vests and carried clip boards with lists of regulations attached. Their job was to validate voter identification, stamp hands with indelible ink to prevent multiple voting, and look over the shoulders of those tallying outcomes.

Janice and I were less official. We chose to comb the streets around the voting areas and report any infractions of external behaviors. In Mexico, it is forbidden to have any political campaign materials visible in the voting area. This ranges from those T-shirts and rubber candidate masks to posters and buttons. It stops short at wearing party colors, but that was pushing the line. It is unlawful to sell liquor. Only one person allowed in the voting booth at a time. No intimidating behavior or crowding allowed.

Again we grabbed our cameras and hit the streets. Our realm covered the Augsburg neighborhood voting base, its stores, and streets up to the 2000 bridge. We were to be incognito, something not easily done for two English-speaking, fair skinned foreigners. As apparent tourists, we warmed up to our jobs by starting our observations in stores. Liquor is sold in small groceries, some hole-in-the-wall family street *bodegas*, and large supermarkets. To prove they were in compliance, swaths of yellow tape, like police use in U.S. crime scenes, were strung across the shelves of Dos Equis, tequila, rums, and *vinos*. In theory, no one was buying booze. In reality, I guessed they had stored up late Saturday night.

Done with that tour, we backtracked to our street and found the voting area set up as had been described. An eight-foot table under a canvas tarp was where the process began. Beneath the flap sat several election officials with pages of voters' names, ages, addresses, and ballots. After showing the officials their photo I.D.s and verifying their residences, they received ballots for each state and federal office.

Twenty feet away, a small table stood along a wall in the shade of a jacaranda tree. On top were three transparent plastic boxes labeled: President, Governor, and Senate. In past elections, solid boxes fell victim to a prevalent tradition whereby one voter stuffed multiple ballots at one time into the prescribed box. At tally time, these boxes were referred to as "pregnant" boxes.

THREE VOTE BALLOT BOXES

People who participated in rigging elections were called *mapaches* or raccoons. Don't laugh. Four months after this Mexican election, the U.S. would coin the phrase "hanging chads."

Janice and I found some shade across the street from this orderly Mexican moment and settled into observing. That was our job, after all. It was mid-morning. A police car slowly perused the line-up and motored on. Above the scene a banner proclaimed "*TU VOTO ES LIBRE Y SECRETO*" (your vote is free and secret). But what's with the four legs stretched underneath the white plastic sheet of that voting booth over there? Was this an infraction? Only one person per booth! Secret vote!

Not so fast. A five-year-old boy emerged from the booth with his mother. Moments before, he had been in tears. He was too young to even vote in the children's election, an initiative to promote voter participation in the future. He looked over at me, smiled, and raised his fingers in a "V", symbolizing "Vote for Change" in this historic election.

"Does that count as an infraction?" Janice smiled down at me. "If he voted for change, it had to be for Fox," she reasoned.

"I think we'll let him go, but look at what is coming down the street. I think that is clearly abuse of campaigning at the voting site. Get out your camera and zoom in."

In front of a well-dressed woman waddled a darling dachshund at the end of its leash. It waddled its way closer, then passed alongside the line-up of voters waiting their turn.

"It's wearing a sweater!" she reported, then added, "In this weather?"

"But it's what the sweater says," I pointed out.

She zoomed in to the tiny letters running the length of the dog. She slowly sounded out the Spanish, "*Vota por FOX*," before exclaiming, "Vote for Fox!"

It was the only direct election violation we witnessed all day.

ELECTION NIGHT

It was after dark when the last of the observers dragged in. You could tell the official ones from those of us on street duty by their sunburned necks and noses, empty water bottles, and the way they sank into their chairs at group sharing time.

Observations were positive. Each polling place managed to keep the peace among the three parties present to count and verify votes. The radio reporters and our Augsburg group witnessed long lines, standing under the hot sun for hours, waiting to exercise the privilege of having their voices heard. I don't know how people did it. The heat, no water, needing to use bathrooms, but not willing to get out of line. We in the U.S. should be so moved.

After all reports were completed, the Augsburg leader stood up and addressed our group.

"We don't know how tonight will turn out. From all indications, PRI is losing. The news journalists are cautious about a change of power. This is big and no one knows if it will go without a fight. We hope Mexico has a strong enough democracy to make this transfer peacefully. However, Latin America does not have that track record. This will be Mexico's test.

With that in mind, we might have to implement a change in your itinerary. Augsburg is prepared to fly you out at the least provocation of unrest."

Janice and I exchanged glances. I have friends in this town. I'd attended several schools here and lived with host families. The idea of violent protests, of an upheaval in these friendly streets, of everything changing overnight . . . I shook the thoughts from my head.

The leader continued. "We recommend you pack tonight in case we need to bus you to the airport in Mexico City tomorrow morning. We won't be driving through the mountains at night. There are snacks in the dining area and you are welcome to join those staying up to hear the results."

Food for thought, but I had no appetite for the news nor the snack. Janice and I returned to our room and packed. Satisfied that we were ready to leave on short notice, we rejoined the others in the common area to wait for more news.

The group mood was more excited than fearful. We knew Mexico was not a beacon of democracy. It just rotated dictators, people who dictate, from the same party. We discussed "pregnant ballot boxes" and election fraud. We spoke of our country, now in the throes of campaigning. We compared their large plantations lording over the people to our large corporations and how CEOs earned in hours what workers earned in months. Mexico had corrupt politicians, bought and paid for by oligarchs. We had lobbyists and special interests.

The conversation whirled around the room between updated tallies. The parallels between our countries grew. How could we point our fingers at their *dedismo* system of appointing the next presidential candidate when our elected officials seemed to come from some sort of pre-connected pool of politicians? How could we judge seventy-one years of same party rule when we had no term limits in Congress nor in the Supreme Court? That night, we were not yet aware of how things might change in Mexico . . . or a few months later for the U.S. in November.

It was nearing midnight when the news came over the radio. PAN had "overthrown" PRI. Vicente Fox was proclaimed the winner. The other two candidates faded into background noise. And there was plenty of noise. It was coming from across the bridge, on the other side of the ravine. Downtown. Explosions. Popping sounds. Everyone's gaze flitted around the room. We froze. In a jolt, some of the group took off for the roof of our building to get a look. Some of us went for our cameras. No one went for their suitcase.

Within minutes the roof delegation shouted down their report.

"Fireworks. It's like the 4th of July!" Followed by a wild Mexican mariachi-type whoop.

With a sigh of relief, Janice and I headed for the front door. "Anyone else want to come along?" I shouted back into the room.

Outside the air was electrified. It was palpable. Doors were opening. People stuck their heads out, then stuck their feet out onto the sidewalk. We sped up, aiming for the bridge. From the guardrail, we could see the sky lighting up. More fireworks burst over the ravine. We passed a young woman carrying her baby. She looked at us with tears gleaming in her eyes and a smile breaking across her face.

"*PAN, PAN ganó!*" she beamed. "PAN, PAN won!" She held out her beautiful baby so we could see it. "*El futuro*, the future!" then she covered its face with kisses.

The fireworks lit up the faces of the crowd congregating in the main plaza. Taxis buzzed around the square. It seemed like all the drivers were honking. People hung out of car windows and their upstairs apartments. Music. Not the week's "battle of the bands" put on by opposing candidates, but music made by the harmony of their jubilation. It felt like bursting free from a tight corset. A release. Being able to take a deep breath. It was glorious.

221

Augsburg did not put us on the morning flight out of Mexico. We gathered at breakfast, weary and jubilant. We came to Mexico with the desire to learn about and join our Mexican neighbors in this moment. It was time to come together and celebrate. If not Vicente Fox, then the ability to transfer power peacefully.

Vicente Fox. Fox? What sort of Mexican name was that? A businessman with Coca-Cola. Former rancher. Accounts for his cowboy boots. Was he qualified? Don't know. Everyone was flashing a "V" hoping for change. Hoping it would be change for the better. That is what we wanted for everyone. The best.

That is what we wished our *compañeros* when we bid each other *adieu* and returned to our U.S. lives. There our own country's election would soon be filled with accusations of fraud, arduous recounts, and a court challenge before the next President took office.

~ *Puente* ~
Reflections on the U.S. Election of 2000 and 2020

When we left for Mexico, Elián González, a young Cuban boy, was the center of an international immigration debacle. This five-year-old, clinging to an inner tube, washed ashore on a Florida beach, had escaped the fate of his mother and other raft companions in their fatal attempt to flee Cuba.

His immigration status caused an outcry and emotional upheaval. There were at least two legal contentions. First, the United States practiced a "Wet foot/Dry foot" policy regarding Cubans arriving by water or land. If they were picked up at sea, that was "wet" and they would be returned to Cuba. If they managed to get to a dock or dry land, they were allowed to apply for asylum. I kid you not.

Second, Elián had U.S. relatives who sought his custody. Certainly, they reasoned, a country that offered Disneyland was the obvious best choice. Back in Cuba, Castro and a million protesting countrymen disagreed and marched to have him returned to his father. The photo of him hiding in a closet with a very large, looming U.S. Federal Agent, complete with military uniform, helmet, and gloves, brandishing an automatic weapon to extract him from his relatives' home, appeared in newspapers and hit all the major networks. This little boy, held in his relative's arms, a look of terror on both their faces, was not good press for U.S. Attorney General Janet Reno nor the U.S. government's humanitarian image. It just looked wrong.

The photo won the 2001 Breaking News Pulitzer and put a little boy's face on the debate. More to the point, politicians now began to sit up and take notice. Not so much about immigration, but about the potential of the Latino vote to sway the Presidential election. This case riled up Jeb Bush's Florida contingency of Cubans. A unified Latino vote merited campaign ads in Spanish—a truly hot-spot immigration moment.

George Bush and Al Gore raced to the finish and beyond, as it turned out. A little review here. The final presidential vote was too close to call. Both candidates had 48 percent of the vote. Enter Florida. It seemed their system had something called "hanging chads"—a computer punch card imperfection. Was the vote for Al Gore or Pat Buchanan? Seriously, did several thousand people in Democratic Dade county vote for Buchanan? Were senior citizens being faulted as confused in their decrepitude or being used as scapegoats? While Florida did a recount, hand-holding ballots up to the light to guess which hole went where, my Mexican friends were having a heyday.

"Looks like we should send some International Election Observers to you all," they quipped. "Antiquated election computers? Sloppy punch card holes? Can't tell who got the vote? Sounds like you need some outside officials to verify your results!"

It was true. The first world country of first world countries couldn't verify its most precious commodity: Our Vote. Streets filled with protesters. Florida called it for Bush, then Gore, then Bush. It didn't sit well that George's brother, Jeb, was the governor of this undecided state. How could that not be a bias? It was over a month before Al Gore conceded and the electoral college awarded George Bush the presidency, with Florida's twenty-five votes going in his favor. This would not be the last time the majority vote would not get their chosen president.

That was in 2000. Bush, from Texas, (formerly part of Mexico, for the record) and Fox, the first ever non-PRI Mexican president, took office on their respective sides of the border. Immigration was a top issue for both. Arrangements were made for both presidents to convene and grapple with the broken and, frankly, harmful system. It took years to process asylum-seekers and people were dying in the desert. Both Presidents made immigration a top priority, arranging to meet in September 2001.

Finally. A coming together of the minds around immigration. No more "kicking the can down the road." A Texas President with border experience might be motivated. A new PAN candidate had things to prove to his base.

In his article for the Schwarzenegger Institute on May 1, 2013, Vicente Fox reflected back:

> "Throughout 2001, President George W. Bush and I spent time negotiating an important bilateral agreement on immigration policies and programs. We optimistically pieced together an innovative framework, and were close to reaching our goals when the terrorist attacks on September 11 derailed our plans."

Yes, they were supposed to meet in late September 2001. But then September 11th happened, the infamous game-changer. Immigration was literally blown off the table, not even on the back burner after the twin towers crashed and burned.

Immigration still waits for revision, innovation, and correction. It continues to be broken and used as a pawn in political elections. In 2016 and beyond, Donald Trump ratcheted up the rhetoric from "illegal immigration" to "invasion." He demonized the immigrant, spread divisive fear amongst the peoples of the northern hemisphere, including the meltdown of NAFTA, imposing tariffs, diverting military funds to build a 2,000-mile border wall, closed the border by an executive order, and created a self-made national emergency. There. I have said it. I don't know how to be gently diplomatic in the face of what I witnessed.

Now contemplate U.S. elections of the future. Mexico was tested in 2000. Its Constitution allows a President one six-year term. They got around that with seventy-one years of same party rule. Fraud was prevalent and proven. Mexico watchers held their breath until PRI peacefully accepted party defeat and transitioned to Vicente Fox, from PAN.

My question to the U.S.: Will we continue to transition peacefully? In 2000, both Mexico and the United States' systems were tested and continued to respect the rule of law, have a sense of honor, and country over personal gain. The transfer of power remained peaceful.

With the rhetoric of "fake news," accusations of fraud in the 2016 elections, sowing seeds of doubt on U.S. intelligence agencies, downplaying the Mueller report, and blocking witnesses for Congressional impeachment hearings, there is reason for concern. When the presidential response to divergent ideas is governing by executive order and tweeting out personal attacks, there is reason for concern. Will the United States' democracy hold up under this barrage? Will term limits be respected? Will election results give the majority of citizens the president they voted for or will we rethink the Electoral College? Will facts even matter if accusations smear and undermine the results? Trump publically said he would accept "dirt" provided by other foreign entities if it would serve his re-election bid.

In 2000, my Mexican friends asked pointed questions about our broken hanging-chad system in jest. It's no longer a laughing matter. Think Russian interference in 2016. Will we need International Election Observers before our precious voting privilege erodes away?

Maybe the International Election Observers should be from Mexico.

Section 8

A Medical Mission
in Guatemala
2003

HELPS MISSION STATEMENT

"Helps International is a non-profit providing enduring programs
of practical, social and spiritual value to people in the developing
world through a system of partnership and mutual responsibility."
Founder: Steve Miller, 1981 "The life you change might be your own."

~ *Puente* ~
# Signing Up

It was a first Thursday of the month, the ritual date of my Cultural Thursday offerings at Central Lakes College. The presenter that day was Sharon, a local RN and repeat medical volunteer in Guatemala. Sharon was part of a large Minnesota contingency led by Dr. Paul Schultz and Cammy Olsen, LPN, of St. Cloud.

Sharon related stories of the Guatemalans, mostly Mayans, who often hiked out of the highlands, traveling through the wee hours to stand and wait in triage lines. Some carried dehydrating babies or held the hands of toddlers with cleft palates. Others hobbled in on legs once broken but never set. Machete cuts from farming and hernias from carrying water and wood were common. Her slides showed patients being treated by the volunteers from Minnesota and Wisconsin contingencies. These volunteers had spent the year fundraising, gathering reading glasses, collecting pharmaceuticals, and checking for bargains on hygiene products to package and distribute. Many of the sixty-some volunteers were "regulars." By 2003, Sharon was going on her 12th mission.

When she left the stage, I was already scrambling to figure out how I might be able to join in. The main obstacle was timing. The trips didn't coincide with spring break. Being at the college meant no substitute teachers. If I took a week off, students would be losing classes they had paid for. Besides, I didn't have medical credentials.

"Well," Sharon informed me, "we always need translators! Dr. Pablo and I would welcome some help."

Dr. Pablo was one of my repeat students. No, he wasn't failing Spanish. He was one of a cadre of community adults who took my evening conversation class every year. His Spanish could do the job just fine, but Sharon insisted, "Jan, we always need more translators. What do you have to do to get out of school?"

The college president "temporarily" reassigned me to Guatemala, according to the paperwork sent to the University of Minnesota office for approval. It was accepted. I prepared myself and some lesson plans to cover the student's classwork.

I attended the local medical group's orientations, was invited to give a presentation on Guatemala's recent history to the medical team, spoke to my local church, rallied my Spanish Club to collect donations, and make some beaded scarves as gifts for a girl's school. In this way, I met others on the team. The final list of volunteers by category included:

Surgeons-3, Anesthesia-4, Pharmacy-2, Medical Clinics-10, Cooks-6, OR-7, OR Scheduler-1, Instruments-2, Triage-3, Translators-7, McGyvers-3, Recovery Room-13, Dental-6, Medical Helpers-1.

Through these dedicated people, I gained a chance to participate in an ultimate intercultural communication experience. Helps obtained Guatemala's government permission to enter, was granted military escorts, formed agreements in local communities, and won the trust of incoming patients.

Once in Guatemala, I watched those patients look up at our team with reverence and awe. In the clinic, soldiers guarded people who had once been targets in the Civil War. The ladino sat next to the Maya despite blatant class divisions. In this moment, they all had to trust—trust the strangers, our medicines, and our translators. We all brought cultural mores, life experiences, and stereotypes to the clinic. What was normal to them was foreign to us. What was normal to us was foreign to them. It takes more than words to build relationships. We proceeded with what we had—a trust in our common humanity.

MEDICAL STAFF GETTING READY TO DELIVER SCARVES

35

Capítulo Treinta y cinco
Barillas

Our plane landed in Guatemala City at 12:30 p.m. after a three-hour flight from Houston. Sixty-seven of us collected our personal items and made our way down the plane's narrow aisle and into the bustling airport. Somewhere in the hub-bub, our Guatemalan contingency waited to help us claim our plastic tubs of medical supplies, crates of surgical instruments and boxes of pharmaceuticals collected over the past year. Our line-up snaked through the crowds, rolling, pushing, and pulling our gear until we reached a short, pudgy man dressed in khakis. He called off our names and waved us through Customs, drugs and all.

Outside the sliding doors, air-conditioning gave way to a wave of heat and bright sunlight. Honking taxis, luggage carts clattering over cement, airport cops blowing whistles, and scurrying travelers engulfed our crew as we wound our way behind the little man headed to the back parking lot. There three vehicles idled, surrounded by several army Jeeps and their commander. When all was loaded, we boarded and sank into our seats. The minibus, a lorry, and a full blown passenger bus inched their way into the capital's chaotic streets. Traffic soon swallowed up the three keeping themselves in each other's rear view mirrors. They caravanned their way out of Guatemala City, destination Barillas, a remote, tiny town near the Mexican border. The military escort, mandated to guide the motorcade safely through the countryside, was under pressure to arrive at our layover hotel in Huehuetenango before nightfall.

The truck and passenger bus sped up when the city morphed into the low hills of the suburbs. But the minibus chugged ever-further behind, belching out clouds of black smoke. One of the military Jeeps slowed down to follow, as if wanting to give it a push. Collecting traffic blared its impatience until the little bus that couldn't edged to the shoulder, creeping along the gravel ascent. I was inside that bus, looking out into the haze of air pollution softening the sunset into other-worldly hues.

I have one simple Latin American night-driving rule: Don't. If that can't be avoided, then stay out of the mountains. Here I was, unable to abide by either. To me, the army escort added a third good reason not to be traveling just now. If these soldiers were still deemed necessary for our protection, then all was not resolved with the war that had ravaged the country for thirty-six years. I wondered how many on this bus full of midwestern medical volunteers knew the history of the 200,000 Guatemalans, mostly of Mayan descent, who died in the long conflict.

In the dusk, car lights flashed, indicating their intent to go through the intersection. Taxis darted in and out of undefined lanes, vying for customers. Brightly painted chicken buses clucked their way past our laboring van, returning *campesino* farmers from the markets to their countryside villages. Semis careened around the mountain curves into oncoming lights. But it wasn't the infamous driving habits that required the presence of soldiers.

On December 29, 1996, a tenuous peace agreement was signed between the government and the so-called rebels, those accused of being "insurgent-communist-sympathizers," often innocent Maya who happened to own land that corporations wanted. The weapons were turned in, but many young, forcibly recruited boys grew into men, without education but with memories of their training. They formed gangs, creating their own little Mafias. Their one-time president, Ríos Montt, once ordered 445 Mayan villages burned to the ground declaring: "To catch the fish, drain the lake." Later, the World Court accurately found him guilty of genocide.

My mind returned to the mechanically-challenged minibus now crawling away from the city lights into the country darkness. Outside, the occasional pedestrian materialized in the low beams. Did they have a war story? Their silhouettes hugged the road's edge or were they ghosts mingling among the living? Our military commander ordered the functioning vehicles to proceed to the hotel, leaving us with a handful of young soldiers in a Jeep. I shut my eyes and directed my thoughts away from the darkening night and its equally dark history.

My bus reached the hotel nearly three hours after the expected arrival time. Earlier in the day, I am sure the banquet room was a cheery sight of long tables covered with fine dishes, local flowers in orderly placed vases, and steaming delicacies. At this hour, we were greeted by bowls of wilted salads, reheated chicken, and a manager wearing a faded smile. Despite our hunger, eating that sad buffet was an act of courtesy and courage.

After a good night's sleep, hope returned. Hope that someone had cured or disposed of the slow bus. It wasn't to be so. There it was. I considered boarding the other bus, but everyone acted as if they had assigned seats. My fears were realized before we got to the highway. My bus was literally left in the dust. Within a few miles the army commander ordered the procession to pull over.

We piled out under a spray of shade provided by some scattered palms. I watched him pace. This tall, wavy-haired, obviously non-Mayan man talked fervently with the bus drivers, then the accompanying mechanic, and back to his second-in-command. Knowing Spanish, I edged my way into hearing range. Evidently, some work had been done on "my" bus, but it obviously wasn't improved. No larger towns were available to switch out vehicles. Another look under the hood involved a lot of head-shaking, gesturing, and wrinkled foreheads. With a shrug, he signaled us to reboard.

The sun rose high and hot. The hours stretched out. We needed a rest stop. That was when the "go-fers" returned from the bus storage bin with bad news. Several cases of bottled water had not been loaded. My half-full bottle now looked half-empty. Hydration was essential to our health, already made unstable simply by being in Guatemala. With the slow bus being the pace setter, it was anyone's guess how long our provisions would have to last.

The bus chatter shifted from rationing water to our food supplies. I opened my backpack to check my stash of dried fruits, cracker packets, and granola bars. I expected these snacks to hold me during the long hours in clinic over the next ten days.

"Well, I don't want to be eating these peanuts," I heard a nurse behind me announce. "They make me thirsty, and with this water situation," she let the thought fade.

"My pretzels will have to wait," moaned her seatmate.

"If you have raisins or dried fruit, you can suck on them," I suggested. "It will hold off thirst for a while."

We did a quick inventory of our collective supplies. I wondered if others were also hoping to avoid an ethical dilemma by not having to decide who would get the last rations!

We twisted our way up into the volcanic mountains. These once jungle-covered landscapes were now scraped bald by slash-n-burn agriculture. A light rain tapped against my window, taking my mind to mudslides. Guatemala has a history of hurricane residue gushing, now unhindered, down these slopes. The forests used to protect the villages that now lay open to burial during torrential rains. The clouds opened, allowing the sun back to steam the pavement. Ahead an oasis of ramshackle buildings and one gas station emerged. We stopped.

BATHROOM BREAKS

Bathroom breaks for women are always a tedious affair. This stop slowed our progress considerably as we waited for this "one-holer." Camaraderie develops when stuck in a line. I got the chance to chat with some local women, albeit about weather, travel plans ,and, in my case, what the heck all these Americans were doing here. A cluster of women dressed in traditional garb stood off to the side. Most Mayans are multi-lingual, due to trading with other villages. I believe these women stayed on the periphery due to social divisions, not lack of language skills.

Our second break on a mountain side went much faster. Men were directed to go to the left and women down the hill to the right. When, at last, my minivan chugged into sight, I got the unprecedented view of dozens of white butts squatting over logs. Fortunately, toilet paper was on our packing list. I edged my way down the slippery vegetation, grateful for my years of hiking in the north woods. This was normal procedure, except in the northland, I knew which plants not to touch and that the snakes were not poisonous!

Back on the bus, stomach troubles began. This was only our second day in Guatemalan back country and the amoeba hit. I suspected last night's wilted salad greens. The present lack of water and abundance of heat, multiplied by exhaustion, were also factors. People popped preventative diarrhea meds, if it wasn't already too late.

I grit my teeth and thought of my happy place. I imagined kayaking on Julia creek in the Nicollet National Forest, floating through the white lily pads and painted turtles. I envisioned the great blue heron swooping ahead, landing in the rushes to catch a frog. I could do mind-over-matter. I just had to. I did not come this far after all these years, with special "reassignment" from my college president, to end up incapacitated! The driver put his foot down hard on the accelerator, bringing me out of my trance. A now familiar cloud of black diesel regurgitated itself out the back pipe. This was not helpful.

I could barely see through the heavy mist. Some roads turned slick with a covering of black volcanic mud producing conditions not unlike icy Minnesota roads. Villages came and went with less regularity. Smaller villages consisted of house clusters clinging to the edges of cracked cement sidewalks, heaved there by one of their earthquakes. Larger towns included a corner gas station, small central plaza, a government building marked by a flag, and an adobe-bricked market with metal laminate roof. Both arrangements included skinny, sleeping street dogs that chose to lift their heads or not when we passed. These rural Guatemalan hamlets were separated by long stretches of ruts, speed bumps, potholes, and patches of remaining rain forest. To exacerbate our delay, we got waylaid by a jack-knifed semi, skewed over both lanes. With no police and no official relief in this remote part of the country, drivers got out of their vehicles, rallied their tools, ropes, winches, whatever they had, and began the communal labor of removing the semi-trailer. An hour and a half later, we continued. At this point we no longer checked our maps nor estimated our time of arrival.

THE HOTEL QUETZAL

It took a total of thirty hours driving time over two days to reach Barillas, a frontier town at the end of a seemingly endless highway. Our caravan carefully descended the switchbacks into the sleepy streets lined with adobe buildings topped by corrugated tin roofs. The last hours were fuzzy memories of self-willed pep talks, rationing, and pit stops for the afflicted. Anything would

CHICKEN BUS IN FRONT OF HOTEL

be an improvement and "anything" it was. The manager of a non-descript hotel waited in front of his emptied property for the Helps entourage takeover.

Seeing three vehicles pull around the corner sent him hustling his helpers into position. They carefully unpacked the surgery instruments, the marked boxes of medicines, the crates of food brought in so we would not get sick, and blue tarps for tents. That night and for the week that followed, this property boasted: No vacancy. The proud owner and his organizational clipboard converted the Helps roommate list into room assignments. I was assigned to Chris, from Detroit. She took the small key, glanced at me and said, "Here we go!" We walked down the narrow hallways between cement walls until we found the wooden door with our number. She wiggled the key into the lock, sang out, "Ta-da," and swung the door open.

It took only a moment to survey. Two army cots snuggled into an 8' by 10' space with a narrow door in one wall. In its favor, it looked freshly painted, or at least, recently scrubbed.

"The walls are the same color as my pajamas!" Chris exclaimed after sizing up the lavender-pinkish paint. "Which cot do you want?"

"The one by the bathroom," I winked at her, noting they were both equal distanced to everything in the room. She plunked her pack on one cot and I on the other.

"You check behind there," she nodded toward the slender door.

I slowly nudged it open. It creaked. I peeked. To the left, a toilet with just enough space to tuck in the mandatory plastic bucket for used toilet paper at its side. Above it, a shower head. To its left, a small sink with a candle on the ledge and a light bulb over the mirror. On the floor, a drain.

"I'm not sure about showering with an electric fixture so close, but come on in," I invited her as I stepped back into the room.

"Do you think we'll have hot water?" she asked.

"You try first," I offered with a bow, then turned back to making my cot into a home.

"Hey, look!" I yelled in to her. "On the pillow! A piece of chocolate! And a hand-written note!" I picked it up and read aloud, *Bienvenidos a Barillas*— Welcome to Barillas.

MOVING IN

"Lavender," Chris said. "Lavender helps to disinfect," she continued, identifying potions as she unpacked. "The Tea Tree Oil shampoo is good for lice."

Clearly I had underestimated my preventative health needs. I looked down at my packets of motion-sickness and diarrhea pills. Wasn't it enough to be with a mobile hospital and traveling pharmacy?

"Put some of this lavender on these cotton balls and lay them on the corners of your cot and the pillow," she directed. "We'll sprinkle some on our bandanas and wear them around our necks. It also helps to reduce fleas," she finished matter-of-factly.

232

This was just the beginning of our attempts to stay healthy among the locals. It isn't that they weren't sanitary, it is just that we are a hyper-hygienic society and, therefore, susceptible to whatever is out there. We wash, we lotion, we medicate, we pre-medicate, we stomp on ants. This isn't a judgment but a method to live in both worlds.

Dressed in our lavender-scented bandanas, anti-fungal powdered feet, with hand-sanitizer tucked into our pockets, we headed to the hotel patio for our supper. The temporary kitchen was set up and the cook ready to give pointers when we all arrived.

"Always wash your hands before eating," he began. "I know your momma taught you, but I am not kidding." He continued, "Only eat off of your plate, never anything off the table."

"We rinse the lettuce with chlorine. Fruits are peeled. We buy fresh produce at the market daily. All the rest was shipped in for our use. The plates are disposed of due to water scarcity for this many dishes. The silverware and glasses are dunked into two buckets, both with chlorine. You can never wash too much."

We hand-sanitized, picked up our plates, filled them with refried black beans, a chicken with rice dish, and before sitting down, dipped our fingers in the chlorine water on the way by, just in case.

The Clinic

After supper, we got our official assignments. Chris was a cook, setting her alarm to the local rooster, around 5:30 a.m. I was the translator assigned to Dr. Pablo and Nurse Sharon, both veterans of multiple Helps Guatemala medical missions. Sharon explained some of the expected routine for the next day before excusing herself to erect a mosquito tent over her sleeping bag. We agreed to meet at breakfast and walk to the compound together.

The next morning I slipped into my newly commissioned hand-me-down scrubs, donated by a petite Brainerd nurse. The cutesy patterned pastel shot my last hope of blending into my surroundings. Usually my height and coloring camouflage me in Central America. However, stepping into the dirt brown streets of Barillas with a flock of folks, mostly tall Scandinavians dressed in a rainbow of scrubs, made for an attention-getting parade. Fortunately, we were preceded by positive propaganda, so townsfolk greeted us with smiles and a wave, not a call to the *Policia*.

The plan to arrive before the patients was a myth. We rounded the last corner and were engulfed by lines forming down the block. Many had walked for miles, starting before dawn, taking the winding foot trails out of their villages, along the cornfields and out to the highway. There they flagged down chicken buses, those infamous North American school buses resurrected, painted over with local colors, and furnished with religious icons dangling from the rearview mirrors.

Most women wore myriad Maya weaves representing their villages through the colors in their skirts, embroidered blouse *huipiles* and folded head coverings. Many Mayan men wore the western shirt and pants used by *Ladinos*, folks who are at least two or three generations removed from their indigenous roots. Those lighter-skinned, Spanish speaking people stood in line, hats in hand. When we passed them on our way to the entrance, the Maya respectfully lowered their eyes and the *Ladinos* tipped their heads. My eyes, however, took a quick sweep of the crowd.

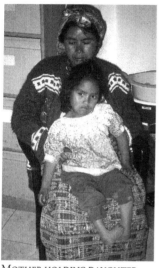

MOTHER HOLDING DAUGHTER

A young boy leaned on a hand-made crutch with a bloody cloth wrapped around his leg. Women with babies bundled on their backs collected in the shade. Old women with bent backs and weatherworn faces stood by old men with gnarled hands curled over their walking sticks. Children with big eyes and cleft palates peered from behind their mothers' woven skirts. Groupings of families clustered around fathers.

We entered the building, passed the tables set up for triage, passed the makeshift pharmacy, passed the waiting room cycling a Helps video on TV, and two exam rooms, before Dr. Pablo ducked into the third. Inside, a gurney table, three chairs, and a shelf full of pill-packed zip-locked bags waited. Before I had time to acclimate, another doctor rushed through the door.

"Can you come with me, quick?" he gave me a tug. I looked over at my team and Pablo waved me off down the hall to my first assignment before the doors even opened.

"We have a woman in labor and she'll need a C-section! We need you to explain that to her, but our real dilemma is the husband," he rattled off as I ran after him.

"Surgery isn't totally set up yet, but I think we can get this in time," he finished as he guided me into a room with a nurse, a very pregnant woman, and her non-cooperating husband.

All my cultural awareness classes kicked in, yet I lacked specifics for this situation. Husbands often make the decisions for the women. I had worked with that. This cultural experience, however, might well involve blood, pain, and potential screaming.

Between contractions, I introduced myself and began to translate. "The baby is breech," was not part of my daily vocabulary. With hand gestures and explanations, I managed to get the husband to realize they wanted to take his wife to surgery for her sake and the baby's survival. After my calm yet strong plea to release her, he nodded his permission.

"*Oh, señor, usted no va a repentir*, you will not be sorry," I told him. "*Todo va a salir bien.* Everything will be alright," I continued, realizing I was reassuring myself more than him. "*Vaya con la enfermera a la sala de espera,*" I gave him what I hoped was a culturally acceptable pat on the back directing him to follow the recovery room nurse to the waiting room. I watched them disappear behind the door. My hollow words echoed back. I had no clue how this would go. My heart pounded. This could easily be a life-and-death situation.

On my way back to Dr. Pablo and Sharon, the gravity of this brief encounter hit me. We were making decisions out of our world view, not theirs. Respecting his masculine role and her lifespan from my cultural bias was not textbook but real life. He gave up his *machismo* for the moment, but at what personal cost? He had to face his community. We, as interlopers, dealt with the moment, not with the fallout. This could get complicated!

"How did it go?" Dr. Pablo asked me with a grin when I returned to our exam room.

"Much blood?" This coming from a doctor who cannot abide the sight of it!

"No, Pablo, they took her to surgery and released me," I said, relieved. "I think the blood might have been easier for me than the husband making decisions for her. I have a hard time with that."

Sharon nodded and put the last Ziplock of meds on the shelf. There were purple pills and red pills for aches and pains. There were bandages, the stethoscope, ointments, vitamins, cotton swabs, and antiseptics. The scraps of paper and magic marker were a mystery to me. No time to ask. Shuffling footsteps headed our way. The doors were now officially open for business.

THE SPIEL

When the go-fer from triage knocked on the door, Dr. Pablo was waiting, perched on a stool by the examination table. Nurse Sharon stood behind it and I stayed to one side. By mid-morning, the clinical visits took on a synchronized dance, each of us reading the other's actions as patients recounted their personal history and medical complaints.

Our first arrivals included an elderly woman, her adult daughter, and a baby girl. They wore the *huipil* and *cortes* of their village mixed with western sweaters. Dr. Pablo greeted them.

THREE GENERATIONS OF WOMEN

"*Buenos días,*" he always began. "*¿Cómo están?*" he asked in his intermediate Spanish. Dr. Pablo was too humble to let on the amount of Spanish he could maneuver.

"*Bien, gracias,*" came the usual answer, followed by names, ages, a few questions about family, how far they had come, and informal niceties. After Pablo's quiet, calm interview he moved on to the reason for their visit.

"*¿Dónde le duele?* Where does it hurt?" Soon the conversations and the body language took on a pattern. Once stoic shoulders slumped, chins fell to their chests, hands clasped into wringing, and a litany of physical complaints trickled forth.

"My head hurts most of the time. And my neck. It is sore."

"Do you wear the *mecapal* when you carry things?" Pablo would ask.

Mecapals are head bands and straps universally used to hoist anything from firewood to small sofas onto their backs for transport. Even if done with proper bending of knees and other people supporting the load as it is put into position, strain is inevitable.

"Do you cut firewood every week?" "Do you carry it yourself?" "Do you go up in the mountains to find it?" Dr. Pablo quietly asked his litany of questions while he pulled back their eyelids to shine a light into their eyes, put his stethoscope to their chests, and massaged spots on their necks and shoulders.

"Yes, my son and I go once a week. He is six years old and helps put the wood in my *mecapal*. We walk about an hour up the mountain. The close wood is already cut and burned."

While I translated, Dr. Pablo motioned to Sharon, who already knew which Ziplock bags of meds to assemble for their symptoms.

At the end of each visit, she handed out a month's supply of vitamins to everyone, sending extras for children who could not make the trip. That is when I discovered the use of the mystery paper and magic markers.

"Jan, draw a full sun and a sunset, like a half circle on a line with rays, and put a slash mark for the number one in red. Or two red marks for two," she indicated the paper and pens. "That means to take one red pill in the morning and another at night. When it is a purple pill, put the slash marks in purple. If they know their numbers, then put the number," she finished explaining. It became my job to literally draw up the prescriptions for each patient.

She ended her pill dispensing with the usual, "Take these pills with a glass of water" and sometimes she added, "Take with food." Easy-peasy? Not so fast.

Step back from this scene for a moment into the world of the Guatemalan Maya Indian woman. She often does not have running water, unless the river has a strong current! Some catch rain water on their roofs, but it isn't potable. Others might go to a spigot alongside the fields where they work the company plantation. Others take containers to the town center for a fill. We just told her to take a pill with a glass of water, clean water. Remember I said things get complicated? Let's follow this thought.

She is likely carrying water on her head in one of those blue and white plastic jugs we've seen everywhere. She walks a mile to her source and another back. The water might not be clean, so she boils it. That takes firewood. Go cut some. Haul it back with your *mecapal*. Half of the water boils away. By this time she has a headache, backache, and leg cramps. Take with water? Not simple.

INVISIBLE INJURIES

Outside our clinic, the sun rose into the heights and the line grew longer, not shorter. Some were brought in on stretchers, carried by the stronger members of the family. A man hobbled in on his bandaged leg, injured by his own machete while cutting wood. Some children had fevers and cold sores while others were sent to surgery to correct cleft palates. And there were those people with no visible ailments at all.

Our next patient was such a case. He was a middle-aged *Ladino* man, accompanied by his daughter. He fidgeted in his chair, babbling incoherently to some unseen entity. Dr. Pablo shook his head, pointed at me and said, "This woman," he paused, "this woman is a psychologist with a specialty in stress." He continued, "She can teach you some relaxation techniques that might help when you get tense." My mouth translated faster than my mind registered what he was saying! He finished his illustrious introduction and motioned for me to take the man to the corner chair and advised us that we'd be spending fifteen minutes together. Another complicated moment?

What in the world was I going to do? Was this man reacting to stress or unknown demons only he could hear? I took a deep breath. That was it! I could try some yoga breathing and simple stretches.

"Inhale," I guided him filling my lungs. Then, "Slow exhale," I said, releasing a long sigh. This felt like malpractice, until I saw him relax. My mind raced from a procedure called "tapping" to Capacitar, a practice of holding on to different fingers, each representing diverse emotions. My friend, Karen, taught it to Guatemalan women for use in cases of PTSD and abuse.

I tried a mixture of ideas as they popped into my head. When our "session" ended, he wasn't babbling. He smiled. Did stress manifest itself this way? Dr. Pablo's quick thinking was insightful, if not brilliant. Perhaps this man's symptoms were related to the years of violence? I turned to his daughter and asked about the civil war.

"He was a civilian guard," she recalled. "He was assigned to watch for any suspicious behavior among his neighbors. You can imagine this was not a comfortable assignment, but he had no choice. He thinks people want to get revenge. He's paranoid. He wasn't like this before."

There is was. Post-Traumatic Stress. How many people were we seeing who suffered physical pain due to emotional experiences? Oh my god, what a can of worms this was turning out to be! This was beyond pills. Mind-body connection made sense to me. And the key: be flexible. Here, we had just combined two cultural approaches for greater healing. Imagine taking the best the world has to offer and combining it for greater good?

WESTERN MEDICINE

The man left my relaxation therapy with his daughter, promising to check local sources for trauma treatment. I couldn't image what might be available at this outpost of a frontier town, but felt that, despite my lack of medical credentials, I needed to give some guidance.

One after another, individuals, spouses, and extended families came to our room after being processed by triage. Dr. Pablo asked what he could and I translated what he couldn't. One story linked to the next, giving us added insight to their lives and causes of their "dis-ease."

Dis-ease. We had these pills to dispense, advising patients to take with water they didn't have for aches we could only try to imagine. I looked again at the purple and red pills zipped into bags by the hundreds. A new thought hit me.

Purple and red, colors of Cold and Hot. Cold and Hot are the two main categories of illnesses dating back to 5th-century Greeks. Headaches, dysentery, diarrhea, and fevers are considered "hot" and need a "cold" remedy for balance. That might be in the form of a bath using 'cold' herbs. Swelling and rheumatism are examples of 'cold' illnesses that might be treated with a *temascal*, a sweat bath. This medical theory stuck around until the 18th century, but the practices live on in shamanistic practices today.

These Maya likely went to shamans! I recalled Calixta at Iximché, a Mayan site outside of Guatemala City. She led healing prayers to the four directions and called forth the ancestors at our sacred fire with sage, smoke, sprinkles of *aguardiente*, colored candles, and incense. She prayed for balance. At some mind-body-spirit level, healing happens. Western pharmaceuticals are based on rain forest remedies (yet, don't compensate for shamans' remedies), but have much to learn about relationships and beliefs. At least some local supermarkets sell medicinal teas!

But this goes beyond echinacea. Shamans live among the communities they serve. They are familiar with their patients. They diagnose with knowledge of family relationships, village dynamics, and personal foibles. They inherently work mind-body healing. And here we were, dispensing plastic bags of purple pills to people who might believe they needed the red ones.

By the afternoon of the first day, I melded into the role Pablo had bestowed on me. While he poked and prodded their bodies, I gently poked into their lives. I went beyond translations, hoping that a smattering of personal questions would give insight to their overall health. They trusted. I hope it was my sincerity and not their awe of our professional position that led them to share their stories.

WHO WERE THEY?

A bent, shriveled woman shuffled in. She was an elder, dressed in traditional garb. Deep lines in her leathery face. No teeth in her weary smile. I had to repeat the questions. She pointed to her ear. Didn't she understand me or couldn't she hear? Sharon propped her up on the exam table, took her bright light and beamed it inside. "Wax," Sharon reported. "Loads of wax."

I thought back to my homeopathic friend, putting a hollow beeswax candle into my ear and lighting the top with a match, holding it carefully, so that we wouldn't set me on fire! Candling. I guess the suction pulls ear wax into the candle. Might be something a shaman would do, but I preferred Sharon's method. With one hand, I kept the ancient one from falling off the table and with the other, gently rolled her head so that Sharon could administer the first of several rounds of ear drops.

"Jan, would you massage her neck right under the ear?" Sharon asked. "This will take a few treatments," she reported and began the extraction. When we finally eased our *anciana* back to the floor, she grinned at us. "I can hear better!" she clasped Sharon's hands in her own and held on. "Oh, *muchas gracias, señora enfermera*, Mrs. Nurse." She wore the look of someone who had met an angel. She had.

Others came in, squinting from all their hours of weaving on back-strapped looms. Women tie looms to trees, sit on their haunches, and send the shuttle back and forth, a thread at a time. It takes approximately a month to weave a length of material for their *cortes*, the long, wrap-around skirts. Some men do embroidery and wood crafts, bent over their workbenches well into the night. Others squint for hours in the fields under a burning sun. When they complained of eye strain, we handed over our box of donated cheater glasses. They tested each pair by looking at a written page. We knew by the women's squeals and the men's sighs that a pair of glasses was the answer. "Giving sight to the blind," Dr. Jerry once said, "is almost like being Jesus!"

One woman arrived with her entire family in tow. She wanted and, in my humble opinion, needed a hysterectomy. She experienced continuous bleeding and had already birthed seven children. The complication once again rested in tradition. Not only her husband, but the entire nuclear family, was included in this decision. Dr. Pablo, always the calm diplomat, methodically reviewed her condition to those filling our examination room. I endeavored not to let my tone of voice influence my translation. Whatever it was, she got their permission and was sent to surgery. Before she left, Pablo reiterated there would be no lifting for six weeks! She alone was pleased with that news.

Many younger women arrived on their own. Some already had children, but others were still children themselves. Often they were raising their siblings, due to the death or disappearance of their own parents. One seventeen-year-old with two children came hoping for birth control advice. She had little knowledge about reproduction and was a product of an arranged marriage. We gave her information on options, but didn't deal in devices or birth control pills. Sex education is a dicey business in every culture, let alone across cultures.

A fourteen-year-old girl came in with complaints of headaches, fainting spells, and general weakness. This combination was so frequent, we invented an abbreviation, TBA, Total Body Aches, for our charts. The additional questions I asked about living situations improved our recommendations. In her case, we discovered that she supported three siblings with her laundry job. She earned fifteen *quetzals* a day, slightly under $2.00. She needed 200Q for monthly rent and 30Q for food. Her parents were dead. We sent her to the in-house social worker, who enrolled her in a food program and got housing assistance.

The note I jotted on an eleven-year-old girl's chart was simply: Overall sadness. "*Estoy aquí sola,*" she began. "I am here alone. It is too much for my mother and my seven brothers and sisters to get here. Besides," she continued, "I don't want them to know that I am here. I have to clean houses to help with our expenses and I go to school."

"How many hours do you work?" I asked.

"I go to school in the morning, go home for lunch, and then work four hours in the afternoon. I still have my schoolwork to do at night."

"What do you eat?" was a question I recently added to my list, discovering their menus to be scarce in nutrients.

"A few tortillas a day."

"Corn or flour?" At least corn had more nutritional value.

"Corn, with salt sometimes."

I wrote on her chart: Headaches likely from hunger and emotional stress. I didn't need a medical degree for this diagnosis. When she got up to leave, I handed her my midday energy bar, an apple, and a bottle of water to go along with a month's supply of vitamins for the whole family that Sharon had bagged. It felt meager. Overwhelming. It was what we had. It was a beginning.

The next girl was twelve and had a large burn on her face. Burns are common around the open cooking fires used in their huts. Little kiddos toddle around and fall in. Others trip into the flames. Some accidently burn fingers when they flip the tortillas on the iron cooking *comal*. This case was different. Her mother had pushed her in as punishment.

Older folks came into our room complaining of "*bolas en el estómago,*" as they crouched over their protruding stomachs. Their years in the fields, cutting wood, placing individual seeds in the ground with a planting stick, or hauling children on their backs all day produced: hernias. After two days of clinics, I began recognizing maladies before Dr. Pablo voiced his prognosis.

There were untreated old injuries, bones that had to be re-broken and re-set, or tumors that had lives of their own. Blisters and bruises were universal. Babies were born. Children got physicals. One man came in with a bullet wound. The dentists peered into mouths that didn't know toothpaste. Some things required surgery and others, bandages and a smile. They always smiled back. They were always grateful.

I was always humbled.

BLOWING BUBBLES

Most of the day I hunkered down beside Dr. Pablo and Sharon, rarely leaving our exam room. One afternoon, however, Sharon sent me down the hall to pharmacy for refills. On my way, I heard children's laughter coming from the inside waiting room area. I took a detour and discovered a mayhem of preschoolers buzzing around the room with toys provided from some donors somewhere.

The air was filled with floating bubbles, usually nontoxic entertainment, but the source stopped me. Not just bubble blowing wands, but bubble guns. These were bubble guns being pointed by kids at kids. I felt sick. I know. At home we pointed squirt guns at each other every summer but here, it took on another level. If not their parents, then their grandparents had surely lived through the recent civil war. Even if 200,000 Guatemalans hadn't died in that thirty-six-year war, why use toy guns when the bubble wands would be perfectly neutral?

Back home, our township had voted down a permit for a paint ball business out in our rural woodlands. We have a culture of deer hunting but not pointing guns at people. I tried to wean my own son off of violent video games for the same reason. Isn't the connection obvious? Point and shoot? My dad taught me to carry guns barrel down, and NEVER, not EVER, point at people.

My focus returned to the scene in front of me. Dr. Pablo told of his countryside visits. He mentioned pre-teens handling real guns, tipping the caps off of their friend's heads with the muzzles of rifles, probably remnants missed during the confiscation process of the Peace Accords. These boys stood grinning proudly with their guns. No gun safety classes during war, a war they were too young to remember.

I shuffled back to the examination room and entered quietly.

"Is something the matter?" Sharon asked.

"Oh, the bubble blowing guns make me sad. Subliminal messages. Synapsis connections routing the brain."

She patted me on the back. "To use your words," she reminded me, "it's complicated."

WHEN SPANISH WASN'T ENOUGH

The younger patients learned Spanish as a second language. Likely, they were attending public schools and assimilated into the dominant culture. Not so for the elderly, who came to us with their TBA, total body aches, plus age-related maladies. Those bent, wrin-

241

kled, and wise ones did not speak Spanish. The elders remembered. They remembered the military coming in, rounding up the men and raping the women. They remembered hiding in the mountains, watching their villages being torched. They remembered the spies and clandestine graves of the past.

Into the present walked a young soldier, short hair, immaculate uniform, boyish face and shy smile. He wore camo-fatigues and preferred to be called Tomás Eduardo instead of by his military rank. The army commander called him in to translate because he spoke *Q'anjobal*, the native Mayan language of this region. He was eighteen and only a toddler during the years when other teenaged boys were forcibly conscripted to fight against their own people. Again, my mind whirled around the past and tried to reconcile it with the present.

TOMÁS (SOLDIER & TRANSLATOR), JAN, & ELDER

Our first *Q'anjobal* speaking patient was likely in her eighties. She was frail, her bones barely allowing her blouse to hang on. Her face was deeply creased, like an ancient pine tree's bark. Her skin, brown leather. Tomás and I would never know her story, but she was wary of a male stranger, military man no less, being in on her physical exam. This was an oversight on so many cultural levels! But what other choices did we have?

I translated Dr. Pablo's questions into Spanish for Tomás and he, in turn, spoke *Q'anjobal* to the *anciana*, the ancient one. He could have been her grandson, such was the likeness and care in his voice. Her body relaxed. She answered him and back down the line we went. Things do get lost in translation. We had three languages going from three very distinctive cultures between three generational groups. Oh, and two genders. Translating words is not enough.

After several sessions with Tomás, my visions of the past had softened into the present. We met several times so he could pronounce some simple phrases into my tape recorder. It was obvious I would not be taking on a third language anytime soon. I never asked him about the military nor its present role. It was enough to be part of this transitional relationship between the military and its ancient culture, the Maya. On that day, at a clinic in Barillas, Guatemala, we were people gathered for a common purpose doing our best.

ONE LAST PATIENT

Our last patient was a timid woman from town. Not a Maya but a Ladina, western dress, educated, soft-spoken. She reminded me of a librarian, if your image includes wire-rimmed glasses, quiet eyes, and a whisper. She just didn't seem to fit in the gathering of brightly dressed Mayan women, surrounded by children, clicking away in their native tongue. She came alone.

She watched me flitting around between doctors, the triage, and people in line. Maybe she heard me going between Spanish and English. Maybe I just didn't strike her as a threat. After a few passes, she got up the nerve, tapped my shoulder as I scooted by, and said, "*Disculpe*, pardon, do you have a minute?"

That is when I fully saw how much she was not part of this group. She was probably an employee in town, making middle-income wages. She might have access to medical care, but something must be of special concern if she was seeking the American team of doctors.

"How can I help you?" I pulled up a chair.

"I want to see a doctor, but I am afraid of men doctors. I just can't go to one," she winced.

"We have that in common," I confided. "I am working with a very nice man doctor now, however," I went on. "I have known him for many years. I am a Spanish teacher and he has taken some of my classes. He tries very hard and wants to be able to talk to the people."

"He speaks some Spanish?" she reconfirmed. "Would you be there?"

"Yes, I am there to help him when he doesn't understand. There is also a very good nurse helping. We will both be with you," I tried to reassure her. "Would you like to tell me what you think is the matter?"

She was worried that she was losing her eyesight. There was a history of diabetes in her family and that might be what was happening. How would she know? What could she do?

"Let's go and see if Dr. Pablo is available now," I said. "The clinic will close soon and I don't want you to miss your chance."

We stood up and she followed me down the hall where we found Sharon packing up. "Is Pablo around?" I asked her. "I am hoping we can see one more patient."

Pablo soon returned and I quickly filled him in on her male-doctor-phobia and back-story. He was his usual kind and understanding self, putting her at ease. He explained some of the causes of diabetes, foods to stay away from, and other symptoms. He took his time and her questions and then it was time to close. I walked her out, as I was now accustomed to doing. She gave my hand a squeeze and whispered, "He is such a nice doctor. I wasn't afraid at all."

I wished her well and told her to get tested to find out for sure. If she was borderline,

243

the diet and exercise could still bring her back from full-blown diabetes. She did have some control over its progress if that was, in fact, what she had. We waved good-bye. Or so I thought.

The next morning the Helps crew was all on site, dismantling the clinic and packing the lorry. I ferried small boxes from our exam room to the entrance where it was parked. On one trip through the waiting room, there she stood with a young girl by her side. The "diabetes" lady. A smile beamed across her face as she stepped toward me, hands tucked behind her back.

"*Buenos días*," I greeted her, before asking about the girl.

"This is my daughter," she indicated with a nod of her head. "I wanted her to come and meet the nice man doctor." Her eyes twinkled. "And," she continued, "I have these for you!"

Out from hiding, she pulled two wooden hand-carved *campesino* statues, particular to this village. I had coveted this art all week but never got time to shop. That very morning, I bemoaned the fact I wouldn't be able to get the one thing that perfectly represented this trip.

MOTHER & DAUGHTER GIFTED JAN LOCAL HAND-CARVED STATUES

"Oh joy!" I burst out, nearly jumping into her open arms. "I love them! I can't believe it! *Gracias, gracias, gracias*," I blurted into her ear as we hugged.

We stepped back and gazed into each other's eyes, a momentary soul connection.

I clasped the hunched over firewood-carrying peasant statues to my heart. One more soft smile; a parting embrace. She turned slowly and walked away, but she has never left me.

BEADED NECK SCARVES

Gift giving was not over yet. Before the journey, Sharon had told me about a girl's orphanage they visited during their last trip. There were forty-some students living there and she wanted to take some sort of gift back. Nothing made in China. Maybe a make-n-take craft we could do.

As advisor of the Central Lakes College Spanish Club, I had access to enthusiastic volunteers. We decided to make "beaded scarves," a recent fad. I purchased bandanas and colorful beads. Volunteers brought scissors. In a few snips, the scarves were ready for decoration. It was exciting to do a hands-on project with a destination connected to our local community.

Now on location in Barillas, it was time to unpack the scarves and deliver them.

Eighteen of us gathered to make a planned presentation. It was decided to each wear a scarf and surprise the girls at the end by gifting them personally. Even Dr. Pablo put on a beaded scarf before joining the group walking down the streets to the school. We stopped outside for a group photo and finalized our plans. Short speeches were expected by the headmaster and the girls, so we came up with a few words of our own.

We were shepherded into a large room where the girls were already gathered. An older girl gave a courteous welcome and thanked us for coming back to visit. A representative from Helps greeted them on our behalf. Up until the last moment, they didn't know the scarves were meant for them.

I told of our college Spanish students making each scarf with them in mind. Some let out a squeal of glee and all applauded as we headed toward them with our gifts. One on one, looking into their faces and asking their names, we said, "*Para ti*–for you." Next they lined up for a photo, including the Mother Superior wearing her scarf. "*Por favor*," she said, "Take this picture back as a thank you to your Spanish Club."

The photos and story ended up in the local papers, strengthening the bond between our communities.

LEAVING BARILLAS

GIRL IN BEADED NECK SCARF

I'd love to tell you that the trip back to Guatemala City was a breeze, but it wasn't. We were on our way before the rooster crowed, but only after an electrical outage slowed our packing. The weather report was for *chipi-chipi*, the sound made when rain hits the window. It had already rained all night. The volcanic soil was at its slippery best. Would the big bus even make it up the switchbacks on the hill out of town?

Ironically, this larger model bus was called in to replace the two passenger vehicles used on arrival. Perhaps the smaller ones would have been better in this weather but there we were, in the bus, planning to go straight through, lunches packed to avoid delaying stops. I recall the hypnotic slapping of the windshield wipers as I attempted to focus on the landscapes through drizzle. The bus lumbered along. . . until we lost traction.

The ruts were deepening and potholes prevalent. The mud was sticky and caked itself to our boots when we descended for our jungle potty stop. We lifted our rain ponchos to step over greasy logs and decided it was best to remove shoes when we reboarded. About five minutes down the road, it was discovered that we were missing four doctors! We had to go back!

On the downhill slopes, the bus driver pumped his brakes and slapped his thigh, which probably had gone to sleep from all the long stretches of descent. At one point, on the ascent, the bus just refused to make it to the top. We all clung to our seats in horror as this huge machine began to slide backward down the highway. The driver maneuvered us to the shoulder. "Get all the women out," he ordered, as if we were on the Titanic. "Men, get to the back of the bus for ballast."

At this point, one doctor who shall remain nameless, stood up and said what most of us were probably thinking. He wanted off. He had not come to Guatemala to die in a bus rolling off the mountainside. The doctors were then directed to evacuate the bus and join the rest of us standing in the wet grass and greasy mud.

Some of our military escort helped place wood logs from alongside the road behind the wheels. The army captain radioed for assistance, but hung up when the driver crawled under his bus pulling a set of heavy chains behind him. Our intrepid driver wiggled his way into place under the watchful wide eyes of all. Several soldiers took positions around the perimeter, complete with their semi-automatics. How was he going to fasten these tire chains to a passenger bus angled down the mountain? I wasn't the only one holding my breath and looking away.

First one wheel and then the other received their set of monster chains. The gallant driver crawled out from under, slapped his hands together, pulled himself into the bus and buckled himself into his cockpit. The key engaged and engine responded.

We walked alongside keeping our ponchos, now dripping with rain, pulled snug around our necks. The chains caught on the pavement. The bus made a motion forward. Slowly it ground its way up the slope. We let loose a wild cheer when the bus cleared the peak. Before reboarding, our amazing driver stepped down, crawled under the bus again, and removed the chains he had just applied. Oh my! We scraped the cakey mud off our footwear. Again we boarded. Again we sank into our seats. Again we were thankful.

As long as we were stopped, it seemed a good time to bring the bag lunches on board. But where were they? Evidently, back in Barillas. A communal shrug and groan went out before we rummaged around our packs for any morsel left after a week of snacking. Our water supplies were also limited, as some water had been requisitioned for cooling the en-gine. The calculated travel time of nine hours was not happening. Now we were hungry and thirsty to boot.

We had left Barrillas at 5:15 a.m. and pulled into Hotel Antigua at 11:30 p.m., dou-ble the official estimate. We entered this luxury hotel in beautiful, colonial Antigua *con ganas*. That roughly translates to: "Oh my God, I can hardly wait to get into that room, that tub, that hot water." But first they offered us a sumptuous buffet, knowing we had not eaten all day.

When Chris and I finally walked into our spacious room we saw white swans formed by folded towels swimming across each of our double beds, recalling then the kind gesture of chocolate on our humble Hotel Quetzal pillows. The bathroom was immense and the water hot. Sleep was quick and sweet. Breakfast time took us back to the ample dining room, filled with platters of kiwis, mango, papaya, and bananas arranged into pyramids. Sweet cakes and flan were followed by strong coffees or sweet wine. We ate. We shopped. Early Sunday, before people hit the streets, Dr. Dave and I took a photo walk. He added to his collection of doors. I helped him ask permission to take people pictures. Our med-ical team shifted into tourist mode.

Barillas was only a matter of hours behind us, but we were a world away. Helps, in its wisdom, scheduled several days of R&R, rest and recoup. The trip had been arduous, the days packed, our emotions on high alert, the responses flexible and caring. This group of sixty-seven medical personnel, translators, kitchen help, and camp go-fers had served 900+ clinic patients, done medical and dental outreach for another 530+, and performed 78 surgeries during five days, the first of which produced an eight-pound baby boy by C-section.

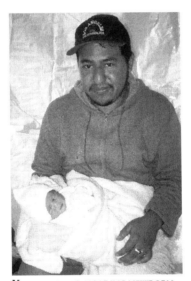

YOUNG FATHER HOLDING NEWBORN

247

Section 9

The Immigrant in Our Midst

~ *Puente* ~
Preparing for Demographic Changes
2003-2013

During my teaching tenure, Liliana and I founded a Latin American Resource Center outside our office. Besides the AFS international teacher exchange, we brought in Mixed Blood Theater, *El Teatro del Pueblo*, Susana's and Maria Elena la Cordobesa's *flamenco tablaos*, St. Cloud's *Pachanga* concerts, Argentina's visiting *Chamamé* musicians, and Juan Acosta's art.

I initiated and hosted sixteen years of Cultural Thursday presentations (still the first Thursday of the month), began and continue to attend the weekly Mesa—a Spanish conversation table, and organized eight annual Festivales Latinos with the help of local community members and resident student volunteers, during Hispanic month. I arranged

JACKIE F. & SONS WITH AL V. AT FESTIVAL

for and guided student travel/study to Spain and Mexico, and continued traveling with Augsburg College, including a trip to Cuba in 2001.

At the college level, I created a new course (1999 to present) called The Many Faces of Mexico. Thanks, a hug, and a bow to Meredith Sommers from the former Minneapolis Resource Center of the Americas and co-creator of the origin curriculum. It is an amazing course, current, and always relevant. It should be required!

While I continued to advocate for language classes, seek technology advancements, and promote cultural exchanges, the outside world was changing.

OSCAR & MICHELLE

250

Neighboring towns were experiencing demographic shifts. Turkey plants and dairy farms were hiring Mexicans, Hondurans and *Guatemaltecos* within a 100-mile radius of the college. Long Prairie elementary had a 52 percent Latino student population. How could we encourage them to be college bound if they didn't have legal papers? They couldn't apply for loans without a social security number. Was it even safe for them to drive in winter, fearing deportation if they slid on the ice into a ditch and were helped by a passing patrol?

The immigrants opened restaurants, bakeries, grocery stores, joined construction crews and took jobs at the meat-packing plants. The local Catholic churches offered bilingual masses. The Fransiscan nuns scurried around to find used clothing, second-hand furniture, and be available to translate at clinics and hospitals.

That is how I met Sister Donna Zetah.

MARGARITA MAKING TAMALES

LONG PRAIRIE VIRGEN DE GUADALUPE CELEBRATION

36

Capítulo Treinta y seis
The Call

PART I: SISTER DONNA

It was 6:30 a.m. My phone rang. That couldn't be good.

"I am sorry for the early hour," Sister Adela apologized, "but I wanted you to know right away. Sister Donna died this morning. Yesterday they covered her with your blanket. It was like a hug from *La Virgen*."

Two weeks earlier, I had been holding Donna's hand, whispering Spanish words of comfort, when a priest arrived with the sacrament. From the convent hallways, a bevy of Sisters appeared and encircled us. I was there to share a cup of tea and now found myself at the center of her last rites.

Sister Donna, however, was not done yet. I checked back a few days later with my manta, a blanket with a life-size depiction of the *Virgen de Guadalupe*, patron saint of the Americas and sainted Mother to the Mexicans. It was perfect for a woman who worked seventy years as a Franciscan Sister with Latinos ranging from Peru to Minnesota.

I spent several years resisting Donna's twinkling eyes and quiet suggestion that I meet folks from her flock. They were mostly immigrants, workers at the

IMAGE OF THE VIRGEN DE GUADALUPE
ON A BLANKET

local dairy farms or the meat packing plant. They needed documents translated, interpretation at doctor's appointments and, occasionally, furniture. I hedged on commitments, as I often traveled out-of-town and didn't feel reliable.

Yet, a week after her death, there I was, saying yes to Jesse's request to go to his farm and translate at his workers' meeting. One disgruntled worker was causing general discomfort for all. It might get heated. The other workers suggested Jesse get a man translator. He informed them that women can be strong, too. "It is their culture," he explained. "A bit macho, but also a relationship and trust thing." I was impressed with his knowledge and wisdom regarding the nuances of his employees.

I drove the muddy backroads until I arrived at their milking operation, walked up the icy steps, and entered a one-time porch turned meeting room. Jesse introduced me to his parents and each worker as they arrived, took a can of pop, and helped themselves to hot pizza. Perhaps having a woman there softened the situation. There was no confrontation. Some housing issues got resolved. The video on pre-milking sanitation was an education . . . for me. Jesse used Google translation for his power point. It was surprisingly adequate. His efforts to work with Oaxacan farmers far exceeded adequate.

I walked back outside and inhaled the frosty air. Cows were bellowing. A big milk truck pulled out. I looked into the bright blue April sky and smiled. Are you watching, Sister Donna? Here I am. Just like you planned.

JAN & SISTER DONNA

PART II: SERVICE CALLS

A call for telephone service brought Rob, the repairman, to my kitchen. After evicting several caches of mouse inhabitants from three telephone boxes along the road, he stopped in to check if the crackling on the line was gone. The subject of mice brought up stories of country living, which led to a story of his growing up on a farm at the Canadian border. He went to school with Indians, which was what you called them in those days. That reminded him of the moment he introduced his Dominican fiancé to his "Archie Bunker" father. His smile changed to a frown when he related his dark-skinned son's experiences at our local elementary. It was nearly noon when he put his hand on the door knob, ending the visit.

I returned to my unfinished list of calls and reached for my cell. A message popped up that was already thirty minutes old. It was Sara from the farm. What could it be?

"Jan," the message began, "one of our workers, Macrina, was kicked in the face by a cow. I was hoping you could talk to her and see what exactly happened. I guess we'll head to the ER. Call me?"

Oh my. I pressed call back and waited. "Sara, where are you?" I started.

"We're on our way to Little Falls. I can't figure out if she was kicked twice or only once and then hit her head when she fell. We can't understand each other," she sighed.

"I'll call the hospital and see if they have translators. If not, I'll meet you." She hadn't thought of that.

I was relieved to find out they have a phone translation service, albeit not my favorite medium. Sara directed me to stay put. "If it doesn't work well, call me back," I said and headed for an appointment in the opposite direction.

Just as I reached my destination, my phone rang again.

"The first interpreter didn't work out," Sara reported. "Talked too fast or something. The second one was a bit better, but there is so much to explain."

"Macrina's first language is Zapotec," I noted, "Or maybe it's the interpreters' accents. It doesn't help that she can't see the speaker or gestures. Should I come?"

"Not yet. The CT scan should be back soon. I wanted to know if you'd be available to take a call and you explain?" she asked.

My heart had been nagging me to go since the first call. Actually, the nagging feeling started two years ago when Sister Donna first looked at me with those twinkling eyes and sent me to Margarita's with some tomatoes from the Convent garden. If there is a heaven and if there is an afterlife, her eyes are sparkling now! My phone rang again, jarring me back to earth.

"Jan, the CT scan shows some slight bleeding on the brain. They can't handle it here and want to send her by ambulance to St. Cloud." Sara paused. I was already walking toward my car.

PART III: CALL THE AMBULANCE

I found Sara wrapped in her winter coat, sitting on a stool in a tiny ER room next to an empty gurney. Her head hung down. Her boots were covered in dried farm mud. Weariness and uncertainty filled the cubicle. We hugged.

"I'm ready to go to St. Cloud," I said, despite my own waning energy. "You've been here for hours and have farm work. I'll text you when we know something."

I heard someone at the door and turned to see the patient being rolled in. A small woman of unidentifiable age lay hidden in an oversized hospital robe. "Here," the nurse said, handing us a new gown, "I found one that will fit better. We called for the ambulance. Please tell her I am going to give her some intravenous pain meds, they're strong but won't last very long. Might upset her stomach."

This is how I met Macrina. A finely chiseled, copper-toned face stoically lifted to meet my gaze. "*Me llamo Jan*," I began, "*Pero, Juanita si prefieres*. My name is Jan, but Juanita if you prefer. May I speak to you using the informal *tú*?" She nodded her permission.

A knock on the door brought in two ambulance personnel. The man greeted Macrina in tentative Spanish, then whispered to me. "I know a little. My wife speaks Spanish, but I mostly know bad words. They are the ones she uses when she's mad at me." He smiled.

"These people will take you to the St. Cloud ER," I translated. "You might want to sleep," I suggested. "Sara will go back to the farm and finish some business, change her clothes and wait for us to call," I continued. "They have translation services, but I will go with you."

Her deep brown eyes locked into mine. The hand without the tubes and clips reached out to me. "I don't want to sleep. I want to know what is happening to me. Please, no operation."

"Macrina, I'll stay with you," I reassured her. And so it was that I headed farther away from home into an afternoon with no time boundaries. It would take as long as it would take.

PART IV: CALL TO THE ST. CLOUD ER

A half-hour later, I rounded the corner to the ER entrance just as the Gold Cross ambulance pulled up. The driver waved and shouted out to meet inside.

I passed through security and was given a tag labeling me: Room #8. She was already there with busy hospital personnel when I knocked.

"Are you a friend or family?" the woman at the computer asked me.

"Friend and interpreter," I responded.

"Whew," her shoulders relaxed. "That will help." She took her clipboard and began a torrent of questions.

"Do you know where you are? What day is it? When did this happen? Where do you hurt? On a scale of 1–10 . . . Are you nauseous?"

Macrina quietly answered. "St. Cloud. April 11. It was at the farm this morning. About 11:00. My lips and teeth. The back of my head. A cow kicked me in the mouth and then I fell down. About a number six on my mouth. My head hurts. My teeth hurt. No, my stomach is fine."

As I translated, our situation sank in. Macrina, out of her country and language, trusting us all. Me, a retired Spanish college instructor, explaining what I couldn't translate, trying to keep up with the barrage of information flying around the room. A petite Asian woman with her registration clipboard waiting patiently. The large boisterous doctor talking fast, I suppose, so he could get a ten-minute speech into five minutes and move along.

"I sure am glad you don't expect simultaneous translation," I finally smiled at him, taking a breath. He slowed down, only to use some highly specific medical terms that meant nothing to me in English. He ordered morphine. The nurse injected it into Macrina's portal, explaining that her mouth was too swollen for a pill. An aide came in with a baggie of ice cubes for her lip. Why hadn't that been done hours ago? It's the first thing a mom would have done.

This is your call button," someone explained. No, Macrina didn't want the TV on. Never likes to watch it. Besides, it's in English. "Well," I confided, "I watch Dish Latino soap operas to help my Spanish."

"Aren't you tired?" I asked. "Would you prefer we didn't talk?"

"If I sleep now," she reasoned, "I won't be able to sleep tonight. It would be a very long night here alone in the hospital. Best we talk." Over the next hours of sporadic medical interruptions, I sat by her bed getting acquainted.

She is from Oaxaca. I was born in Illinois. She was widowed more than 15 years ago. I was widowed thirty-nine years ago, but remarried. She has five kids. I have one. Three of her children are still in Mexico. My son lives in Minnesota with his family. She has a two-year-old grandchild. I have two grandchildren. Her parents aren't living anymore, but Sara is like a mother to her. My mother is ninety-two years old, lives alone, and is always busy. I showed her a photo in my phone.

The woman with the ice bags returned with a refill and Doctor #2. "Your pain number now?" he wanted to know. "Your job is to tell us before it starts again, so we can manage it," he gave her a serious look and then asked if she needed anything.

"Water? May I have some water?" She had been told hours ago that she could not have water or food. I wondered why they hadn't offered a blanket, but that thought got buried when the aide presented two glasses, one with and one without ice. She drank them both.

Another knock and Doctor Fast-Talk was back. "The x-ray seems to show an air bubble by the shoulder. We are sending you back to the lab. Want to be sure it isn't anything." He vanished.

Even though my thoughts ran wild, going places I hoped reality wouldn't, I calmly relayed the message. I walked alongside the gurney as she was pushed down the hall. One technician talked of growing up on a farm. She understood the seriousness of cows. Macrina smiled through her swollen lips. Smiling was good. The doctors asked her to smile after each test.

The technicians took me behind the protective wall and directed me to say "*respira profundo*," breathe deep. The x-rays showed a funny spot. "Not again," the man exclaimed. Before I could get too concerned, he added, "Her hospital gown has snaps and they keep showing up." I wonder if she will be charged for multiple x-rays.

Back in Room #8 we continued to wait for "the" doctor. Evidently, we hadn't heard from the one in charge of test results and decisions. Our afternoon was now slipping into early evening. I wanted to be home before dark.

We tried the red button. The "ice-bag" aide responded and went off in search of answers. Soon a tall woman with a flowing skirt, black net stockings, long, curly hair, and a stethoscope entered the room. "*Buenos días!*" she chirped. "*Hablo español un poco*, I speak a little Spanish." She repeated all the tests. "Follow my finger. Look into the light. Push against my hand. Smile.

Lift your leg against my push." I kept up with her commands and pantomimes.

Between translations, she talked of going on a medical mission to Guatemala. Was it the same organization I had traveled with in 2003? Her long hair flowed behind her as she circled the bed. She wished she knew more Spanish. Her fingers were gentle on Macrina's skin. She moved with determined expertise, yet with the touch of a butterfly. She looked at Macrina with a soft smile and took her hand.

"*No operación; concusión, no más.*" She continued with limited, but warm and comforting Spanish. You will stay tonight for observation and have another CT scan in the morning. We will compare. You will not be able to work for several weeks. You might be easily frustrated, but this is the concussion." Before leaving, she went over all the medications, the "do's and don'ts," and what to watch for in the coming days. It was time to call Sara.

"Macrina," I translated, "Sara will wait and come in the morning. Then she can get the test results and take you home. Is there anything else I can do before I leave?"

"I need to know how to ask for more water and the bathroom. And could you hand me my sweater?" So she was cold!

I asked the doctor for a piece of paper to write the phrases in English and Spanish, before getting her sweater.

When the doctor returned, she handed me a sheet of paper. On one side, she had drawn a glass of water with a straw and, on the other side, a toilet!

Brilliant! We thanked the lovely doctor. We held hands. I tucked her into her sweater and dimmed the light.

Her eyes were closed before I shut the door.

Section 10

Future Hope

37

Capítulo Treinta y siete
Nana and Ella Go to Spanish Camp

We met midway between our cities at a McDonald's to make the connection. Daughter-in-law Cindy transferred the backpack and a bag of comfort toys from her trunk to mine under the watchful eye of nine-year-old Ella, standing rigid, clutching a little stuffed elephant singing "You are my Sunshine" to her face.

"I don't want to go. I did not agree to this," she directed a snarled whisper through clenched teeth at her mother.

I held my breath on two accounts. One, would Cindy hold her ground and two, would Ella forfeit hers?

"Ella," Cindy cooed, "here is your pink monkey and silky blanket. You'll be fine." She shut the trunk.

"I need your hoodie, too," Ella pouted. It has the scent of her mother on it and comforts her through her potential bouts of homesickness.

Cindy looked down at her daughter. "I forgot it at home," she shrugged, then began to take off her shirt right there in the parking lot. "Good thing I'm wearing two shirts today!" she laughed, pulling it over her head and placing it into Ella's outstretched hands.

Thus began my journey into the north woods of Minnesota to Concordia Village Spanish Family Camp with my granddaughter, Ella. My dream, not hers.

Ella sat in back, quietly hugging her elephant and monkey. I wondered if I would be able to stay awake through two-and-a-half hours of silence.

"Ella?" I asked, "would you like me to put on some music?"

To my surprise she handed me a cord and said, "Plug this in. We can listen to my music. Daddy put a bunch on my iPod." Ice broken.

"I'll play a song and you guess the singer," she reported, making rules for her newest game. Our generational gap was quickly exposed as one song after another went unrecognized.

"Don't you really know any of these songs?" she groaned. "Try this one."

Thankfully my son, Greg, is a great fan of the Beatles and Frank Sinatra and Ella had the idea those might be of my vintage. "How about this one, Nana?" she chirped.

"That's Sergeant Pepper!" I exclaimed, "by the Beatles." Finally I began to win a few points in this game and with her. The music trivia lasted half an hour before the proverbial question arose.

"How much longer 'til we get there?"

"About another hour. Do you want to stop and walk around?"

"No, but I do want to ask you something."

"Like what? About camp?" I asked, hoping to lead her into my pep talk orientation.

"Nana, do I have to speak Spanish?"

"It won't be speaking so much as learning new words. We'll learn songs, words for foods and practice what you already know, like: '*hola, gracias, adiós*' and numbers from 1 to 10."

"Mommy said I can go home Wednesday if I don't like it!" she stated firmly.

Cindy and Greg would be back from Colorado by then, but this was news to me. I had no intention of going home early.

"Ella, we aren't making plans to leave before we even get there. This is new for both of us. I've never been to family camp. I used to take high school students for Spanish weekends at the Norwegian Village and those kids had fun. I think we will, too."

"Now would you help me look for the turn off? We should be seeing a sign soon," I asked, hoping to redirect her attention.

"Here's the clipboard with the directions," I continued, handing it into the backseat. Without a whimper, she turned off her music and took a tone of co-pilot. "We're looking for County 75, then we take a right. We cross the Mississippi. . ."

After numerous rights and lefts, we saw the sign announcing: "Concordia Language Villages" and two rows of flags. "There's the U.S. flag," she pointed. "And there", I said, "is the Mexican one. See the eagle with the serpent in its mouth?"

We followed the signs posting "Spanish Family Camp" and wound our way to what was actually the Finnish Campgrounds, as the Spanish Village was occupied by middle schoolers that week. We slowed at the last turn and were waved over by our first official.

"*Buenos días*," the young woman greeted us. "*¿Quiénes son ustedes?*" I gave her our names, she checked us off the list, pointed to the parking lot, and continued, "*La Aduana está por allí.*"

"*Gracias*," I said, nodding and smiling back at Ella.

"Nana, what did she say?"

"That Customs is over there by the parking lot. Here we go!"

Before I had the trunk open, two counselors were at our sides asking if we wanted help moving our bags to the cabin or to go through Customs first.

"Ella, what do you think?" I deferred to her as part of my plan to have her make decisions. She chose moving in.

Leonardo, from Uruguay, and Fito, from Argentina, hoisted our sleeping bags and suitcases while we followed with our backpacks. We passed the Finnish-styled lodge, log cabins labeled *Casa Iguazú, La Pampa, Machu Picchu*, and stopped at *Casa Cusco*, a cabin located in the Swedish Village! The white walls, simple design, and five cubbies of two bunks each reminded me of European hostels.

261

Ella walked down the row of cubbies, peeking behind each curtain, before choosing the one closest to the back door.

"Do you want the top or bottom bunk," I asked, recalling that she had done some sleep walking. "Top!" she said without hesitation. I had discussed this possibility with her parents and received approval. I was off the hook.

In no time we made the beds, hung up clothes, put shoes below and swim needs in the box above. She plopped her six comfort animals by her pillow, seven if you include Cindy's shirt, and declared that we were moved in. Time to take our passports to Customs.

At the red and white canopy, we found four tables. The first was for passport review and to choose our Spanish names. I'm always Juanita and she picked Estrella. Estrella is "Star" in English, the name she uses when she pretends to be a horse. Was her choice a coincidence? How would she have known?

At the second table we were separated for short interviews that would help them discern our language ability level. Table Three checked our health documents and allergies. Table Four listed family activity options. I was relieved when she chose *arte* and *música* over soccer. I was unsure of my kick-and-run abilities.

After the simulated *Aduana*/Customs area, we located the *Tienda* and went in. The store offered Guatemalan hacky-sacks, bilingual books and games, T-shirts with Spanish logos, and candy. Never-ever-in-her-life-tasted-before candy! Her eyes widened. There was a *Banco* window in the back of the store where dollars could be exchanged for pesos, but she didn't have time for that. She was already headed to the cashier with candy in hand.

After some taste testing, I suggested we walk it off. We had an hour to explore before supper. I gave Ella the camp map.

"What is *la playa*?" she asked, pointing to a sign. We followed the arrows to the beach. Along the way, we peeked into a Finnish *Saami* Hut where we were sure Bilbo Baggins must have stayed at one time. We passed the sauna and a boat house full of canoes, paddle boards, life preservers, and kayaks. No time now. The bell rang, calling us to our first dinner.

Emilio, the meal-time leader, raised his hand in the camp sign for silence. He then yelled down the stairwell, and up ran a half-dozen counselors dressed in improvised costumes, ready to start the pre-meal skit, introducing us to that dinner's Spanish vocabulary.

A uniformed man blew his whistle. Two counselors put their hands together to make a barricade. In front of them, a Custom's official stood behind a small table blocking the entrance to the dining area. One by one the costumed counselors passed through the arm barrier to the inspection table.

When the buzzer sounded, each incoming traveler was stopped and searched. If caught sneaking in food, the item was held up in the air while the Customs official yelled out its name. We all shouted the word back at him, thus learning our menu. The skit ended with Customs officials taking away a loaf of bread from the last man but allowing him to pass through with his Paul Bunyan ax. Some kiddos didn't get the joke, but the adults pointed and yelled at the official to chase him down.

Every meal was preceded by a crazy skit involving everyone. *Super Español* swooped in, sniffing the aromas emanating from each main dish before repeating its name for us to learn. *Super Española* flew over the tables to see if you were ready for dessert and if you wanted to take the camp *Todo Español* pledge, All Spanish . . . all day!

Ella tentatively tried each dish. There were *medianoches*, a Cuban cheese and ham sandwich on freshly baked buns. The *milanesas*, a slice of beef with cheese and tomato was too chewy for her braces, but the fruit salads, strawberry crepes, *churros*, fresh peas and *ñochis* (gnocchis) went down for seconds. One morning Ella cleaned up five pancakes, tried vanilla yogurt with fresh blueberries, uncurled a croissant, ate a hard-boiled egg (well, the whites!), and drank her *jugo*, juice.

Everything was served family style. If one table ran out of anything, you checked with another table or the kitchen for more. Cleanup was also a community event. The silverware was sorted into cups, the plates cleaned into a bucket, the liquids into a pitcher, and back to camp only after the table was wiped clean. The camp subliminally taught recycling, cutting food waste and modeled everyone working together.

Telenovela, the traditional Mexican soap opera, followed breakfast. This week, Shrek was presented in an abbreviated, onstage play format by an array of the counselors. Donkey, a.k.a. *Burro*, wore a fur covered winter hood. Shrek wore a green Mexican wrestler's mask. Pinocchio held a stick up for his long nose. To Ella's surprise and my delight, they all spoke Spanish. She knew the movie. I knew the Spanish. We both understood.

After the *novela*, counselors trouped onto the stage with drawings of animals posted on sticks. "What is happening?" Ella pulled on my sleeve.

"We're being separated into groups. You'll do activities and I have class. In an hour we'll break for snacks." I heard them call out, "Estrella." I waited. She stood up and left me!

Our days were filled from wake-up to *fogata*, the evening bonfire. Ella and I walked hand-in-hand through the forest. Sometimes she skipped, came to a halt and asked me to listen or look. The eagle above, the frogs in the leaves, the two deer behind our cabin, the fifteen baby snappers that hatched the last day. "*Tortugas*," I pointed at the critters toddling toward the lake. "*Tortugas*," Ella yelled to the kids coming up the path, and they all ran to watch. We were learning Spanish in the heart of northern forests.

At 3:30 it was beach time. I'd tip-toe behind her into the cold waves. She counted to ten in Spanish, the sign to dip in up to our necks. When she saw the other kids float away on a paddle board, she asked if we could. Well, a role model can't say "no" now can they? Next thing, we were both on our knees, balancing our way through the reeds. The following day she went off with another girl her age.

Thursday morning, we awoke in a loud crashing thunderstorm around 5:30 a.m. I heard a knock on the headboard and saw her little fingers wriggling around trying to get my attention. I gave her hand a squeeze and then got out of bed.

"Ella," I whispered, "would you like to come down with me?" She nodded yes and began handing me her seven comfort items. I placed them on my pillow and helped her down the ladder. We pulled up the sheet and straightened out her sleeping bag on top of us. We were scarcely cuddled in when a loud snort from the snorer in the next cubbie sent Ella's muffled giggles into her stuffed elephant. Snoring, the one thing I had not anticipated at camp.

That afternoon she came to me and asked, "*¿Cómo se dice 'knees' en español?*" I nearly dropped. "*Rodillas,*" I answered, and I joined in singing, "Head and shoulders, knees and toes" in Spanish.

Friday morning she looked at me and asked, "Is this our last day?"

"Yes, Ella, tomorrow, we leave after breakfast."

"Already? I feel like I am in a time-warp! How can that be?"

"Welcome to the grown-up world, Ella. Days are full and they go fast." I smiled at her. "You've done so much this week!"

"Remember, you didn't want to come, but you did? We met lots of new people all the way from Illinois, California, Tennessee, and Connecticut to Argentina, Uruguay, Spain, and Mexico. You even ate Cuban food. You loved your activities with Vicky. I met Sabrina, a former student of mine! What next?"

"The Feria tonight!" she grabbed my hand. "What are you going to wear?"

We put on our only dresses and joined the scattered groups headed toward the main lodge. Inside, the tables were set up banquet-style, allowing for a big center stage. They served *ñoquis*, of which Ella ate three servings even though it meant she had to ask at another table.

After the meal we watched the adult class dance the salsa, the kids showed their paintings, demonstrated their crafts, and filed up in groups to receive *certificados de participación*. With each presentation, the crowd chanted. "*Foto, foto, foto*" until everyone

smiled. Gustavo, Dean of Spanish Camp for his twenty-fifth and, now last, year, was honored with a tasty cake, baked and rolled out to the center of the room by Sabrina. Another relationship come full circle. Between hugs, tears, and cheers, the chant rose again. "*Foto, foto, foto*" as we all gathered together and smiled for our global family *FOTO!*

ELLA & NANA JAN

La Despedida
Fare Well

In Spanish, the word *Adiós* stems from *"Vaya con Dios"* or "go with God." It is generally used upon departing, but also as a greeting, accompanied by a slight nod of the head in passing. Either way, it is a blessing.

On the *Camino de Santiago* pilgrimage throughout Europe, hikers greet each other with: *"Buen Camino*-Good Roads." It is said with a sincere sense of camaraderie, identifying and connecting pilgrims sharing this human endeavor. Hike the path. Discover your truth. Hike some more.

I am still hiking. My northern footsteps have trod Spain's Roman roads, walked in solidarity with Central American refugees, and stood by the weary, waiting to connect with a doctor, all given deeper dimensions through familiarity with language and culture. Spanish opened multi-faceted levels of comprehension.

Yet it was that syncretic combination of cultures, from which I picked what suited me, that gave me a new way to maneuver through life. My culture did not offer solace when Jim was killed. My "northern-sauerkraut" foundation supported me, but the "southern-salsa" side provided a way to grieve and, finally, to celebrate.

I learned that language requires cultural context the day our Mexican waiter turned heel and brought *leche*, not *agua*, for Lorraine's burning throat. Furthermore, that adult waiter heeded my rudimentary utterings. A new code unlocking another world like magic! Powerful.

Words create or destroy, define and confine, liberate or imprison. Words open new worlds, add extra dimensions, provide more understanding of others and ourselves.

Think "melting pot," the concept that everyone coming to America gets thrown into a simmering assimilation stew resulting in the "look, act, think, and talk alike" recipe. Why not envision instead an *Ensalada Mixta*—a tossed salad? Bring me your spinach, your jicama, your pomegranate seeds. Better yet, let's have a potluck. Bring your sushi, your paella, your naan. . . Serve up your unique background and homeland flavors. Take a taste.

Words matter. Yes, English is a common denominator in the United States, but ENGLISH ONLY? What is the advantage to being one-dimensional? Teach English as the binder, but encourage immigrants to maintain their native languages and share traditions. Learn the difference between *lutefisk* and *lefse* at Minnesotan Christmas feeds!

Words matter. As I write, we are heading into another election cycle. The Latino vote is finally being taken seriously. Some politicians are speaking in Spanish. Those who don't are hiring interpreters or trusting their Google translators. Googlers beware. Remember context and culture? One young lass handed me an essay where she planned to say she enjoyed "practicing her tennis ball strokes" and got "liked to caress balls." Now take these mistakes to the world leader level.

Jimmy Carter's 1977 greeting in Poland went from "liking" the Polish people to "lusted after the Polish people" caught too late by the translator. One can snicker, but it gets serious. In 1956, Russia's Cold War Nikita Khrushchev was mistranslated from stating that capitalism would "bury itself from within" to "We'll bury you," sending out worldwide fear of impending nuclear war.

Even exact words from the dictionary don't guarantee clear communication. The house in Saltillo, Spain's ninth-floor apartment, Guatemala's mountainsides of wooden pallets covered with corrugated steel are all images of "home." Politicians meet in high-rise hotels looking down on Central America's capital cities with their bellies full and after-dinner drinks in hand. Their words have different definitions than the conversations in the streets below. I recommend that they do a homestay in a refugee camp or hike a few miles with the immigrants to the U.S. border to improve communication, amplify insights, and expand human relations.

My maze. A hike through Mayan highlands taught me about Eastern and Western medicines. The path leading me to border detention camps and Central American refugees brought true empathy. There is a place for *pupusas* and strawberry Jell-O on the same plate. The U.S. eagle and the Latin American condor fly in the same sky.

Two visions. Varied viewpoints. Expanded options. Enrichment. Revelations. Combining cultures creates something new, innovative, maybe improved. What a concept.

I leave you with that thought. *A Despedida.* Go forth with a curious mind. Gifts await you... many just outside your comfort zones.

Buen camino and *Adiós,*
Jan

ACKNOWLEDGEMENTS

First gratitude goes to my parents, Donald and Phyllis, for providing a loving base, family forays out of our comfort zones and the north woods cabin. My father died before the inception of this book leaving my mother to be the president of my fan club. Her daily encouragement buoyed me through. My husband, Robert, supported my endeavor through pancake breakfasts, nature walk breaks, and protecting my writing time from interruptions. To my son, Greg, for reading the manuscript with a caring yet critical eye of a bookseller and avid reader.

To Donna Salli, author of *A Notion of Pelicans* and member of our Homer's Writing group, the midwife in this birthing process. Each essay received her guidance, gentle nudging and firm critique. She generously offered her time and expertise until this book came to life.

To the readers who reviewed "their" sections: Edith Alvarez—The Presbyterians; Dr. Dave Boran—Barillas; Sister Adela Gross—The Call, and to Sister Mary Obowa for assembling six Franciscans to read the book in its entirety, with special thanks to Sister Jan Kilian for her diligent feedback. To Jan and Paula, two of my Mom's book club friends, for their input and enthusiasm generously given at each step.

To my editors, Angela Weichmann of A.M.W. Editing, for her formative recommendations and passion for the core human story. Her energy was invaluable in keeping me moving forward. To Tenlee Lund, for meeting me in the north woods and in my mother's living room to edit grammar and clean out obscure passages. And to Lois Hollingsworth, my *amiga*, my travel companion and, in this adventure, a proof-reader. That feat goes beyond words!

This editing was supported, in part, by a grant provided by the Five Wings Arts Council, with funds from the McKnight Foundation supplemented with Legacy funds. Thanks, Vicki.

Special mention goes to Heather Felty, Publisher of Inner Peace Press, for supporting me to keep my website (janetkurtz.com) updated and being my go-to guru.

My book finally entered the world thanks to the creative expertise and with the lov-ing touches of Chip and Jean Borkenhagen of Riverplace Press. Their personal commit-ment, talent and patience carried me forward as we chose photos, art and a new title.(Formerly known as: *Sauerkraut & Salsa*). They work from the heart and brought out the soul of my story. *Mil gracias amigos.*

Finally, my gratitude to Maribel Adame for sharing Spain with me since 1976; to all the friends appearing in my stories and to those behind the scenes—the volunteers and participants in my cultural events, community members, and the strangers that became my friends. We are all woven together through our stories. Time to again walk through the door and ripple outward.

MAPS OF MEXICO, GUATEMALA & SPAIN

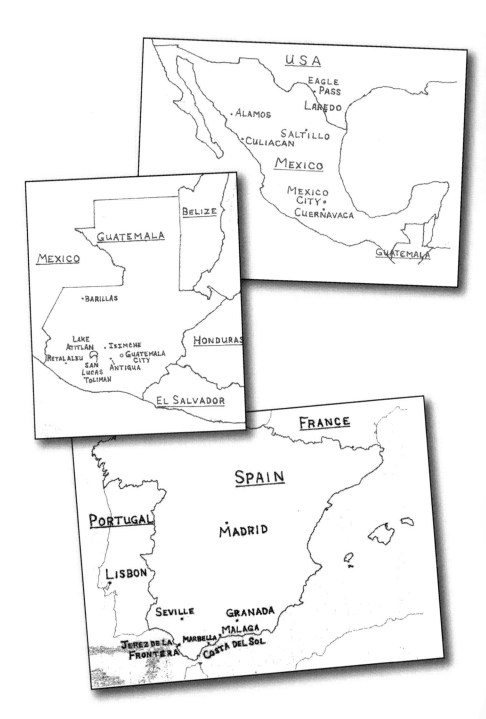

RESOURCES

RECOMMENDED READINGS:

- **Sanctuary: The New Underground Railroad** by Renny Golden and Michael McConnell, Orbis Books, 1986 ISBN: 0-88344-440-2

   Refugee stories document their dangerous situations and courageous decisions as they struggle to live amidst or flee their government's atrocities during the twentieth century.

- **Inevitable Revolutions: The United States in Central America** by Walter LaFeber, W. W. Norton & Company, New York, London; 1984 ISBN: 0-393-30212-1

   LaFeber lays out the long and often untold historical interventions of the United States into Latin America, resulting in the current, misrepresented events regarding immigration today.

- **Bitter Fruit: The Story of the American Coup in Guatemala** by Stephen Schlesinger and Stephen Kinzer, 1982, First edition
ISBN–13: 978-0674019300   ISBN-10: 067401930X

   Bitter Fruit details the CIA's overthrow of the democratically elected government of Jacobo Arbenz of Guatemala in 1954, resulting in a continuous breakdown of U.S./Central American relations.

- **I, Rigoberta Menchú** by Elisabeth Burgos-Debray and Rigoberta Menchú, Verso Publishing, 1984, First edition ISBN–10: 0860917886   ISBN–13: 978-0860917885

   Rigoberta Menchú Tum, a Guatemalan K'iche' Indigenous feminist and human rights activist, came to public attention during the 1980's Guatemalan Civil War, receiving a Nobel Peace Prize in 1992.

- **What You Have Heard is True: A Memoir of Witness and Resistance** by Carolyn Forché, 2019, Penguin Press, NY, ISBN: 978-0-525-56037-1

   Carolyn Forché tells her true story of following a mysterious invitation into El Salvador's Civil War, thrusting her into the center of revolutionary change. Perfect timing for understanding today's news.

- **Travel as a Political Act** by Rick Steves, 2009, Nation Books, NY
ISBN: 978-1568584355

   Rick Steves shares his worldwide travel with this philosophy, "Travel connects people with people . . . we can't understand our world without experiencing it . . ."

- **Roads Less Traveled: Dispatches from the Ends of the Earth** by Catherine Watson 2005, Syren Book Company, Minneapolis
ISBN-13: 978-0-929636-45-0   ISBN-10: 0-929636-45-7
"Catherine Watson leads us gently by the hand to unusual places—and new understandings." Catharine Hamm, travel editor, The Los Angeles Times

- **With Our Own Eyes: The dramatic story of a Christian response to the wounds of war, racism, and oppression** by Don Mosley with Joyce Hollyday, 1996, Herald Press, Scottdale, PA   ISBN 0-8361-9050-5
"*With Our Own Eyes* is the inspiring story of what can happen when a group of Christians takes seriously Jesus' call to be peacemakers in a world full of violence." Jimmy Carter
Website: https://www.jubileepartners.org/

- **The Faces of Change** by Joan Jarvis Ellison, 2007, Otter Tail County Historical Society, Fergus Falls, MN   ISBN: 0-9658782-2-8
"The story of Pelican Rapids is complicated, yet hopeful... It helps us understand how people from divergent backgrounds can build a vibrant community." Mary Pipher, *The Middle of Everywhere*

- **Village Assignment: True stories of humor, adventure and drama in Guatemala's highland villages** by Dave Huebsch, 2004, Highlight Publishing, Little Falls, MN
ISBN: 0-9741734-0-1
Dave Huebsch left his successful career in 1984 and traveled to Guatemala where he spent his life creating with Common Hope and later, Rising Villages. His projects included schooling, sponsorships, building homes and relationships. His insightful vignettes are both heartwarming and thought-provoking. Books available through: https://www.abebooks.com

RECOMMENDED VIDEOS:
- **Jaunty Fashion, Proud Cultures, and Fighting Hunger in Guatemala and Ethiopia** Rick Steves,
Insight into Guatemala, guided by Fidel Xinico Tum from Augsburg Global Education (also led my group). https://blog.ricksteves.com/blog/guatemala-ethiopia-ngos/

- **A Day W/O a Mexican**, 2004, Rated R. Actors Caroline Aaron, Tony Abtemarco and Sergio Arau (Director, Producer and Writer). Listed as: Comedy, Drama, Mystery & Suspense, Science Fiction & Fantasy, something for everyone. I call it a "pseudo-documentary" including pointed factual data sprinkled amidst a green fog that whisks away all the Latinos in California, leaving residents reeling among drippy faucets, rotten fruit and lack of Big League players. A "tongue-in-cheek" movie offering serious talking points.

About the Author

In theory, I have always been connected north to south. At age six months, my mother dipped my toes into Lake Julia, a body of water joined in a chain of northern lakes that flow into the Wisconsin River before joining the Mississippi, ever widening southward until emptying into the Gulf of Mexico. In theory, I could paddle my kayak from the family cabin to all points south. In reality, I am connected to the world via travel, friendships and activism, all enriched by the ability to speak Spanish and my belief in the Golden Rule.

I am a cheerleader for language learning, an advocate for the joys of diversity, and a supporter of cultural outreach. I live in a northern Minnesota woods with my husband, Robert, in a house that we built. . . I'm talking hammers and nails. My home is wherever I am.

Made in the USA
Middletown, DE
18 October 2023

41042710R00152